THE MAD EMPEROR

HELIOGABALUS AND THE DECADENCE OF ROME

HARRY SIDEBOTTOM

ONEWORLD

A Oneworld Book

First published by Oneworld Publications in 2022
This paperback edition published 2023

Copyright © Harry Sidebottom, 2022

The moral right of Harry Sidebottom to be identified as the Author of this work has
been asserted by him in accordance with the Copyright, Designs, and Patents Act
1988

ISBN 978-0-86154-685-5
eISBN 978-0-86154-254-3

Maps © Erica Milwain

Typeset by Tetragon, London
Printed and bound in Great Britain by Clays Ltd, Elcograf S.p.A.

Oneworld Publications
10 Bloomsbury Street
London WC1B 3SR
England

Stay up to date with the latest books,
special offers, and exclusive content from
Oneworld with our newsletter

Sign up on our website
oneworld-publications.com

Praise for *The Mad Emperor*

'We are used to being told that the historical truth is less exciting than the myth. But, as Harry Sidebottom's *The Mad Emperor* demonstrates, this is one of those rare cases when the history does not fall short... Sidebottom presents a picture of third-century imperial Rome that is, if anything, wilder than the popular imagination.'   *Telegraph*

'An enjoyable romp through the few highs and many lows of Heliogabalus's fleeting four years as emperor... Throughout Sidebottom showcases the historian in action, assessing his sources, trawling through prosopography and carefully identifying marble portrait busts. He offers a scholarly but readable biography of an emperor who has been rather short of such attentions.'   *TLS*

'*The Mad Emperor* recreates the Ancient World with the eye of a poet and the sure hand of a scholar.'
                                        Barry Strauss, author of *Ten Caesars*

'Harry Sidebottom skilfully juggles what to believe and what not to believe... The racy story is told with the vivid phrasing and descriptive powers of an accomplished novelist... a well-illustrated and absorbing read.'   *BBC History Magazine*

'Sidebottom brings [Heliogabalus] vividly back to life. His prose feels vibrant and effortless but also rewards close reading.'
                        Daisy Dunn, author of *In the Shadow of Vesuvius*

'A scholarly but highly readable account of the teenager who became classical Rome's most reviled emperor, but who may be viewed with a touch more sympathy now.'
             Matthew Kneale, author of *Rome: A History in Seven Sackings*

'A riveting and rollicking account of a much maligned but truly thrilling era in Roman history.'
                                              Emma Southon, author of
                      A History of the Roman Empire in 21 Women

About the Author

Dr Harry Sidebottom teaches Ancient History at Lincoln College, Oxford. Since the publication of *Fire in the East* in 2008, he has written and published a novel each year, all of which have been *Sunday Times* top five bestsellers. His *Warrior of Rome* series has been published in fourteen countries. *The Mad Emperor*, his first work of narrative non-fiction, was a *Financial Times*, *BBC History* and *Spectator* Book of the Year and shortlisted for the *Slightly Foxed* Best First Biography Prize. Harry is also the editor of the *Blackwell Encyclopaedia of Ancient Battles*.

To the three women who make the books possible:
my wife Lisa, my mother Frances
and my aunt Terry

HELIOGABALUS FAMILY TREE

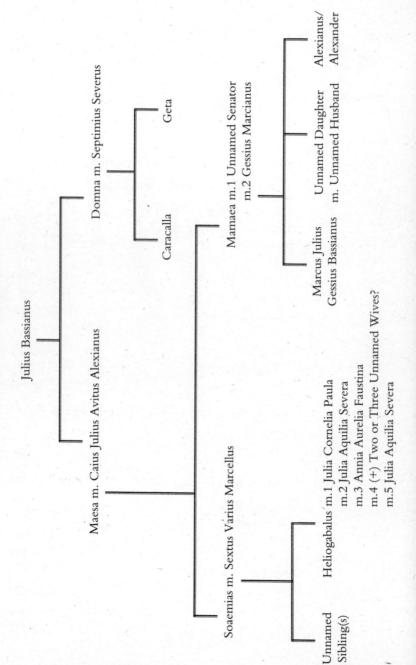

CONTENTS

97

97
101
108

119

119
122
125
129
136
138
143

150

150
153
159

168

168
173
178
201

203

203
206
209
219
227

232

232
240

North Sea

ANGLES

Atlantic
Ocean

BRITANNIA
INFERIOR

BRITANNIA
SUPERIOR

FRISII

GERMANIA
INFERIOR

Colonia
Agrippinensis

Mogontiacum

BELGICA

LUGDUNENSIS

Elbe

Danube

Rhine

GERMANIA
SUPERIOR

RAETIA

NORICUM

Carnuntum

AQUITANIA

1

Mediolanum

2

Aquileia

PANNONIA SUPERIOR

NARBONENSIS

3

DALMATIA

ITALY

HISPANIA
TARRACONENSIS

LUSITANIA

Tarracona

Rome

BAETICA

Mediterran

MAURETANIA
TINGITANA

MAURETANIA
CAESARIENSIS

Carthage

NUMIDIA

AFRICA
PROCONSULARIS

1   ALPES GRAIAE
2   ALPES COTTIAE
3   ALPES MARITIMAE

0   500   1,000 miles

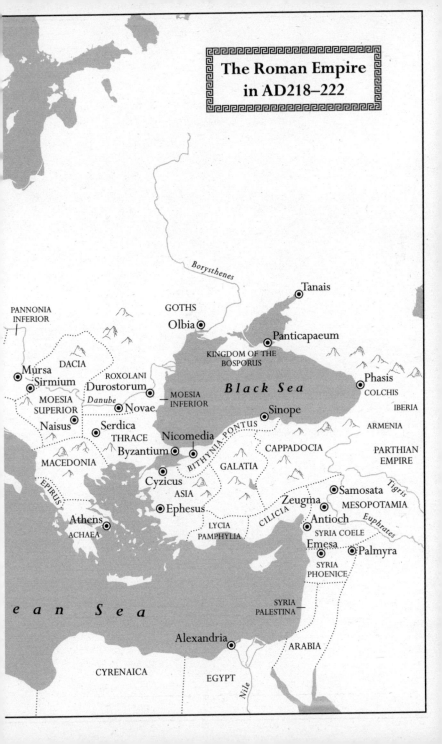

The Roman Empire in AD218–222

PANNONIA INFERIOR

GOTHS

Olbia

Tanais

Panticapaeum

KINGDOM OF THE BOSPORUS

Mursa

DACIA

Sirmium

ROXOLANI

Durostorum

Danube

MOESIA INFERIOR

Black Sea

Phasis

COLCHIS

MOESIA SUPERIOR

Novae

IBERIA

Naisus

Serdica

THRACE

Nicomedia

Sinope

ARMENIA

Byzantium

BITHYNIA-PONTUS

CAPPADOCIA

PARTHIAN EMPIRE

MACEDONIA

GALATIA

Cyzicus

EPIRUS

ASIA

Ephesus

LYCIA PAMPHYLIA

CILICIA

Samosata

Zeugma

Tigris

MESOPOTAMIA

Antioch

Euphrates

SYRIA COELE

Emesa

Palmyra

SYRIA PHOENICE

Athens

ACHAEA

Borysthenes

e a n   S e a

SYRIA PALESTINA

Alexandria

ARABIA

CYRENAICA

EGYPT

Nile

LIST OF ILLUSTRATIONS

Image 11: Domna and the Altar of Elagabal. Bronze Coin of Julia Domna, Emesa, AD 193–217, 1944.100.66178, courtesy of the American Numismatic Society.

Image 12: Heliogabalus and his God, photograph courtesy of Numismatica Ars Classica NAC AG, Auction 29, lot 596.

Image 13: The 'Horn' of Heliogabalus, photograph courtesy of Numismatica Ars Classica NAC AG, Auction 54, lot 514.

Image 14: Relief Sculpture of Elagabal, photograph © Clare Rowan.

Image 15: Reconstruction of the Temple of Elagabal on the Palatine, drawing reproduced by kind permission of Patrizia Veltri and Françoise Villedieu.

Image 16: Reverses of Silver Coins of Heliogabalus Found in Hoards, from Clare Rowan, *Under Divine Auspices: Divine Ideology and the Visualisation of Imperial Power in the Severan Period* (Cambridge: Cambridge University Press, 2012), p. 166. Reproduced with permission of The Licensor through PLSclear.

Image 17: Cameo of Heliogabalus? Bibliothèque nationale de France, camée.304, 'Elagabale sur un char traîné par des femmes'.

Image 18: Heliogabalus in Carnuntum. Gewandstatue mit Kind, 3.-4. Jh. n. Chr., Kalksandstein, InvNr CAR-S-1328, © Landessammlungen NÖ, Archäologischer Park Carnuntum (Photo: N. Gail).

Image 19: A Statue of Heliogabalus Remodelled as Alexander. National Archaeological Museum, Naples, Italy, © Album / Alamy Stock Photo.

Image 20: *Caracalla and Geta* by Lawrence Alma-Tadema (1907), courtesy of Wikimedia Commons.

Image 21: 'A Roman Lady'? Photograph by Mr R. Laev, reproduced by permission of Forschungsarchiv für Antike Plastik, Universität zu Köln: arachne.dainst.org/entity/148607.

INTRODUCTION

The Roses of Heliogabalus

Image 1: *The Roses of Heliogabalus* by Alma-Tadema

The false ceiling moved and the rose petals began to fall. Did the diners have any warning: a click or a whir of machinery, or perhaps some hint from the young Emperor? Certainly, they were on edge. Heliogabalus' banquets were notorious for surprises. Often these were humiliating or frightening. Couches were rigged to tip their occupants sprawling onto the floor. Wild beasts were released among the tables. Imperial Rome had a history, by turns pleasant and sinister, of false ceilings at dinner parties. A dining room in Nero's Golden House had revolving panels in the ceiling to sprinkle the guests with perfume and flowers. In the reign of Tiberius, informers secreted themselves in the hollow between the false and real ceiling to eavesdrop on any senators lulled by wine and trusted companions into treasonous chatter.

At what point did Heliogabalus' guests realise they were in danger? How soon did the scatter of rose petals become a deluge, which threatened to smother them? When did they begin to struggle, start to fight for their lives? When did they realise they were going to die?

The Roses of Heliogabalus by Sir Lawrence Alma-Tadema was first exhibited in 1888 at the Royal Academy in London. In the painting, everyone appears strangely calm. Heliogabalus, clad in golden robes at the head of the dais, looks on impassively. His interest seems less piqued than the others reclining in safety on the high table. They, at least, lean forward for a better view. Even odder are the reactions of the victims down below. Two women in the centre move, but languidly: more as if luxuriating in the flowers than trying to avoid suffocation. Two other women gaze out at the viewer. Far from terrified, their faces betray no flicker of emotion. Perhaps the awful realisation has not yet dawned. Although, given that the woman looking out from the left of the picture is already so submerged that her pink face has almost disappeared into the pink of the flowers, that seems improbable. More likely their lack of reaction is intended to be understood as the end result of Roman decadence. They are all so sated with luxury and sensuality that any new experience, even the threat of death, provokes nothing but boredom: the particularly Victorian emotion of ennui.

Never mind that *The Roses of Heliogabalus* is complete fiction. Alma-Tadema took the story from a late antique historical novelist. He altered the 'violets and other flowers' of the original to roses (and, incidentally, replaced the mechanical ceiling with an awning). For Victorians, roses symbolised both sensuality and decay. Always obsessive about detail, and working in the chill of an English November, when roses do not bloom, Alma-Tadema imported at vast expense thousands of fresh flowers to his studio. An extravagance redolent of his subject. Alma-Tadema's source, the unknown author of the collection of lives of the Emperors known as the *Augustan History*, adapted the anecdote from the dinner of Nero, which he had found in Suetonius, got rid of the perfume, and added the lethality. There is much more to say about *The Roses of Heliogabalus* and we will return to it in the final chapter (in preparation, you might want to check out the ornaments in the room, and the man on the right with the elaborate hairstyle, and maybe take a look out at the landscape). For now, it is enough to note that while Alma-Tadema's painting may be a complex, multi-layered fiction, it perfectly encapsulates Victorian ideas about the decadence of imperial Rome, and the young Emperor as its lowest point.

Fast forward over a hundred years to the twenty-first century, and in general Roman decadence is still going strong. The cruelty and depravity of Caligula and Nero are embedded in popular consciousness (there is plenty of evidence on the internet). But Heliogabalus has almost completely disappeared (again, we will study this disappearance in the final chapter). The young Emperor can still be found, among the piles of notes and ziggurats of books, in the studies of a few scholars. Actually, a very few scholars, as academe largely ignores him. Otherwise, he has withdrawn to the margins. Sometimes he makes an appearance in the counterculture at the wilder edges of the LGBT+ community. Now and then he can be glimpsed (always through the prism of Alma-Tadema's painting) in contemporary art and its often overblown criticism. Once in a blue moon he is paraded (again always mediated via *The Roses of Heliogabalus*) in the vacuous publicity of fashion houses. But in the mainstream, like a god abandoned by his worshippers, Heliogabalus has vanished into thin air.

In the Roman world Heliogabalus always remained centre stage. This is ironic, as after his death his memory was formally condemned. *Damnatio memoriae*, as scholars frequently remind us, is a modern term. But the concept was Roman, and its penalties were rigorously enacted in the case of Heliogabalus. Some of his statues were carefully taken down and stored in warehouses, waiting to be remodelled as someone else, while the rest were mutilated. The hammer blows were aimed at the sensory organs: eyes, ears, nose and mouth. Then the battered statues were dragged off to be reused as building materials, or ignominiously discarded. Some, or all, of his official names – Marcus Aurelius Antoninus – were chiselled off inscriptions, and crossed out on papyri. Even his coins were not exempt. It is probable that many were melted down. Some that survived were counterstamped with the initial of his successor. A few, like his inscriptions, were defaced with a sharp instrument. Paradoxically, this thorough *damnatio memoriae* actually helped preserve the memory of the Emperor. He became a significant presence by his very absence: the empty plinth and the blank space on the inscription.

The dead Emperor remained distinctly alive in the Roman imagination. He acquired a wide range of nicknames. Despite the brevity of his reign (AD 218–22), many are known, more than for any other Emperor. They are all derogatory, mocking his illegitimacy, his effeminacy and sexuality and his race and religion, as well as the fate of his corpse: False-Antoninus, Unholy-little-Antoninus, Gynnis ('womanish-man'), Bassiana (the female form of a family name), Koryphos ('virgin-rapist', or perhaps 'catamite'), the Assyrian (i.e. 'oriental'), Sardanapalus (after a mythical Assyrian king), Tractitius ('the dragged', from the treatment of his dead body), Tiberinus (from the river where his remains were thrown), and Elagabalus and Heliogabalus (both derived from Elagabal, the god he worshipped).

This is a good place to pause and consider his names. As a child, most likely, he was Sextus (or Caius) Varius Avitus Bassianus. When he came to the throne he became Marcus Aurelius Antoninus. After he was dead, he got all those other names. As far as he is remembered at all in the modern world, usually he is Elagabalus or Heliogabalus. What should we call him? Marcus Aurelius Antoninus risks confusion with two other Emperors with the same names (either his supposed father, also known as Caracalla, or the famous philosopher, the author of the *Meditations*). Elagabalus, the nomenclature commonly employed by academics, hardly distinguishes him from the deity Elagabal. It leaves a text littered with near homonyms. One scholar has championed the use of Varius. This has the disadvantage that neither his subjects nor anyone now would know who it was meant to identify. Heliogabalus was a made-up name. The god Elagabal was identified with the sun: Helios in Greek. Combining the two produced Heliogabalus. 'A monstrous name for a monstrous Emperor', as has been noted. Say it aloud: *Heliogabalus*. It sounds like the gabbling of a turkey, or a barbarian. The latter was the intention. The name Heliogabalus was not created until the Emperor had been dead for almost two centuries. It is not ideal, but it is distinctive. People know who you are talking about. It is what we will use. Well, most of the time...

The injunctions of *damnatio memoriae* did not cover works of literature. Which is odd, when you stop and think about it. Sometimes ancient writers expressed their reluctance to record the vices of bad Emperors before, with the morality of a tabloid journalist, going on to elaborate every nuance of depravity. 'My page is dirty, *as was his life*, but my life is clean', as they might have expanded the standard excuse of Latin erotic poets.

There are three main surviving literary accounts of Heliogabalus, all in varying degrees salacious. Two of them are by contemporaries. The first is Cassius Dio, who wrote a history of Rome from the arrival of Aeneas and the foundation of the city to his own lifetime under the successor to Heliogabalus. Unlike the majority of the text, which is extant only in later epitome, the section on Heliogabalus survives in the original (although there are lacunae in the manuscript). A Greek from Asia Minor, Cassius Dio had a successful career in Roman politics. He was twice appointed consul, the highest magistracy, and served on the council of at least two Emperors. His work is that of an informed insider, whose interpretation is filtered through the outlook of the senatorial class. Complicit in the regime of Heliogabalus, in retirement he sought to distance himself from the dead Emperor.

The second is Herodian, another Greek, a younger contemporary of Cassius Dio. His history of the Roman Empire from the death of Marcus Aurelius (AD 180) to the accession of Gordian III (AD 238) survives intact (unless a final book or two is missing). Herodian was of less exalted status than Cassius Dio (it has been suggested that the author was an ex-slave), and his history contains fewer details, especially on senatorial matters. Yet, with his interest in religion and the imperial women, he provides an alternative viewpoint, essentially that of an educated Greek subject.

The final major source is possibly the most perplexing in all Classical literature. It is the *Augustan History* (the name is modern: in Latin *Historia Augusta*, and also in older scholarship the *Scriptores Historiae Augustae*), which gave Alma-Tadema the story of the fatal dinner party. The *Augustan History* is a series of biographies of Emperors from Hadrian (AD 117–38) to Carinus

(AD282–5). They claim to be written by six different men around AD300. In fact, the lives were the work of one writer living about AD400. Despite over a century of intensive modern scholarship, no consensus has emerged concerning the motives of the unknown fraudster (anti-Christian propaganda or sheer devilment are the leading interpretations). The life of Heliogabalus is best interpreted as an ancient historical novel, which mixes reliable information with generalisations, wild invention and sly, scholarly literary allusions and jokes.

It is worth remembering that the vast majority of Classical writers do not survive by chance. They survive because they were copied and recopied by generations of scribes across the Middle Ages. The reason they were copied is that their works were recognised from the start as high-quality literature. Of course, chance played a large part in survival: a fire in a monastery; a philistine using the only manuscript to wipe his arse. Yet the worse the writer the more susceptible his works were to such accidents. They had been less copied in antiquity. There were fewer manuscripts. The Classics that remain are classics not just because they are very old, but because their writers were literary artists. Part of that artistry was their deft handling of themes that illuminated their own age and had resonance in later times. If Heliogabalus was the worst of men, he made the best of subjects. Cassius Dio, Herodian and the *Augustan History*, although with varying emphases, depict the Emperor as the most monstrous tyrant ever to ascend the throne. Cruel and bloodthirsty, profligate and perverse, the devotee of a barbaric god, the transgressor of every social and cultural boundary: Heliogabalus was a terrible warning to rulers and the ruled, both contemporary and in the future, against the ultimate excesses of autocratic power.

Another part of the literary artistry that preserved these three Classical writers – two historians and a biographer/novelist – was their narrative skill. Cassius Dio, Herodian and the author of the *Augustan History* were great storytellers, and the life of Heliogabalus was a mine of great stories.

A Syrian youth (just thirteen or fourteen years old) was against all probability victorious in a civil war started by his aged grandmother. His reign opened with a spate of killings: that of his tutor was by the Emperor's own hand. In the four years of extravagant misrule that followed, the Emperor elevated lower-class favourites to positions of prominence and appeared to go out of his way to humiliate the established elite. He was married to at least four women, and, to the outrage of traditional sentiment, twice to a Vestal Virgin. Again flouting Roman conventions, he openly enjoyed the passive role in male–male sex and it was said that he married a man, worked as a male prostitute and asked doctors about the possibility of a physical sex change. His ancestral god, manifested as a large, conical black stone, was imported to Rome and installed in a lavish temple on the Palatine. Another temple was built in the suburbs. The Emperor, disdaining the dignity of a Roman toga and dressed instead in 'barbaric' robes and wearing make-up, danced in public ceremonies worshipping his god. Linked to his religion were rumours of magic, even necromancy. Other deities had to make way for Elagabal. Two goddesses were married off to the newcomer. Much worse, Jupiter Optimus Maximus was deposed. Henceforth, Elagabal, the deity from the East, was the head of the state pantheon. The temples, weddings (human and divine), ceremonies and the Emperor's lifestyle consumed immense sums of money. Ignoring the normal duties of an Emperor, it was said Heliogabalus devoted himself to driving chariots, sometimes pulled by naked women, sometimes by dogs or even less likely animals. And there were the dinners: all the food of one colour, the courses served in different palaces, pimps and buffoons as guests and the notorious one with the deadly cascade of flowers. Finally, the Emperor was assassinated, along with his mother, by the Praetorian Guard. The coup was again orchestrated by his grandmother. The corpses of Heliogabalus and his mother were stripped naked and dragged by hooks through the streets of Rome. To deny it burial, that of the Emperor was weighted down and thrown into the Tiber.

Many of the stories, not just the roses, appear implausible. Historians like Cassius Dio and Herodian were far closer in their methods to a modern historical novelist than to a modern historian. In antiquity, the genre of history writing was very different from that of the modern world. It discouraged the naming of sources and insisted on the invention of dialogue, in the form of formal speeches. It was relaxed about chronology and even the invention of entire episodes. Classical biography might include documents, letters and the like, but it was even less constrained by factual accuracy than history. Amid the exuberant fictions of the *Augustan History* are many evidently spurious documents. Our sources were not attempting a dispassionate reconstruction of the past on its own terms. Instead, they drew on its material for their contemporary purposes. They told stories either to make serious political and cultural arguments or to provide entertainment. Ideally, they did both.

So many stories swirl around the figure of Heliogabalus. To complicate matters, our three main sources are not completely independent of each other. Herodian had read Cassius Dio, although the level of his dependence on his predecessor is controversial. In turn, the author of the *Augustan History* had read both Cassius Dio and Herodian. Here the question is to what extent the mischievous biographer deliberately altered what he found in the accounts by the Greek historians. To make sense of all these interlocked stories, modern scholars have created a rule of thumb: Cassius Dio is more reliable than Herodian, with the *Augustan History* tailed off last. Except that, when we come to the reign of Heliogabalus, a few scholars reverse the top order: Herodian becomes more trustworthy than Cassius Dio. The *Augustan History* remains a distant third, until we reach the last months of the reign, when there is a strange unanimity that it begins to follow a good, now lost, source and so becomes extremely plausible.

This hierarchy of reliability should be abandoned. Instead, to try and judge which stories are true, or at least plausible, each must be considered in the light of the aims and methods of its teller. Each must be measured against all the surviving evidence. Like a detective, we need to evaluate each piece of evidence without preconceptions, on its own merits, before we attempt a reconstruction.

We will investigate our sources and explore different inter-pretations. This history with the top off, revealing its workings, shows what historians actually *do*. This detective work – part forensic examination, part intuition – is one of the keenest pleas-ures in thinking about the past. Sometimes the journey is as important as the destination.

Not just literature will come under the microscope. We will be looking at inscriptions, coins, papyri, archaeology and many works of art, including several statues and portrait busts, a couple of relief sculptures and an extraordinary cameo.

As well as sex and death and decadence, the story of Heliogabalus is an ideal prism through which to view other questions which were central to imperial Rome. What were the limits of political power? How far should a ruler intervene in the life of his subjects? What was an Emperor actually expected to *do*? What constituted religious extremism? When did admirable piety tip over into superstition and dangerous zealotry? How was ethnicity constructed? Was Heliogabalus hated because he was Syrian? Were the Romans racist? Such questions – changed, but not out of all recognition – are still vitally important today. When we illuminate the past we are shining a light upon ourselves: in what ways are we different and what ways the same? Rome, as it is often said, is always 'good to think with'.

Enough about roses and false ceilings, about sources and methods. It is time to tell the story of Heliogabalus. We need to start at the beginning. How did this unlikely boy ever become Emperor of Rome? We need to go back to a mild spring night in Syria, back to the night after the Ides of May AD218.

CHAPTER I THE REVOLT

Syria: May AD218

I *The Flight*

After nightfall, they took the boy and slipped out of the Syrian city of Emesa. Time was not on their side. It was the night after the Ides of May: only ten hours of darkness and over twenty miles to the fortress at Raphaneae. A very long walk for a child, even tougher for an old woman. They could have ridden in a carriage, but that might have made their departure more conspicuous. A senior officer was close to the town, with troops known to be loyal to the Emperor. The conspirators had to avoid detection and reach the fortress well before dawn.

Emesa was a walled city, more from civic pride than for defence. It was over two centuries since barbarians had raided these upper reaches of the Orontes valley and Rome's recent eastern wars had been fought either away in the north of Mesopotamia, or far off in the east, in the territory of the Parthian king. The gatekeeper might have been bribed to turn a blind eye and let them pass, or perhaps the local status of the family had secured their discreet exit.

Immediately outside the gates was the necropolis, the city of the dead. Both sides of the road would be lined with tombs. They could take different forms, resembling towers or pyramids or houses. The architecture might vary, but the practice was normal for any settlement. Yet at night the respectable and the superstitious avoided such places. Prostitutes, down on their luck and lacking a room, plied their trade in abandoned sepulchres. And there were endless stories of the unquiet dead walking. It was only two nights since the last *Lemuria*, when the gates to the underworld stood open. The boy, Varius, was fourteen (or perhaps still thirteen) and fascinated by the supernatural. If he dwelt on such things, as he passed the gloomy structures, it could be forgiven.

Our two contemporary sources differ on who was hurrying through the darkness. Cassius Dio says Varius was taken to the camp by his tutor Eutychianus, and that the young *grammaticus* (almost certainly an ex-slave) did so without the knowledge of the family. Herodian, not mentioning the freedman, claims it was the boy's grandmother, Maesa, along with his mother, Soaemias. An attempt could be made to reconcile the versions: the initiative lay with the women, who sent Eutychianus but themselves remained in Emesa. Such a course, however, brought no advantage. Anyone left behind was in great danger, as would be shown by the tragic events of the following day. Modern scholars often downplay the evidence of Herodian, pointing to his dramatic desire to emphasise the role of the women. Yet that ignores the equally strong literary aim of Cassius Dio to stress the disreputable and lower-class nature of everyone involved in the revolt. Furthermore, Cassius Dio was writing in the next reign, when his career flourished under a regime initially controlled by Maesa. It would have been tactless to remind his readers of her role in bringing to power a now deposed and disgraced young Emperor.

Oracles had spoken of change, among them the patron deity of Emesa. Their ambiguous utterances might have encouraged Eutychianus to act alone. Young men still do extraordinary and terrible things in the name of God. But Eutychianus was a creature of the family. He had been raised in the home of the grandmother (and thus we assume his servile origins) and was the lover of the mother. Although Soaemias was widowed, the affair was shocking to contemporaries, even more so as the man she took to her bed had been a slave. No matter how close to the family, in ways conventional or otherwise, Eutychianus was unlikely to have access to either their closely guarded coffers or their most treasured heirlooms, and tonight both would be required. Neither woman was given to shying away from direct participation in desperate political events.

Cassius Dio says that Eutychianus had the help of just a handful of others in the plot: some town councillors of Emesa (perhaps just six men of equestrian status, the second rank in Roman society, but the manuscript is defective), and a few freedmen and soldiers. One of these individuals can be identified as Festus, a freedman, who would be given an important role at Raphaneae by Eutychianus. Among the town councillors was one Aurelius Eubulus. From Emesa, Aurelius Eubulus was later a close companion of Heliogabalus and entrusted with a post of equestrian status crucial to the Emperor in Rome.

According to Herodian, the soldiers acted as guides and two others were included in the expedition. Maesa had another daughter and grandson. The boy, Alexianus, was even younger than Varius, about nine. Alexianus and his mother Mamaea were not central to the drama that was planned, but the perils of leaving them behind were evident. At least one other grandchild, but most likely two, who lived nearby, were left to their fate. Maesa was ruthless. If the gods were kind, they could be summoned in the morning.

So a small and unimpressive party then – three women, two children, a few ex-slaves and soldiers, and perhaps half a dozen locals – set off into the country. The path to Raphaneae ran north-west from Emesa. A medieval copy of a late Roman map, the so-called Peutinger Table, shows a road connecting the two places. The going was not difficult, across rolling hills and through olive groves. And the night would be mild, in the mid-fifties Fahrenheit (about thirteen Celsius). But the countryside was an alien environment. In bucolic poetry and novels it was a place of antique innocence, where rustic swains sought the love of virginal shepherdesses. In reality, it was something the elite rushed through to get from the safety of one town to another, or to the security of a landed estate. The countryside was infested with brigands. Across the empire tombstones were inscribed *interfectus a latronibus* (*killed by bandits* in Latin), or the like. People just vanished. It was advisable to make a last will and testament before setting out.

Worse than brigands haunted the countryside at night. It was then that the membrane that separated humanity from the denizens of the other world was especially porous. Daemons, vampires, werewolves, all sorts of creatures, were imagined to roam the dark hills and fields. Crossroads were especially bad. Travelling in the East, the philosopher Apollonius of Tyana had encountered a shape-shifter. It had fled at his shout. But Apollonius himself was touched with the divine and his was an unsuitable solution for those travelling covertly.

There was much more to unsettle the boy Varius than just the darkness and the countryside. He was wearing someone else's clothes, and he had a new name, a whole new identity. The man who had raised him had died a few years ago. Now he was told that the man had not been his father. No longer Varius Avitus Bassianus, the son of a Roman senator from Syria, now he was

Marcus Aurelius Antoninus, the illegitimate child of the murdered Emperor known as Caracalla. A far more dangerous inheritance. The boy knew, as did the adults, that if things did not go well at the camp, none of them would live to see another night.

II Domna's Plot

On the night of 15 May AD218 the stakes could not have been higher. There could be no hope of clemency. This was not the first time a woman of the family had conspired against the Emperor.

Julia Domna, the sister of Maesa, had been the wife of the Emperor Septimius Severus (AD193–211) and mother of the Emperor Caracalla (AD211–17). In the last three years of his reign, while Caracalla had been campaigning against the Parthians, Domna had remained in the Syrian city of Antioch. All correspondence to the Emperor had gone first to Domna. She had decided what should be forwarded to Caracalla. The rest she dealt with herself. In an autocracy, access to the ruler was power. Apart from the field army, all other aspects of imperial government in effect had been controlled by Domna.

The message, totally unexpected and devastating, had reached Domna by courier. Her son was dead. On 8 April AD217 Caracalla had left his winter quarters at Edessa in Mesopotamia to sacrifice at the Temple of Sin outside the town of Carrhae. Suffering from an upset stomach, he had dismounted to relieve himself. To give him some privacy, his escort had withdrawn and looked away. A soldier called Martialis approached, as if summoned by a nod. Martialis had a concealed dagger. Caracalla's back was turned, his trousers around his ankles. Just one blow was struck, catching the Emperor near the clavicle. Reaching his horse, Martialis tried to escape, but was brought down and killed by the javelins of Caracalla's barbarian bodyguards. Senior officers, including the praetorian prefect Macrinus, ran to the stricken Emperor. It was too late. The wound was fatal. Macrinus wept and lamented. The Emperor had been killed by an individual with a grudge. That, at least, was the official story.

Learning of the murder of her son, Domna resolved to die. Beating her breast, she inflamed a quiescent tumour. Refusing food, she began to starve herself. Macrinus, now proclaimed Emperor, sent her, along with the ashes of her son, a kindly letter of condolence. No change would be made to her royal retinue, or her guard of Praetorians. Domna rallied and took food. Yet she did not write back to the new Emperor. Instead, far from expressing any gratitude, she began to intrigue with the soldiers against Macrinus.

There was another version of the story of the assassination of Caracalla. The blow of Martialis had not proved fatal and he had not acted alone. Pretending to rush to the aid of the wounded Emperor, two brothers, Nemesianus and Apollinaris, tribunes of the Praetorians, had finished him off. Most of the headquarters staff were implicated in the plot, including Agrippa, the commander of the fleet, and Triccianus, the prefect of the Second Parthian Legion, who was seconded to the mounted escort. The whole conspiracy against Caracalla had been masterminded by his successor Macrinus.

Cassius Dio and Herodian both subscribe to the latter story: Macrinus was responsible for the assassination. It has been suggested that they merely reproduce the propaganda spread in the reign of Heliogabalus. This seems unlikely. Both historians detested Heliogabalus. Writing after his death, they had no reason to produce any version that might help to justify his uprising. Almost certainly, the rumours that Macrinus had been behind the killing of Caracalla flourished from the start. They would have reached the ears of Domna. Cassius Dio says that as soon as she heard of her son's death, Domna had indulged in bitter abuse of Macrinus.

Revenge on the killer of her son gave Domna a strong motive. A fragmentary passage of Cassius Dio adds another: fear that she might be deprived of her title of Augusta and that she might be forced to return to her native city of Emesa. As we will see, status was everything to the women of this family.

The intrigue of Domna was not to be dismissed lightly. Caracalla had been loved by the common soldiery. For almost a quarter of a century, the troops had taken their military oath to the 'Divine House' of the Severan dynasty. Honoured as 'Mother of the Camp', Domna was the central member of the imperial family. Funds were available. Apart from her own fortune, and that of her relatives, Domna was in wealthy Antioch, the imperial capital in the East. Detachments of many units, as well as the Praetorians assigned to Domna, would be stationed in the city. From its port of Seluceia Pieria, supplies and reinforcements flowed through Antioch to the field army with Macrinus in Edessa. Disaffection might easily spread.

Macrinus was decisive but circumspect. The open execution of Caracalla's mother would provoke unrest among the troops. Instead, Domna was ordered to leave Antioch and go wherever she wanted. If Praetorians still attended her, no doubt they were carefully chosen to watch her. To add to her misery, word reached Domna of rejoicing in Rome at Caracalla's death. Unlike the soldiers, the Senate and people in Rome had hated her son. There was no point in living. Although she was dying from cancer, she now went through with starving herself to death. Such is the account of Cassius Dio. That of Herodian is briefer and more sinister: 'she committed suicide [the Greek verb can mean either by starvation or hanging], perhaps without any prompting, or perhaps because she was ordered to do so.'

What had been the aim of Domna's intrigue? A recent study suggests that, as 'a woman could not rule', she had actually intended to put on the throne her great-nephew Heliogabalus (as we will now call Varius). A previous plot, a year before the flight to Raphaneae, is an intriguing idea. Yet, ultimately, it does not convince. Heliogabalus might not have been the obvious choice in the family. His father had died some years before, his maternal grandfather very recently, and an unknown sibling (we do not know if it was a brother or a sister) at some time between those dates. Yet other male relatives were alive. There was an uncle by marriage who had two children. One was a married daughter. The other, if blood was what mattered, was a son. This man, known via an inscription, and probably mentioned in a fragmentary passage of Cassius Dio, had been co-opted into the Arval Brethren, a college of priests, in AD214, three years previously. Thus, unlike Heliogabalus, he was an adult and a senator.

Other candidates aside, if Domna had advanced Heliogabalus as a pretender it is probable that he would have suffered the normal consequences of failure: death, or, at the very least, exile to a secure prison island. As we will see in the next section, Macrinus left Maesa in full possession of her wealth and sent her to live in Emesa with Heliogabalus. That would have been an act of immense political folly if her sister had just attempted to start a rebellion in his name. Summing up the reign of Macrinus, Cassius Dio wrote that he had been 'overthrown by a mere boy of whose very name he had previously been ignorant'.

Finally, it is worth looking closely at what Cassius Dio says about Domna's motives. 'She hoped to become sole ruler [*autarchese*: literally "independent of others"] like Semiramis and Nitocris, inasmuch as she came in a sense from the same parts as they.' Semiramis and Nitocris were legendary rulers in the East: Queens of Assyria and Egypt respectively. By pointing to her Syrian origins, Cassius Dio intended to ease his Greek and Roman readers into believing that Domna was aiming at such a 'barbaric' role. In fact, no woman would rule the Roman Empire in her own right for centuries; not until Irene, the widow of Leo IV, took the masculine title *Basileus* (AD797–802) in Constantinople, long after Rome itself was lost. Yet that does not automatically mean that Domna did not aspire to sole rule. From the inception of the Roman Empire, for two and a half centuries, no Emperor had been from an equestrian background, until Macrinus ascended the throne in AD217. Yet as early as the reign of Tiberius, the second Emperor (AD14–37), the equestrian praetorian prefect Sejanus was believed to have schemed to take the purple for himself.

Although it may have been unrealistic, after twenty-five years at the heart of the imperial court, the last three effectively running the empire, Domna might have sought to grasp sole power. Cassius Dio may not have been totally wide of the mark. As we will see, several factors in Domna's background in the East encouraged her ambitions. And the women of the Emesene dynasty were to confound contemporary expectations repeatedly.

III   *Maesa's Plot*

Maesa, although married to a leading senator, had lived at court with her sister throughout the reigns of Septimius Severus and Caracalla. She was with Domna in Antioch during the last fraught months. We are told nothing about her role in events, but she suffered in the aftermath. Macrinus ordered her to depart and live in her home town of Emesa. Ironically, it was the fate

Domna had feared for herself. Maesa was allowed to keep all her possessions, including the vast wealth accumulated in her decades close to the throne.

Maesa's husband, the senator Caius Julius Avitus Alexianus, had died recently of old age, serving as an adviser to the governor of Cyprus. So it was as an elderly widow that Maesa returned to the provincial town of her birth. At first glance it was an unpromising position from which to plot the overthrow of the Emperor. What induced her to take the terrible risk?

Maesa might have considered herself lucky to have survived the failed intrigue of her sister, but she was far from safe. In Roman law there were two types of exile. Those condemned under the harsher *deportatio* were confined to a specific place, usually an island. Their civic rights were removed, and, almost always, their property was confiscated. The milder penalty was *relegatio*, which entailed banishment from Rome, Italy, and, if applicable, their native province. Those suffering *relegatio* normally kept their estates, as well as their status and citizenship. Evidently, Maesa does not fit either of these categories. The will of the Emperor had legal force and overrode the niceties of temporal law. No formal sentence may have been passed on Maesa, but she can have been under no illusion that her condition was anything other than a form of internal exile.

There was serious cause for concern. All too often, the executioner followed the exile. A prominent person was got out of the way before being killed quietly off stage. The death sentence might arrive quickly, or after years of anxiety. Maesa knew this well from the experiences of her own family. Plautilla, the wife of Maesa's nephew Caracalla, was divorced and banished to Lipara in AD205. For the next seven years she lived in 'great fear and wretchedness', until the order for her death reached the island in AD212.

Maesa's vast fortune only added to the anxiety. Perennially short of funds, Roman Emperors frequently succumbed to the temptation of unjust condemnations of members of the elite in order to confiscate their wealth. To create a fictional rural idyll, the philosopher Dio Chrysostom imagined two peasant families left to their own devices when the Emperor executed the owner of the estate of which their smallholdings had once formed a remote part. No Emperor was specified. There was no need. His readers knew it was just what Emperors did. They killed the rich for their money. Rather than the aberration of tyrants, such behaviour can be interpreted as a structural part of imperial finances. Again, Maesa was all too aware of this threat. Her brother-in-law Septimius Severus had been notorious for convictions motivated by gain.

The two fears were inextricably linked. If Maesa were executed, her family would be reduced to penury. Together they made a potent incentive. But other factors urged her to take the ultimate gamble.

Maesa, quite rightly, held Macrinus responsible for the deaths of her nephew and sister. Revenge (*ultio*) was an honourable ambition, even a duty, in Rome. Emperors commonly killed the families of those executed for treason, not just out of wanton cruelty or greed but to safeguard their own future. Although it might be tempered by clemency (*clementia*), taking justified revenge was embedded in the value system of the Roman elite. It was the flipside of their much-vaunted giving of benefits to the deserving. The Dictator Sulla had inscribed as his epitaph that no one had outdone him in doing good to his friends, or harm to his enemies. Here, yet again, Maesa had the example of her family. Both Septimius Severus and Caracalla had praised to the Senate the severity of Sulla and Caracalla had restored the tomb of the Dictator, epitaph and all.

Fear and revenge were keen spurs to act. Another is given by Herodian. Maesa 'would rather have risked any danger than live as an ordinary person, apparently rejected'. She had a straightforward desire for status: the same motive ascribed to Domna by Cassius Dio. Living in a less hierarchical culture, we might be tempted to dismiss the idea. It could be written off as nothing more than a rhetorical flourish. Perhaps it was just a literary *topos*, borrowed from Cassius Dio by Herodian, and transferred to another character. Taking such a line would be a mistake. By the standards of their culture, both Cassius Dio and Herodian were acute judges of motivation. In many ways the Romans were similar to us, but in others they were very different. That was as true of their thinking as of externals like clothes or food. For them, the core of status was the concept of *dignitas*. Dignity in English is derived from the Latin word but does not convey its importance. For us, dignity is vaguely suspect, something to stand on, easily slipping over into self-importance and pomposity. For the Romans, *dignitas* was a key element of their identity. Famously, embarking on his own insurrection, Julius Caesar had announced that *dignitas* meant more to him than life itself. It was a sentiment Domna and Maesa might have echoed. And Maesa was about to put it to the test.

In many ways the time was promising for a rebellion. The new Emperor Macrinus was not yet settled on the throne. The army disliked him. As Caracalla's successor, Macrinus had inherited his war with Parthia. It had not gone well. In the summer of AD217, a battle at Nisibis in Mesopotamia had cost huge numbers of Roman casualties but brought no decisive victory. The latter, rumour had it, was because Macrinus had lost his nerve, and fled the field. His previous career as a lawyer might not have fostered physical courage and did nothing to endear him to the troops. Negotiating a peace treaty – one widely regarded as unsatisfactory to Roman interests – had necessitated keeping the army in the field over the winter of AD217–18. Short of supplies, and many living in tents through the inclement weather, the soldiers became resentful. Especially as Macrinus himself was said to be living in luxury in Antioch, cultivating his beard and discussing philosophy. Barbarian incursions into the province of Dacia caused unrest among the detachments of the field army drawn from the garrisons along the Danube. Their families were at risk and they demanded to go home. To make matters worse, Macrinus decreed that new recruits would not receive the increases in pay and privileges awarded the troops by Caracalla. The attempt at budgetary restraint might have been necessary, but it could not have been more untimely. Unsurprisingly, serving soldiers saw it as the first step to removing their own grants. And behind it all ran the story that Macrinus had been responsible for the death of Caracalla, their fellow-soldier.

If any of the Emperor's subjects ever compiled a handbook on insurrection, explaining in detail how it must be undertaken, his work of practical instruction has not survived. Modern scholarship has attempted to fill the gap. Successful military rebellions – as opposed to assassinations or palace coups – were led by men with great names: senators at the least, much better aristocrats, especially those commanding armies. First they got their own entourage and those serving in their province onside. Oracles might be consulted. Their predictions were always ambiguous, but if useful could be circulated. Divine favour counted for a lot. Enough to outweigh the risk of being denounced, or blackmailed by unscrupulous priests. Letters would be sent to the powerful: men who, like the sender, had troops. They contained promises of career advancement, both personal and for family and friends. More letters would go to rich provincials and important cities. Status and material rewards were offered. Finally, clandestine distributions of money were made to the soldiers. Every step was treasonous, and every step carried the death penalty. But the broadest base of support was needed.

Maesa arrived in Emesa in August AD217, at the earliest. She set off to Raphaneae with Heliogabalus in mid-May the following year. At most, nine months to organise an uprising. She would not have started planning straight away. Time was needed for her to identify her opportunity.

The patron deity of Emesa was Elagabal, a sun god, manifested as a large black, conical stone. The temple of Elagabal was wealthy. Herodian tells us that every year the governors of neighbouring provinces and barbarian kings sent costly offerings. The priesthood was controlled by Maesa's family. Once they had been kings of Emesa. When their monarchy had been abolished by the Emperor Domitian some five generations previously, her ancestors had channelled their energies into the cult, perhaps importing the god, to maintain their primacy in the city. The current priest was her great-nephew. Soldiers regularly came from the local garrison to worship. The Third Gallic Legion had been based at Raphaneae for well over a century. The majority of its recruits were Syrian. Elagabal was the ancestral god of some and culturally acceptable to all. Some of these soldiers were already clients of Maesa's family. A customary aspect of Roman society, the relationship of client and patron was reciprocal. The client showed respect to the patron and supported their aspirations, while the patron gave benefits to the client. Herodian implies that the soldiers frequenting the temple also had non-religious motives, taking erotic pleasure in watching young Heliogabalus officiate at the ceremonies. Given Roman sexuality, which we will explore in chapter 10, this is quite likely.

Here was Maesa's opportunity. A direct line into Raphaneae, and from there to all of the camps of the army in the East. She knew that the soldiers were dissatisfied with Macrinus and revered the memory of Caracalla. As Heliogabalus was chief priest, favourable oracles were not hard to produce. That similar utterances were forthcoming from other shrines is an indication of the influence of the family throughout the region. Maesa told the soldiers that Heliogabalus was the illegitimate son of Caracalla. Never mind that it branded her daughter an adulteress. Given the affair with Eutychianus, even had she wished Soaemias was in no good position to object. Maesa also took the irrevocable step of promising the troops money if they would restore the throne to her family.

We cannot be sure if Maesa spoke to the soldiers herself. Given their later prominent roles with the troops, Eutychianus and Festus might have been her envoys. That some of the soldiers were already clients of the family would have facilitated the approach. By the spring of AD218, several of the essentials of the revolt were in place. Maesa had obtained divine backing, although one assumes it had the enigmatic nature of all oracles. She had secured the support of the freedmen of her own entourage, as well as certain notables in Emesa, and had offered at least some of the nearby garrison money. Yet it was still a small group, with none of them senior officers. A worryingly narrow foundation for an armed insurrection.

A fascinating papyrus recording an attempted rebellion survives from Egypt. Although brilliantly reconstructed, the text is so fragmentary that the effect is like watching a damaged DVD: the picture pixilates, freezes, then jumps to a moment of clarity, before vanishing again. It is an official document: the account of the revolt being added to the morning report of a Roman army unit. The year is uncertain. We shall return to that (in chapter 5), as it may be in the reign of Heliogabalus himself. Most likely the rebellion was in Egypt, but again we cannot be sure. The report may have come from another province. Yet some specifics can be picked out. Timing was important. The coup was launched during a festival, when the troops were on holiday and discipline relaxed. Religion was repeatedly stressed. The standards, the shrine of the camp and the military oath are mentioned. As well as the troops, an attempt was made to win over civilians. The uprising was launched by an officer referred to as 'that prefect' (*ille praefectus*). Perhaps he was the prefect of Egypt, or of the Second Legion Triana Fortis stationed there, or of an auxiliary unit? Whatever his rank, it seems he acted with one centurion and ten soldiers. It shows that a rebellion could be started by a small group, without powerful backers. Yet the careful avoidance of the name of 'that prefect' also indicates that he failed.

The evidence of the papyrus points to the odds being very much against Maesa when she took Heliogabalus to Raphaneae. Like 'that prefect', she had the support of no men of high rank and influence. Why had Maesa not enlisted the governors and the barbarian kings with connections to the temple of Elagabal? The recruitment of the latter in a Roman civil war might have been unwise. Several barbarian monarchs offered their aid when the Emperor Vespasian made his bid for the throne. It was held to his credit that Vespasian had declined. Emesa was in the Roman province of Syria Phoenice. The governor, Marius Secundus, was away on official business in Egypt. Secundus, not long appointed, was loyal to Macrinus. The absence of Secundus actually allowed the plot to incubate. Yet we hear of no approaches to other governors. Later, after the outbreak of the revolt, when both sides sent letters trying to rally the provinces to their cause, Cassius Dio implies it was for the first time. A quarter of a century at court had taught Maesa the importance of the legions and their commanders. Something had brought the timing of the rebellion forward.

Ulpius Julianus, one of the two praetorian prefects recently installed by Macrinus, had arrived in Syria Phoenice. We are not told why he was there. With Secundus away, Julianus may have been given the task of overseeing the province and inspecting the troops in their winter quarters. Later, we hear of many deserters in the region, so perhaps Julianus was rounding them up.

It has been suggested that when Maesa set off to Raphaneae she was unaware of the proximity of Julianus. This is extremely improbable. A praetorian prefect travelled in some style. Julianus was accompanied by a unit of Moorish auxiliaries and had an escort of his own guardsmen. As well as being predominant in Emesa, Maesa's family had relatives and estates in the neighbouring cities of Apamea and Arca. As we will see, Julianus was in the vicinity of Arca. Maesa would have been informed of the arrival of the praetorian prefect.

Julianus, even before being rumoured to be implicated in the murder of Caracalla, had an unsavoury reputation. One of his previous posts had been commander of the *frumentarii*. Despite their anodyne name – which implied something to do with the grain supply or rations – the *frumentarii* were the nearest thing Rome had to a secret service. They were the Emperor's confidential messengers. More sinisterly, they were his spies and assassins. As praetorian prefect, Julianus remained responsible for their activities.

The appearance of Julianus in Phoenice terrified Maesa. At the least, he was well placed to uncover her treasonous intrigues. At the worst, news had already leaked and the praetorian prefect had orders for her arrest and execution. Maesa had intended to strike while the army was still in winter quarters, and before the return of Secundus. Many parts of the plot were in place: the oracles, her freedmen, a few local dignitaries and some legionaries of the Third Gallica. But she had yet to secure the adherence of a single army commander. There was no time for that now. The arrival of Julianus precipitated her frantic nocturnal flight from Emesa.

IV *The Acclamation*

Maesa, with Heliogabalus and the rest of her ragtag little party – tired, travel-worn and apprehensive – reached Raphaneae well before dawn. The approach was forbidding. In the gloom, as they came down from the eastern hills, the slope on their right was pitted with dark quarries, the skyline notched with tombs. Raphaneae lay in a valley dominated by a sanctuary – to what deity we do not know – on an eminence to the west. As far as we can tell the town was unwalled. They went through the quiet streets of the civilian settlement to the walls of the legionary fortress. Arriving, they found that the gates were shut. This was a moment of the gravest danger. If they were not admitted, the revolt was over and their lives would soon be forfeit.

The fortress was the home of *Legio III Gallica*. It was a legion with a long and proud history. Founded in the 40s BC by Julius Caesar, partly from veterans of his conquest of Gaul, hence its name, it had fought in Spain at Munda, the final battle of the civil wars that had brought him to sole power. A decade later it had campaigned under Mark Antony at the far end of the empire, against the Parthians beyond the Euphrates. The legion remained in the East for a century and acquired permanent eastern ways. Briefly returned to the West during another civil war, in Italy at the second battle of Bedriacum in AD 69, as dawn broke the soldiers of the Third turned to the East and hailed the rising sun. This Syrian religious ritual was thought by the rest of the army to herald the arrival of reinforcements.

The misinterpretation lifted morale and was pivotal to victory. The following year *Legio III* was sent back to the East to make its base at Raphaneae. And there it had remained for almost a hundred and fifty years. By AD218 the vast majority of its recruits had long been locals: the sons of soldiers, or easterners with Roman citizenship.

To the relief of Maesa and her adherents, the gates swung open. Herodian says the garrison immediately saluted the boy as Emperor. Most likely this is a simplification. Not all the soldiers were in the plot, and the events of the next days show that the legion was unprepared for revolt. There would have been negotiation.

Who did the rebels negotiate with? We hear nothing of any mutiny, so it would have been the officers. Syria Phoenice was a one legion province, so the commander of the Third Gallica was the governor, Marius Secundus. But, as we have seen, Marius Secundus was away in Egypt. In theory, in the absence of the legate, the next most senior officer was the senatorial military tribune. There were six tribunes in a legion: five equestrians, and one from a senatorial family. For all his high social status, the latter was a young man doing military service at the start of his career. In practice, command devolved onto the *praefectus castrorum*, the prefect of the camp, an ex-centurion. A minority of centurions were equestrians, who entered the army at that rank. The vast majority, however, were soldiers who had risen through the ranks: tough professionals in late middle age. There is a temptation to identify the prefect of the Third as one Publius Valerius Comazon. We will meet Comazon again, but at Raphaneae there is a better candidate. Subsequently in the revolt the rebels promoted men within their units. By the end of the year the legate of *III Gallica* was an ex-centurion called Verus. Events would prove that Verus was both ambitious and a risk-taker. As the governor of Syria Phoenice usually would have been based in the capital of the province, probably the city of Tyre, the legionaries at Raphaneae would have been accustomed to taking orders from the prefect of the camp. Verus was the key man who had to be won over.

In the last hours of the night, who undertook the delicate task of persuading Verus and the rest of the legion? The army was, in the phrase of sociologists, a 'total institution'. For a recruit, the identity of 'soldier' largely superseded any previous affiliations. Soldiers had little sympathy for outsiders, like those in Maesa's party. They had no time for civilians. When the philosopher Dio Chrysostom – old and unarmed and with no official position – visited an army camp on the Danube, he was amazed they could even stand the sight of him. Women, obviously, had no role in the army. When Agrippina 'acted as a commander', and quelled a panic on the Rhine, it earned her the lifelong mistrust of the Emperor Tiberius. When Narcissus, the freedman of the Emperor Claudius, tried to address the troops before the invasion of Britain, they refused to let him speak, shouting '*Io Saturnalia*', from the festival where slaves were allowed to dress as their masters.

Despite such prejudices, the attempt had to be made. Perhaps the freedmen spoke first – Eutychianus of course, possibly Festus – then the women – Maesa and Soaemias. Soldiers could be sentimental about children of the imperial family. Maybe Heliogabalus was coached to make a speech. If so, we have no record of what he said. But Maesa had been in Rome seven years before, when her nephew (and now the supposed father of Heliogabalus) had spoken to the troops at a similarly fraught moment. After murdering his brother, when the loyalty of the soldiers was uncertain, Caracalla had gone to the Praetorian camp and said, 'I am one of you, and it is because of you alone that I care to live, that I may confer on you many favours; for all the treasuries are yours.' At Raphaneae something on those lines would have chimed well with Maesa's promises to distribute all her wealth to the troops.

At sunrise, the soldiers acclaimed Heliogabalus as *Imperator*. The time was propitious both for the sun-worshipping legionaries of the Third and the young priest of the specific solar god of Emesa. The youth was draped in a purple cloak. Had the family brought it with them, or was it found in the shrine of the camp? In some impromptu acclamations a cloak had to be stripped from the shoulders of a deity in a nearby temple. There was other paraphernalia of an Emperor: a diadem or even a crown, special clothes and boots. But it was the cloak that mattered. Heliogabalus added a personal touch. He strapped on a sword. A nice touch that symbolised both a transition to manhood and his fellowship with the soldiers.

After the acclamation the soldiers took the *sacramentum*, the military oath. The wording varied over time. In the previous century, the crucial element of the oath had been to 'value the safety of the Emperor above everything'. Only one man in each unit recited the entire formula: the rest in turn just said '*idem in me*' (the same for me). Although to us the ritual might appear slightly comical – all of those soldiers parroting *idem in me, idem in me...* – and in the third century soldiers often broke their oath, it should not be dismissed as a piece of meaningless theatre. The Romans believed in their gods (as we will see in chapter 8), and modern studies demonstrate that the military oath remains important to contemporary servicemen and women.

What had induced the men of *III Gallica* to break their oath to the reigning Emperor and throw in their lot with a fourteen-year-old boy? On any calculation, it was a reckless move. There were some thirty-three legions in the army. Stories of Caracalla's newly discovered son might be circulating, but there was no certainty that any other legion would follow the lead of the Third at Raphaneae. Several interlocking motives had come together. There was dislike of Macrinus, who had displayed cowardice in the field, was living in luxury in Antioch, was thought likely to remove their recently granted extra pay and privileges and was rumoured to have been behind the murder of their 'fellow-soldier' Caracalla. Then affection for Caracalla, loyalty to his dynasty and perhaps sentiment towards his child. Perhaps shared religion played a part. And then there was money. Modern scholars often downplay money. If they valued it highly, they would have chosen a different profession. Contemporaries, albeit members of the elite, had no doubt of its importance to the Roman soldiery. They wanted cash, vast amounts of cash.

The first public step of the revolt had been a triumph for Maesa and her wealth: *idem in me, idem in me…*

V Maesa's Face

What was she like, this aged woman who had started a civil war and put her entire family at risk to place her grandson on the throne? We will form an estimate of her character from her actions, but somehow that does not seem enough. We need to put a face to the name. What did she look like?

A beguiling answer has been offered: a portrait bust from Hierapolis in Syria, usually dated on stylistic grounds to about the right time (*c.*AD218–35). A motif of a stylised acanthus leaf, common on funerary monuments, joining the bust to its pedestal suggests a posthumous image.

This is just how we feel Maesa should look: large, protruding eyes, sunken cheeks, a great, humped beak of a nose, a strong,

Image 2: A Portrait Bust of Maesa?

jutting chin. Gaunt and fierce, this is a woman who would sacrifice any number of her grandchildren to her indomitable will.

Unfortunately, beyond coming from Syria (and Hierapolis
is a long way from Emesa), and, as we will see, *possibly* dating to
about the right time, actually there is very little to connect the
bust to Maesa.

We need to bring out into the open two seldom mentioned
motives for identifying Classical portraits with known individuals. First – and it is very understandable – a portrait of an
empress or the like just seems more exciting, somehow more
significant than one of a nonentity. Second – and much more
dubious – in the modern antiquities market (a notoriously venal

and unprincipled place) a portrait of a well-known individual is much, much more valuable. Some art historians *need* to put a name to the face.

Let us compare the bust to a portrait of Maesa on an imperial coin. We will explore later (in chapter 9) the fascinating issues of who chose coin types and how they were 'read' by different groups in the empire. For now, it is enough to note that this is an 'official' image put out by the regime that was expected to bear a definite resemblance to reality.

Image 3: An Official Portrait of Maesa and the Virtue of Chastity

Maesa's image on the coin – at least to my eyes – looks rather different from the bust. Her nose is straight and her chin is less pronounced. Her face is plumper, with fuller cheeks and a roll of flesh on the neck.

If we look at their hair styles (although we can't see much on the bust, as she wears a veil) both women have a central parting. This can lead to a circular argument. Ordinary women are thought to have copied the hairstyles of members of the imperial family (although how long was it before such imitation took place – a year, two, maybe twenty, and how long did they continue the fashion?). As the hair of the sculpture is somewhat like that of Maesa on the coinage, the bust must date to roughly the same time. Then the argument is flipped. As the bust dates to the right period, and has the same hair style as the empress, it must be Maesa.

Maesa's hair on the coin is modelled on that of her sister, the empress Julia Domna, and hers in turn looked back to that of an earlier empress, Faustina the Younger. It stresses continuity. Nothing innovative here – just another female member of the imperial house.

There is a danger of importing our anachronistic value judgements to such things. Back in the reign of Trajan, when we know from literature that the public role of imperial women was at its most circumscribed, their elaborate coiffures can seem to us to indicate flamboyant self-advertisement. Yet, despite the risk, it is hard not to see Maesa's hair – carefully ordered, scraped back into a sensible bun – as indicating reticence and an almost self-effacing modesty. This image is supported by the labelled personification on the reverse of the coin: *Pudicitia*, Bashfulness or Chastity. *Pudicitia* features on forty-six percent of Maesa's known issues. Her other main types – *Saeculi Felicitas* (the good fortune of the age, twenty-eight percent) and *Pietas* (Piety, thirteen percent) – are equally traditional. The image of Maesa put out by the imperial mint was conservative and uncontroversial: a respectable Roman matron, a repository of antique virtues. As we will see, that image, perhaps deliberately, was deeply misleading.

VI *The Siege* – 1

The praetorian prefect Ulpius Julianus was 'at no great distance' from Raphaneae: probably at the town of Arca (also known as Caesarea ad Libanum). It was about forty miles south-west of

Raphaneae. News of the uprising could have reached him by sunset of 16 May, but certainly within a couple of days.

A praetorian prefect was second in power only to the Emperor. By the early third century the prefects had acquired wide legal and administrative authority. Yet the crucial element of their power remained military. The only men allowed to be armed in the presence of the Emperor, the prefects commanded the nine thousand or so bodyguard of the Praetorians. The danger they posed was evident. Who guards the guards? (*Quis custodiet ipsos custodes?*), in the famous phrase of the satirist Juvenal. The Emperors tried to minimise the risk. They almost always appointed two prefects. Should one turn traitor, the other might remain loyal. With only a couple of exceptions, they selected men from the equestrian order rather than senators. The hope here was that should a prefect attempt to set himself on the throne the traditional elite would offer him no support. Although the Emperor Commodus had been killed by a prefect, and rumour had it that Tiberius had been finished off by another, in general the checks had worked well for two centuries. The reigning Emperor Macrinus was the first prefect to usurp the man he had sworn to defend.

Ulpius Julianus was loyal to Macrinus. His first known post was *princeps peregrinorum*, commander of the *frumentarii*, the imperial secret service, which indicates that Julianus was a military man. At the end of Caracalla's reign, he was in charge of the census in Rome (*a censibus*). From that position he had written to warn Macrinus that he had been denounced, and thus precipitated the plot which led to the death of Caracalla. As the new Emperor, Macrinus rewarded Julianus by making him one of his praetorian prefects. Julianus' colleague, Nestor, was with Macrinus in Antioch. Interestingly, Nestor had also once commanded the secret service.

Julianus acted decisively. Two members of the Emesene family were caught and executed. Maesa's daughter Mamaea in turn had a married daughter, whose name we do not know. The latter woman, and her husband, were the unfortunate victims. Mamaea's husband, Gessius Marcianus, came from Arca. Most likely his daughter was apprehended on their family estates.

Julianus knew that the revolt of *III Gallica* had to be stopped quickly, before it had any chance to spread to other units. Cassius Dio tells us that Julianus collected 'as many of the remaining soldiers as he could in the short time at his disposal'. As prefect, he would have been accompanied by a detachment of Praetorians. We know that at Raphaneae he led Moorish troops. Sent to serve in the Roman army in fulfilment of a treaty with Caracalla, these Moors would have been tribal levies rather than regular units of auxiliaries. As the imperial field army had wintered in Syria, there may have been other troops quartered near Arca. Having gathered what forces were available, Julianus set off to Raphaneae.

The rebels at Raphaneae had not been inactive. Raphaneae was an unusual garrison town. In the eastern provinces, legions were stationed in existing cities. At Raphaneae there is no literary or archaeological evidence for a settlement before the arrival of *Legio III*. As was common in the western provinces, the city of Raphaneae grew around the fortress of the legion.

Although, in a sense, it was *their* city, the civilian town was unwalled, and the legionaries of the Third Gallica made no attempt to defend Raphaneae. Instead, Herodian tells us, 'they moved all their supplies and children and wives from the settlements and land nearby into the camp, before shutting the gates and preparing to withstand a siege'.

The actions of the rebels are revealing in two ways. First, the majority of *Legio III* was not prepared for the uprising. Second, the rebels did not feel strong enough to face Julianus in the field. A legion had a paper strength of about five thousand men. But natural wastage – retirement, death, desertion and detached duties – meant fighting strength was usually lower. Most likely, the rebels thought they would be outnumbered by the forces of the praetorian prefect.

When Julianus marched down into the valley of Raphaneae he would have summoned the Third Gallica to hand over Heliogabalus and Maesa and the others. The summons was refused. Lacking a siege train, Julianus could not batter down the walls of the camp, and he did not have time to starve its occupants out. He decided to assault the gates. Battering rams were easily improvised. The troops chosen were the Moors.

There is something odd here. In ancient battle the Moors were light troops: either unarmoured javelin men, rushing forward on foot to hurl their missiles, then sprinting away, or dashing horse-men, riding without bridles, controlling their ponies with a stick and wheeling back and forth as they harassed more ponderous foes. They were not intended for work close to the steel, and not ideal for storming fortifications defended by legionaries. But, like them, Macrinus was from North Africa. Julianus thought they would fight bravely for an Emperor who shared their ethnicity. Morale trumped tactical experience.

Julianus was right. The Moors broke open the gates. And then, with the camp at his mercy, Julianus called them back. A modern theory asserts they were recalled because the rest of Julianus' troops were mutinous and refused to enter the camp. It exemplifies 'knowing more than our sources'. Cassius Dio gives alternative explanations. Either Julianus 'was afraid to rush in', or he now expected the defenders to surrender. Because Cassius Dio thoroughly disapproved of Julianus, the latter is to be preferred. As dusk fell, Julianus was confident that the rebels would be in his hands the next day. It was a fatal mistake.

In the night, no overtures were made by the besieged. By the light of early morning Julianus saw that the gates had been barricaded during the darkness. He ordered another assault. This time it accomplished nothing. An extraordinary procession appeared on the battlements: soldiers carrying pictures and heavy purses and a youth in a purple cloak. The soldiers brandished the purses, calling out that they were full of money. Perhaps they gestured at Heliogabalus and the images of Caracalla as a child. 'Why do you do this, fellow-soldiers?', Cassius Dio tells us they shouted, 'Why do you fight against your benefactor's son?'

VII Finding a Father

Where had they found these paintings of a young Caracalla? It should not have been difficult. Images of the Emperor were ubiquitous: 'in all money-changers booths, shops, bookstalls, eaves, porches, windows, anywhere and everywhere'. Fearing the army, Macrinus had not condemned the memory of Caracalla. Images of Emperors, past and present, were kept in the shrine of legionary camps. Perhaps the images of Caracalla resembled that on a famous painting.

There is the young Caracalla: curly-headed, plump-cheeked, lustrous-eyed. He is watched over by his father, Septimius Severus, crowned, tanned and with neatly parted beard, and his mother, Julia Domna, adorned with earrings and necklace, and with the carefully arranged hair and paler skin appropriate for the indoors life of a woman. The picture of a model family. Except our eye is drawn to the missing figure, to that brown blur. After the death of their father, Caracalla had his brother Geta murdered and his memory condemned. The official story was that Caracalla had been saved from a plot against his own life. The unknown

Image 4: The Severan Dynasty with Geta Removed

owner of this tondo – some well-off subject in Egypt – had demonstrated his loyalty by having Geta expunged. That had not been enough. Where Geta's face had been was smeared with human excrement. The brown blur is shit.

The disappearance of Geta helped open a conceptual space for the discovery of a new member of the dynasty, for a previously unsuspected son of Caracalla, for Heliogabalus.

Roman families were very different from modern western ones. Let's not even consider the slaves and freedmen included in the *familia*. Let's stick to the nuclear family: those publicly acknowledged by blood and marriage. Its boundaries were less rigid, its composition potentially more fluid. Some individuals suddenly vanished, while others just as suddenly appeared.

A husband wrote a letter to his wife: 'If you bear a child, if it is a male, let it live; if it is female expose it.' Unwanted babies – both boys and girls, and not always those of the poor – were left to die on dung heaps or out in the wilds. Some were 'rescued' by dealers to be reared as slaves. Then again, people of all ages and classes could walk out of the door and never be seen again: especially if they went to sea or ventured into the countryside. Their fate remained uncertain. Some just chose to disappear. But others were lost to illness or accident, were *interfectus a latronibus* or kidnapped by those same bandits to be sold into slavery. Their families never knew what had happened to them. They were just gone. Another category of the 'disappeared' was those in the imperial family, or among the elite, who were declared guilty of treason (*maiestas*). Their memory was condemned. Officially they had never existed, but they at least left a presence by their very absence: the chiselled off letters of an inscription, the faint smell of shit on a work of art.

While individuals might drop out of a family, others jumped fully formed into its ranks. The root cause was inheritance. A Roman *pater familias* was expected to divide his estate equitably between his sons and provide lavish dowries for his daughters. Fearing division of his family wealth, and his descendants' loss of status, he sought to limit the number of his heirs. There were inefficient methods of contraception, involving sponges, pessaries or magic. A more certain form of family planning was for the *pater familias* to have sex with his slaves, not with his wife. Should pregnancy result, he gained a valuable slave rather than another expensive and unwanted heir.

In an age of high mortality, of frequent lethal fevers – let alone execution and murder – there was a serious danger that the one or two legal heirs might predecease the father. To prevent the family dying out the Roman elite turned to adoption. Stemming from different causes, and fulfilling different emotional needs, this also was quite unlike the modern western practice. The adopted son was an adult, sometimes little younger than his new father. The Emperor Septimius Severus – who now at Raphaneae was claimed as the natural grandfather of Heliogabalus – had stretched the already flexible boundaries of Roman adoption when he had himself declared the son of Marcus Aurelius, the Emperor who had been dead for some fifteen years. A senator, known for his biting wit, had the audacity to congratulate Severus on 'finding a father'.

Adoption – real or fictitious – was not the only way to enter, or 're-enter', a family. There was also identity theft. The first Emperor Augustus was confronted by a man claiming to be his dead nephew. The impostor said he had been switched with another child in infancy. Augustus condemned him to be chained to the oar of a galley. In his *Memorable Deeds and Sayings*, Valerius Maximus devoted a whole chapter to 'People who were born very low but tried to insinuate themselves into glorious families by lying'. After the death of Nero at least three men won a brief following by claiming to be the returned Emperor.

Like *The Return of Martin Guerre*, we only hear of those Romans whose imposture was exposed. Assuming the identity of another was easier in ancient Rome. Lacking photographs, the appearance of a long-lost relative was harder to judge. Without modern mirrors, when only the rich caught a blurred and distorted reflection of themselves in expensive polished metal, individuals could not even be certain of their own image. The miraculous reappearance of the long-lost child was deeply embedded in the culture of the Roman Empire. It was widespread in myths, including those about the origins of Rome: Romulus and Remus. It was also the standard plot of almost every Greek novel of the first three centuries AD. A shepherd and a shepherdess (or some other roles equally humble and bucolic) are kidnapped, and after a series of picaresque adventures they return home and are revealed as the misplaced children of two elite families. Novels shape our expectations. These Greek novels, denigrated as *Romances*, were once dismissed as read only by adolescents and women. Now they are considered to have been written by and mainly for adult males of the elite. The inhabitants of the empire – of all ages and classes – were more predisposed than us to accept the reality of the unexpected revelation of a long-lost relative.

The scrubbing out of Geta created a gap in the imperial house. Septimius Severus' posthumous adoption by Marcus Aurelius, and stories like those in the Greek novels, eased Heliogabalus into that opening.

VIII *The Siege – 2*

'Why do you do this, fellow-soldiers?' they shouted, 'Why do you fight against your benefactor's son?'

The soldiers of Julianus held back. Cassius Dio claims that, unhappy with Macrinus, they were looking for an excuse to mutiny. To their eyes the boy up on the ramparts did resemble the young Caracalla. It was, Herodian says, what they wanted to see. While their centurions and other officers tried to keep the soldiers loyal, the rebels in the camp seized the initiative.

Eutychianus sent the other freedman Festus out to persuade them to come over. Any soldier who killed a recalcitrant officer was promised the dead man's wealth and rank. (This, it should be noted, is the evidence for the rebels promoting men within their units.)

Cassius Dio tells us that Festus was named after a favourite freedman of Caracalla: the *a cubiculo* who had looked after his bedchamber. It has been suggested that there was more to it, that Festus actually was pretending that he *was* Caracalla's *a cubiculo*. It would be a sort of double identity theft: Maesa's freedman masquerading as Caracalla's freedman, while attempting to persuade the soldiers that Marcellus' son was that of Caracalla. At first glance the idea seems unlikely. The *a cubiculo* had died in AD214 on Caracalla's final journey to the East. Caracalla had buried him at Troy with elaborate and eccentric ceremonies. The dead Festus had played Patroclus to the Emperor's Achilles: yet another identity theft, this time posthumous. However, as we saw in the last section, there was a readiness to accept men back from the grave, and popular knowledge of recent history was often in error. We will explore the latter in chapter 13. For now, it is enough to note that if contemporaries were often mistaken about something as significant as how an Emperor had died, the soldiers might have been unaware that an ex-slave who oversaw the Emperor's bedroom had died at all.

Whatever role Festus was playing at Raphaneae, it took courage to leave the relative safety of the camp and put himself in the hands of the besiegers. With the vagaries of our evidence, this is the last thing we know about Festus.

From the walls of the camp young Heliogabalus also harangued Julianus' soldiers 'with words that had been put into his mouth'. Who had placed them there: Eutychianus or Maesa? In a fragmentary passage, Cassius Dio tells what he said in reported speech. Heliogabalus praised 'his father' and almost certainly criticised Macrinus, whose name appears in a gap of about fourteen lines. When the text partially resumes, Heliogabalus appears to be talking about restoring the privileges of the soldiers – deserters will resume their rank – and promises to recall exiles.

The words of Heliogabalus and Festus were effective. Coming over to the rebels, the soldiers turned on and killed their own commanders, 'with the exception of Julianus, who escaped in flight'. The praetorian prefect got away – for now…

CHAPTER 2 THE BACKSTORIES

Rome and Emesa: 753BC to AD218

How did a Roman legion come to acclaim a Syrian youth as Emperor? We could point out, as we did in the last chapter, that most of the legionaries of *III Gallica* were Syrians themselves. But that just sidesteps the question. It does not explain the Praetorians, mainly recruited from the Danube, or the Moors at Raphaneae, or the other units that went over to Heliogabalus later in the revolt. The sidestep raises other questions. How had *Legio III*, raised long ago from the Italian veterans of Julius Caesar, ended up being staffed by soldiers born along the Orontes? How had Heliogabalus' family become Roman citizens? To answer these questions we need to explore Rome's openness to outsiders – an openness almost unique in the Classical world – and first we need to go back to Year One, the founding of Rome, all the way back to Romulus and Remus.

I *Rome: The Children of the Wolf*

The story is well known. Or, rather, the stories. Writers from the first century BC on have many variants. Here we will give the commonest version (with just the occasional alternative).

Aeneas, having escaped from the sack of Troy, founds a dynasty at the Italian town of Alba Longa. A later king dies and his bad son, Amulius, deprives his good son, Numitor, of the throne. To secure his succession, the bad king deals with the children of the good one: the son is killed and the daughter is either locked up or consecrated as a Vestal Virgin. Despite these precautions, Rhea, the daughter, becomes pregnant by the god Mars (or maybe by a spark from the sacred hearth fire), and gives birth to Romulus and Remus. Amulius has the cradle of the twins thrown into the Tiber. It snags on a wild fig tree at the foot of the Palatine Hill. Romulus and Remus are suckled by a she-wolf (or, perhaps, a prostitute – in Latin, *lupa*, she-wolf, was slang for a street whore). A good shepherd finds the boys and brings them up. As they grow their bravery makes them leaders of the local shepherds. Learning their true identity, the twins overthrow Amulius and restore Numitor. Deciding to found their own city, they turn to augury (observing the flight of birds) to learn the will of the gods: Remus on the Aventine, Romulus on the Palatine. Remus sees six vultures, but Romulus trumps him with twelve (both the number and type of bird are variously recorded). With a plough, Romulus lays out a plan of the walls. Remus laughs and jumps over the furrow. So Romulus kills his brother. To populate his new foundation, Romulus welcomes paupers, debtors, criminals and runaway slaves. Lacking females, Romulus invites a neighbouring people, the Sabines, to a religious festival, which is a ploy to abduct their women. The ensuing war is ended by the women reconciling their kinsmen and their new 'husbands'. The two peoples merge into one community, jointly ruled by Romulus and Tatius, the Sabine king. After the death of Tatius (killed by Romulus in some tellings), Romulus rules alone. The death of Romulus is mysterious. Either, out of sight of mankind, the gods take him up to heaven, or the senators murder him in secret, chop up his corpse and smuggle out the body parts in the folds of their togas.

Whether any of this bears any relationship to real events is not the point. The name Romulus looks like it is made up from the name of the city, Roma. After much debate, the Romans settled on the year of the foundation as our 753BC, but archaeology reveals settlement on the Palatine from about 1000BC.

And whether the Romans really believed these stories were true is also not the point, though quite probably many did. What matters here is that these were the stories that later Romans told about their own origins. These stories both reflect and shape Roman views of themselves. They encapsulate their identity.

It is an extraordinary set of foundation myths. Yes, it shows the Romans supported by the gods (the paternity of Mars, the possible ascension of Romulus), and that they heeded the gods (the birds over the Palatine); or, at least, most of the time (inviting the Sabines to a duplicitous festival?). It reveals the Romans as tough, even ruthless, warriors (the twins become leaders of the shepherds because of their courage), ready to start aggressive wars, although with good cause (the deposition of bad Amulius, fighting the Sabines to ensure the continuance, or safety, of Rome). The story of the murder of Romulus indicates a commitment to political freedom, and – worth bearing in mind in the reign of Heliogabalus – gives a mythic justification for tyrannicide. But the myths also have a very dark side. They seem to condone criminality, rape, murder, even fratricide. At the beginning is a wolf (the ravening enemy of mankind and its flocks), or a prostitute, and the dregs of humanity: all those paupers, debtors, criminals and runaway slaves. Those incomers are most important for us here. The Romans thought that right from the foundation of the city Rome had welcomed outsiders. Granting Roman citizenship, albeit very much on Rome's terms (remember the Sabine women!), was enshrined in myth.

Moving from myth to history, Rome's extraordinary willingness to grant citizenship, as much as the legions' proficiency in warfare, underpinned her rise to empire (the Romans personified Roma as female). It gave a reserve of manpower unmatched by her adversaries. In ancient wars, rather than specific battles, the gods were on the side of the big battalions. Under the Republic (509–31 BC) grants of citizenship were made to individuals and groups, usually for exemplary service in war. For communities there was an institutional 'halfway house' to citizenship in Latin rights. It took three methods, the implementation of which varied over time. The two annual leading magistrates of Latin towns became Romans. The children of a Roman who married a Latin became Roman. Latins had the right to migrate to Rome, and, providing they left someone to fulfil their duties in their hometown, they could take up Roman citizenship. Originally, the Latins were the inhabitants of Latium, around Rome. Later the status was awarded to towns throughout Italy. As their power spread, the Romans settled veterans in colonies, with either full citizen or Latin status, throughout Italy. There was another Roman social process at work: one noted by the Greeks, who found it very strange. Compared with most ancient cultures, the Romans freed many slaves. They did so for personal aggrandisement or profit and to act as a pressure valve, reducing the chances of servile insurrection. What was yet more unusual among ancient polities, and what really caught the attention of Greek observers, was that these slaves, if manumitted in proper legal form, became Roman citizens. A freedman was a citizen, although debarred from serving as a magistrate, or joining the army. His sons were full citizens.

The spread of citizenship was not always a harmonious development. In 91–87 BC Rome faced a revolt by her Italian allies: the so-called Social War (after *Socii*, the Latin for allies). Some of the rebels fought for independence from Roman domination. But the motives of the majority were different. The war ended when the Romans offered citizenship: first to those who had not yet joined the rebellion and then to those who would lay down their arms. Only a few fought on. After the Social War all Italians south of the river Po were citizens. In the 40s BC Julius Caesar extended citizenship to Sicily and those across the Po.

Under the rule of the Emperors, these processes spread citizenship beyond Italy and out into the provinces. After the reign of Augustus (31BC–AD14) new colonies tended not to be settlements of veterans but grants of status to existing towns. The professionalisation of the Roman army added a new and important engine of inclusion. To join a legion a recruit had to already be a Roman citizen (at least in theory). But almost all the auxiliary units were composed of non-citizens. On discharge, after twenty-five years with the standards, all auxiliaries were awarded a diploma (many of which survive) proving their new status as Roman citizens. Given it has been estimated that there were between 130,000 and 220,000 auxiliaries serving at any one time, the numbers involved were large.

In AD212, Caracalla – the Emperor claimed in 218 as Heliogabalus' father – granted citizenship to all the free subjects of his empire. Only a mysterious group called the *dediticii* (the Latin might suggest they were surrendered barbarians?) were excluded from what is now known as the *Constitutio Antoniniana*. What were Caracalla's motives? Just two ancient sources mention the edict. One, Cassius Dio, dismisses it in one sentence: a money-raising measure, as some taxes were not paid by non-citizens. The other appears to be an extract of the actual imperial decree preserved on a damaged papyrus. In Caracalla's own words (or those of an imperial secretary?) the motivation was religious:

so that the Emperor could lead all to the gods, to share in his victory. The latter, presumably, being his preservation from the 'conspiracy' of his brother Geta, whom he had recently murdered. Modern scholars add a wider motive – to create a Roman unity in the face of the increasing barbarian pressures of the third century.

That the edict leaves so few traces in our sources might encourage us to see it as merely the uncontroversial culmination of a long process. But the choice of Roman names (what scholars like to call onomastic practice) points in another direction. A Roman had three names (Caracalla's official name was Marcus Aurelius Antoninus). It was customary for a new citizen to take the *nomen* (the middle, family name) of the man who had secured his citizenship. After AD212 there was a flood of men called Aurelius. For example, a papyrus from Dura-Europos on the Euphrates lists soldiers from an auxiliary unit. From AD193 to 212 there are eight Aurelii, twelve other Romans and thirty-three non-Romans. From AD212 to 217, when they are all citizens, there are fifty-five Aurelii and just nineteen other names. Clearly, before the *Constitutio Antoniniana* most inhabitants of the empire were not citizens. Although largely ignored by our sources, and no matter how short-term Caracalla's intentions, the huge numbers of new citizens would have had a significant impact, especially in Roman law, which everyone now had to use.

Heliogabalus was eight when Caracalla issued the *Constitutio Antoniniana*. As we will see in the next section, his family had held Roman citizenship for many generations. The edict will have made little mark on the child. His adult kin, however, may have found it slightly disconcerting. The tenants on their estates, their clients and the free among their household servants now shared what previously had been a privilege reserved for the family.

For those families that were rich, educated (in Latin and Greek) and well connected, citizenship could lead to further increases in status. Every freeborn citizen who possessed an estate worth 400,000 sesterces – a very substantial sum: a legionary under Septimius Severus probably received 1,800 sesterces a year – became an equestrian, the second-highest tier in Roman society. The Senate, the summit of the social pyramid – some six hundred of the richest landowners in the empire – were largely recruited from the equestrian order. The senatorial order was not a closed, hereditary aristocracy. It has been calculated that at any given moment about two thirds to three quarters of senators were *novi homines*: the first members of their families to enter the curia. Many established senatorial families failed to produce further generations of senators. They had no heirs, or their descendants either chose not to enter the Senate – under the eyes of suspicious Emperors, it was a dangerous eminence – or fell below the wealth qualification of one million sesterces. *Novi homines* also might suffer a certain disdain, especially if they were from the provinces (we will look at that in chapter 4). Yet generally, the non-reproduction of existing senatorial families eased the acceptance of these newcomers.

Over the centuries, membership of the Senate had rippled out from the centre: from Rome to Italy, and from there to the civilised provinces: to southern Gaul, Spain, Africa and the Greek East. In the reign of Vespasian (AD69–79) under seventeen percent of senators whose origins are known were from the provinces, the rest being Italian. By the time of Heliogabalus and his successor (AD218–35) this had increased to over fifty-two percent. Provinces considered less civilised hardly produced any senators: just three are known from Mauretania and none at all from Britain.

Where senators led, Emperors followed. After producing their first senators, a few generations later the same areas saw members of the local elite (albeit descendants of Roman immigrants) elevated to the throne. In AD69 Vespasian hailed from backwoods Italy. The hometown of Trajan (AD98) and Hadrian (AD117) was in Spain. Septimius Severus (AD193) was born in Africa.

The first known Greek entered the Senate in the 50s AD. Many of the early senators from the East, as descendants of dynasties of now abolished client kingdoms, had long-standing links with Rome. By AD218, easterners made up over half of all senators of provincial origin, and thus about a quarter of the Senate. Yet the East had only produced one short-lived pretender: the Syrian Avidius Cassius (AD175). On this line, the acclamation of someone from Heliogabalus' background might seem nothing at all abnormal; perhaps even overdue. But that might be to seriously underestimate the peculiarity of the family from Emesa.

II *Emesa: The Children of the Sun*

A Phoenician from the city of Emesa, one of the clan of Descendants of the Sun.
(Heliodorus, *Aethiopica* 10.41)

The history of the family starts, as Heliogabalus' story will end, with treachery and murder. In the 60s BC Sampsigeramus, the first securely identified ruler of Emesa, summoned King Antiochus XIII, the distant descendant of Alexander the Great's general, Seleucus. 'Sampsigeramus acted the part of a friend, but placed him under arrest, and though for the time being he merely held him closely guarded in chains, he later put him to death.'

Sampsigeramus – the name itself sounded funny to Roman ears. Maybe it was all those sibilant Ss. After Pompey's eastern campaigns, Cicero mocked the great Roman conqueror as an oriental potentate by nicknaming him Sampsigeramus. Looking out from distant Rome, senators, like Cicero, seldom had anything but disdain for petty eastern dynasts like the ruler of Emesa.

It was sometimes different in the East itself, where local dynasts could prove extremely useful. Iamblichus I, the son of Sampsigeramus, sent troops to Egypt in 47BC to help Julius Caesar, who was in dire straits, besieged by an uprising in Alexandria. The Emesene family were soon given Roman citizenship. On an inscription, Iamblichus' great-grandson has all the three names of a Roman: Gaius Julius Sohaemus. That the brief mention of his father, Sampsigeramus (II, companion of the Roman prince Germanicus in AD18/19), does not include his full name does not prove the family did not already have citizenship. The recipients of citizenship not only took the *nomen* (family name) of the patron who had got them the award, but also membership of his voting tribe in Rome (a leftover from the days of the free Republic, before Emperors made such things as people voting immaterial). On an inscription dating to AD78 or 79 Gaius Julius Sampsigeramus, also called Silas, boasts that he belongs to the Fabian voting tribe. If, as seems most likely, this Sampsigeramus/Silas was a scion of the dynasty, membership of the Fabian tribe indicates their citizenship was a gift of either Julius Caesar, or, at the latest, of his adopted son Augustus (31BC–AD14).

Sampsigeramus/Silas is interesting – we will return to him (below and in chapter 4).

The Emesene house was embedded in a network of eastern royal families. Modern scholars call them *client kings* of Rome: the Romans themselves, more politic, called them *friends and allies*. The network stretched from the shores of the Black Sea to the deserts of Arabia. Sampsigeramus II, the great-grandson of the first Sampsigeramus, married the daughter of the King of

Commagene, beyond the headwaters of the Euphrates. Two of their offspring, a son and a daughter, married into the royal house of Judaea to the south (the boy had to be circumcised). Another possible daughter, named Mamaea, married the King of Pontus, up in northern Anatolia.

The kings of Emesa played politics at a high level. In 64/63BC Pompey granted (or confirmed?) their rule over the Greek city of Arethusa, some twenty miles down the Orontes. In 36BC Mark Antony took it away. Under Nero they ruled the city of Arca, just over forty miles to the south-west, and in AD 54 the Emperor gave them the territory of Sophene, far away to the north-east, beyond the Tigris. Neither possession lasted. Much later, after the end of the kingdom of Emesa, in AD 164, Marcus Aurelius made a man called Sohaemus (an Emesene dynastic name) King of Armenia, a very long way from home. This surprising geographic mobility was aided by the marriage connections of the Emesene royal house, but perhaps also by Roman disdain: *all those oriental kinglets are much the same.*

As well as providing a pool of loyal client kings, the rulers of Emesa gave the Romans military aid. We have already seen Iamblichus I sending troops to help Julius Caesar in Alexandria in 47BC. Earlier, in 50BC, Cicero, as governor of Cilicia (modern Mersin Province in south-eastern Turkey), thought Iamblichus would provide support in the event of a Parthian invasion. Later, Sohaemus twice provided forces to help the Romans fight the Jewish Revolt. Substantial numbers were involved: four thousand in AD 66 and three thousand the following year. In AD 72 Sohaemus sent soldiers for the Roman campaign to abolish the kingdom of his fellow client king, and kinsman, Antiochus IV of Commagene.

Playing high-level politics was dangerous. At any moment the Romans could take back what they had given. Losing additional territory was but a minor danger. In 31BC Iamblichus I was executed by Mark Antony. He was succeeded by his brother Alexander (or Alexios). After the Battle of Actium Octavian had Alexander paraded in chains through the streets of Rome, as part of his triumphal procession, then strangled in the gloom of the state prison beneath the Forum. It is ironic that Sohaemus helping crush Antiochus IV is the last time we hear of an independent Emesa. We do not know when the Emesene Kingdom was abolished. Most likely it happened not long after AD72, as part of the trend to incorporate eastern client kingdoms into Roman provinces by the Flavian dynasty (AD69–96). On the inscription, mentioned above, in AD78/79 neither Gaius Julius Sampsigeramus, also known as Silas, nor his father, Gaius Julius Alexio, are described as king. Although, of course, they could have been members of a still independent royal house, neither of whom was on the throne.

Now, with the end of the kingdom, we must face an inconvenient modern argument that the Emesene royals were not, as most scholars have thought, the ancestors of the family of Heliogabalus, as no ancient source makes the link explicit. It is inconvenient, because it would make the preceding paragraphs, and much of what follows, largely irrelevant to this biography. ('Here are some stories about people from the same town a long time earlier' carries far less clout than 'Here is what his ancestors got up to'.) Yet the argument is reductive – making history less interesting than before – and, based on silence, ultimately not compelling. As the jangling cliché goes, absence of evidence is not evidence of absence. There is no *direct* evidence of descent, but there is circumstantial. Both families occupy the foremost place in the city of Emesa and they both have the *nomen* Julius. Okay, that might not amount to all that much, but they also share variants of certainly two, and quite possibly four, *cognomina*: the third Roman name, that tended to run in families. Alexander/Alexianos/Alexios and Sohaemus/So(h) aemias are certain for both. The case for Iamblichus as a name in Heliogabalus' family will be given below. The argument for Mamaea is circular – as Heliogabalus' aunt was called Mamaea, the woman of the same name who married the King of Pontus must be a member of the royal house – but that does not necessarily mean it is untrue. There is enough to indicate that the family of Heliogabalus *claimed* descent from the royal house. Given their pre-eminence in Emesa, we can assume their claim was accepted by contemporaries, and, of course, it may well have been based on reality.

An anecdote reveals that the family had enemies in Emesa. In about AD 190 the Emperor Commodus sent men to kill Julius Alexander of Emesa. His crime, according to Cassius Dio, was to have brought down a lion with a javelin while hunting on horseback. The *Augustan History* says it was a genuine revolt. Alexander did not go quietly. 'When he learnt of the arrival of the assassins,' Cassius Dio says, 'he murdered them at night, and also destroyed all his enemies at Emesa.' Taking with him a boy-favourite, he mounted a horse and set off to seek sanctuary with the Parthians. An excellent horseman, he would have escaped, but the boy grew tired. Unable to bring himself to abandon the object of his affections, as the pursuit overhauled them he first killed the boy and then himself.

After the abolition of their kingdom, the Emesene family still had wealth and estates, good marriage connections across the region and the fading glamour of royal ancestry. But, in the face of enmity within the town, that was not enough to maintain their pre-eminence. To shore up their position, in modern terms, they diversified. The diversification involved three areas: imperial service, intellectuality and religion.

First, imperial service. To earn the suspicion of Commodus – let alone to embark on a revolt against the Emperor – Julius Alexander must have had an elevated Roman status: at least that of a leading equestrian, much more likely a senator. A legal text gives us the disputed will of Julius Agrippa, a *primipilarius* (leading centurion). Eventually, his property was inherited by his grand-niece, Julia Domna, Heliogabalus' great-aunt. In endless modern historical novels every centurion is a gruff NCO, risen from the ranks, always breaking his vine-stick on the backs of his men. In Roman reality, many equestrians went straight into the army at that rank. Julia Maesa, Heliogabalus' grandmother, married a kinsman from her hometown, Caius Julius Avitus Alexianus, who entered the equestrian imperial service, and commanded three auxiliary units, before being placed in charge of the grain supply in Ostia, the port of Rome. Later, after his brother-in-law Septimius Severus became Emperor, he would enter the Senate and hold high office, including that of consul. Julia Mamaea, Heliogabalus' aunt, first married an unknown senator. Her second marriage was to Gessius Marcianus, an equestrian procurator from neighbouring Arca, who was killed at the outset of Heliogabalus' revolt. Their eldest son, Marcus Julius Gessius Bassianus, entered the Senate and became *Magister* (presiding officer) of the priest-hood of the Arval Brethren in Rome. Heliogabalus' father, Sextus Varius Marcellus from Apamea, had an extraordinary equestrian career, ending up as a senator. But we will hold him back until chapter 4, when we look back at Heliogabalus' childhood. For now, the Family Tree at the start of the book should help sort all these people out.

Second, intellectuality. In the reign of Marcus Aurelius (AD 161–80), one Iamblichus wrote a novel in Greek entitled *Babyloniaca* (Babylonian Story). Although the two Latin novels, the *Satyricon* of Petronius and the *Golden Ass* of Apuleius, are better known today, there was a flourishing genre of Greek prose fiction under the Roman Empire (always a surprise to English faculty members, wedded to their orthodoxy that the novel was invented in early modern Europe). The Greek novels were love stories, set either in the past or in a strange version of the contemporary world, with the Roman Empire edited out. In modern terms, they are historical novels or alternative history fiction. A pair of lovers get separated and endure picaresque adventures, before being reunited.

The *Babyloniaca*, originally a very long novel, survives only in a brief summary by Photius, Patriarch of Constantinople in the ninth century AD, and even shorter extracts in the tenth-century encyclopaedia known as the *Suda*. The King of Babylon falls in love with a beautiful married woman. When she refuses his approach, he orders her bound in gold chains and her husband crucified. The couple escape, and are pursued by two eunuchs – who have lost their noses and ears, as well as their testicles. The fugitives are arrested for grave robbery, tried for murder, nearly starve and just escape being burnt alive. Then the woman is accosted by a goat-like spectre, and forced to have sex with one man and to bigamously marry another. Characters are beheaded, hanged, crucified and drowned by a camel. One is eaten by a dog. There are more mistaken identities than in a Shakespearean comedy. Despite suicide attempts, the couple survive and are finally reunited, when the husband improbably (probability is not big in the Greek novels) becomes King of Babylon. You really cannot say not a lot happens. With its erotic theme, the Christian Photius describes the novel as shameless. A more robust pagan medical writer prescribed it as a stimulant for sexual impotence.

Photius claims Iamblichus was a Babylonian magician who had acquired Greek culture. The *Suda* adds he was born a slave. In the tenth century, the scribe of the oldest manuscript of Photius corrected the Patriarch in a marginal note. 'This Iamblichus was a Syrian by race on both his father's and his mother's side, a Syrian not in the sense of the Greeks who have settled in Syria, but of the native ones, familiar with the Syrian language and living by their customs.' The scribe goes on to give the framing device of the novel, which inspired the mistakes of Babylonian and servile origins. Iamblichus was taught the Babylonian language by a slave, formerly a royal secretary, who had been captured by the Romans when the Emperor Trajan sacked Babylon.

Photius has Iamblichus date his own lifetime first by reference to Sohaemus, the King of Armenia, 'the descendant of Kings' (the Emesene rulers), before he mentions the more obvious reigning Emperors of Rome. It indicates the priorities in his identity: Emesene first, Roman second. Together with the novelist's geographic origins, and the dynastic names, it suggests kinship with the family of Heliogabalus.

At another point, Photius mentions an Iamblichus who was descended from Sampsigeramus, presumably the first known ruler of Emesa. The context – impious pagan philosophers – suggests that this kinsman of Heliogabalus' family is not the novelist, but a rather better known Iamblichus, the third-century Neoplatonist from Chalcis ad Bellum, not far from Emesa in the Orontes valley.

Apart from the novelist and the philosopher, two more intellectuals can be canvassed. There is another novelist, Heliodorus, author of the *Aethiopica*, of uncertain date (third or fourth century?). As in the quote at the beginning of this section, he was proud of his origins as a Phoenician from Emesa. Nothing else, however, connects him to the family. The other is more surprising: Papinian, praetorian prefect under the Severans and famous Latin jurist. The *Augustan History* says he was a kinsman of

Septimius Severus' second wife. As far as we know, Julia Domna was Severus' second wife. Yet it might be unwise to put too much faith in the 'most mendacious' author in antiquity.

The third area of diversification was religion. It is easy to assume that the kings of Emesa had also been high priests (or maybe priest-kings) of the god Elagabal, as later Heliogabalus was high priest and priest-Emperor. But this casual assumption of continuity might be to succumb to the Victorian myth of the unchanging Orient. You know the picture: an Orientalist painting, where the colours are more vibrant than the people – black guards half-asleep at the gate, odalisques languorous in the harem, a eunuch dreaming on the roof, the stem of his hookah slipping from his mouth. The evidence for Elagabal can support an altogether more dynamic recreation.

Nothing suggests that the kings of Emesa were priests of Elagabal. One piece of evidence might point in the opposite direction. As we saw earlier, to marry a Jewish princess, a member of the Emesene royal family had to be circumcised. As high priest of Elagabal, Heliogabalus was circumcised.

The earliest evidence for the god Elagabal is not in Emesa, but some fifty miles to the south-east, on an inscription in the desert. This deity is named and pictured: a rock or mountain with an eagle perched on top. The date – sometime in the first century AD – roughly coincides with the abolition of the Emesene monarchy. That Elagabal was imported to Emesa from somewhere else is undeniable. The etymology of the Aramaic name of the deity – 'LH'GBL, in Palmyrene lettering – means 'God of the Mountain', or 'God Mountain'. Emesa has a *Tell*, a man-made mound, in the centre of the town, but the location lacks anything like a mountain.

Elagabal is first found in Emesa in the reign of Antoninus Pius (AD 138–61). It was then that the city began to issue coinage, and the reverses of the coins are almost monopolised by the image of the black stone of the god. Julius Bassianus, the great-grandfather of Heliogabalus, was alive in the reign of Pius: perhaps he was already an adult. Certainly, he was fathering children under the next Emperor, Marcus Aurelius (AD161–80). Bassianus is not only the earliest securely identified ancestor of Heliogabalus, but he is also the first known high priest of Elagabal. It is not until Caracalla was sole Augustus, free of his father and brother (AD211–17), that we have evidence of the great temple of Elagabal at Emesa, again from images on the civic coinage. By the time of the revolt of Maesa, the temple was drawing the crowds: not just locals, but also the soldiers from nearby Raphaneae, and satraps and barbarian kings from further afield.

A narrative can be constructed. After the abolition of the monarchy, under pressure from other Emesene families, Heliogabalus' ancestors import the black stone and manage to have Elagabal recognised as the patron deity of Emesa and themselves appointed as high priests. Eventually a grand temple is built, and worshippers and pilgrims come from far and wide.

Set out like that, it all sounds a bit cynical: a manipulation of religion for social and political gain. But that is not necessarily so. Belief – and we will have a good look at belief in chapter 8 – is a tricky subject. Piety and ambition can often go hand in hand. And, once again, the family of Heliogabalus had something other Emesene families did not. This time not royal majesty, but something better: divine authority. As they cared for the temple, Elagabal cared for them.

The three areas of diversification – religion, intellectuality and imperial service – came together to elevate the family from provincial notables to actors on an empire-wide stage. The instrument was Julia Domna's horoscope. The stars were interpreted to predict that she would marry a future king (*Rex*). That was why Septimius Severus – still an unimportant senator in AD 187 (an ex-praetor, governor of the unarmed Province of Gallia Lugdunensis) – married the woman from Emesa. Modern scholars doubt the story. Such ambition was unrealistic, meddling in the future too dangerous. Domna's horoscope gets watered down to propaganda invented after Severus became Emperor. But this may not be right.

Belief in astrology was widespread in all levels of society. Severus was a firm believer. We are told he consulted the horoscopes of all his potential second wives. Some years earlier, when he consulted the oracle of Bel at Apamea, he had received some lines of Homer originally addressed to Agamemnon, the leader of the Achaeans at Troy, that compared Severus to the gods: *with eyes and head like Zeus who delights in the thunder*. The mortal most often compared to the king of the gods was the Emperor. Later, Severus would have his own horoscope painted on a ceiling in the imperial palace, with the sensitive parts deliberately obscured. After his marriage, when governor of Sicily, he was indicted for consulting seers and astrologers about the imperial power. Severus was acquitted and his accuser crucified. Such things were dangerous for all concerned. The law was unambiguous: 'Whoever consults (astrologers and similar) concerning the health of the Emperor, or the destiny of the state (i.e. "Will I become Emperor?"), shall be executed together with him who responded.' How many undistinguished senators harboured dreams of great destinies? The question is unanswerable. We only hear of those who succeeded and those who were executed. Certainly, for some, like Severus, ambition and belief in predestination could trump caution. Severus would have encountered Domna's family a few years before, in the 180s, when serving in Syria as Legate of *IV Scythica*. Her name might itself have chimed with her horoscope. In reality, Domna was derived from the Arabic Dumayna. Yet in

Latin it sounded a lot like *Domina*, the respectful address to an empress.

The first two spheres into which the family diversified – imperial service and intellectuality – were unexceptional: they were even to be expected of descendants of eastern royalty. Take two famous monuments featuring their distant kin: a brother and sister from the ex-royal family of Commagene. In Athens, at the summit of the Hill of the Muses, facing the Acropolis and looking down over the city, is the tomb of Caius Julius Antiochus Epiphanes Philopappus, grandson of the last king. Its sculptures proclaim both his Greek and his Roman identity, the latter linked to success in the service of Rome. In the centre of the upper storey, Philopappus is seated wearing Greek costume. In the lower storey Philopappus rides in a chariot, accompanied by twelve lictors, draped in the toga as a consul of Rome (AD 109). In Egypt, across the Nile from Thebes, is the 'Colossus of Memnon' (actually a seated figure of Pharaoh Amenhopis III). Every morning, at dawn, the statue 'sang'. On one of its legs, among other poems, are inscribed four by Julia Balbilla, sister of Philopappus. One of them reads: 'Memnon the Egyptian, warmed by the rays of the sun, spoke from his Theban stone.' It is not great poetry, but better than some of the other verses left by Roman tourists. The third area into which the family diverted their energies, religion, was not itself abnormal. Again, the family of Commagene almost all held priesthoods, both local and Roman. What was exceptional about the Emesene family (and we will return to this) was their self-conscious insistence on the Phoenician – that is to say, deliberately non-Roman and non-Greek – ceremonies of their god.

The god had supported the family for generations. Maesa's revolt at Raphaneae owed much to Elagabal. The god's oracles had prepared the way. The ceremonies at his temple had brought the soldiers to Emesa. At sunrise he had been present both at the acclamation of Heliogabalus and the desertion of Julianus' troops. The rebels would have prayed that Elagabal would continue to watch over them. For now, they had to confront the Emperor.

CHAPTER 3 THE BATTLE

Syria: May to June AD218

I *Macrinus' Beard*

The news of the revolt reached Macrinus in Antioch. There had been many portents. Cassius Dio reports an eclipse and two comets, the tail of one 'extended from the west to the east for several nights'. Such things presaged the death of rulers. But Macrinus was not unduly worried. Raphaneae was the best part of a hundred miles away. Minor insurrections were not uncommon. More like mutinies, they were usually quickly crushed, and whoever had been clad in the purple was killed. According to Herodian, Macrinus 'discounted the affair as child's play'. Cassius Dio says that to Macrinus Heliogabalus was a 'mere boy of whose very name previously he had been ignorant'.

Macrinus had an unconventional background for an Emperor. Born into slavery, as a young freedman he had performed menial tasks in the imperial palace, fought as a gladiator and worked as a prostitute. His ancient biographer expresses a measure of doubt about these stories, which he had found in 'various writers'. As well he might. For in his life of Macrinus the unknown author of the *Augustan History* has invented every element. The servitude, drudgery on the Palatine, the amphitheatre, prostitution and the 'various writers': all are complete fiction.

In reality, Macrinus was a lawyer from the Roman colony of Caesarea in the province of Mauretania Caesariensis in North Africa. Although Cassius Dio does claim Macrinus was the 'son of most obscure parents', probably his family was equestrian. It takes money to train in the law and second-generation senators, like Cassius Dio, could be very sniffy about the origins of those now below them in the social pyramid. A performance in court won Macrinus the patronage of Plautianus, the praetorian prefect of Septimius Severus. That connection was enough to earn him the enmity of the Emesene family. Julia Domna and Plautianus loathed each other. When Domna's son Caracalla engineered the death of Plautianus, his protégé Macrinus was saved by the unexpected intervention of an influential senator called Fabius Cilo. At this point the *Augustan History* claims Macrinus was exiled to Africa. There is no need to take it seriously. Probably it was invented from nothing more than Macrinus' origins. Cassius Dio is quite explicit: Fabius Cilo not only saved Macrinus but got him the post of superintendent of the Flaminian Way, the great northern highway out of Rome. After the death of Septimius Severus, Macrinus briefly held several procuratorships (posts either overseeing imperial estates, or the collection of taxes), before Caracalla appointed him praetorian prefect, perhaps as early as AD212, but certainly by AD214.

The *Augustan History* paints Macrinus as a complete villain: 'shameless in spirit, as well as looks'. He treacherously murdered Caracalla and took his place, for no other motive than ambition. Once on the throne his cruelty was such that the blood-splattered walls of the palace earned it the nickname of 'the meat market'. Yet again, this is not history, but late antique fiction. The contemporaries Cassius Dio and Herodian provide a very different picture. For them, Macrinus' coup was motivated by self-preservation.

Cassius Dio gives some guarded praise of Macrinus. He was a man of integrity. As praetorian prefect he acted as justly as was possible under Caracalla: 'His knowledge of the law was not so accurate as his observance of it was faithful.' And what exactly does that mean – that Macrinus was plodding and ill-informed? Despite such lukewarm approval, Cassius Dio did not think that Macrinus had what it took to make a good Emperor. His move to reduce the pay and privileges of the recruits was well-intentioned, but, as the army was still gathered in the field, disastrously ill-timed. In war, Macrinus was a coward. For Cassius Dio it was not altogether his fault: Macrinus was a Moor and they were notoriously timorous. We will return to such ethnic stereotypes in the next chapter. Seeking to put his own humble origins in the shade, Macrinus advanced base and unworthy men to high office. But Macrinus' worst sin in the view of a senator, and Cassius Dio never entertained any other, was that he had taken the throne as an equestrian. Far better if he had killed Caracalla and then organised the succession of a senator.

Herodian was not a senator and judged Emperors differently. A Greek, not as emotionally invested in Rome as his fellow Greek, the senator and twice consul Cassius Dio, Herodian mainly measured Emperors by their attitude to Greek culture (*paideia*). Macrinus failed to disband the army, or make haste to Rome. Instead, neglecting affairs of state, he lived in luxury in Antioch, wasting his time on mime shows and 'cultivating his beard', walking about very slowly and speaking laboriously in a low voice. Some of these criticisms are unfair. The peace negotiations with the Parthians dragged on into the winter of AD217–18. Macrinus could not leave for Rome, or send his western troops back to their permanent bases, until they were over. Both had to wait for the spring. Other criticisms – of his gait, speaking voice and facial hair – seem odd to us. It is time to look at Macrinus' beard.

Image 5: The Emperor Macrinus

Accentuated by short hair, receding at the temples, Macrinus' beard is a fine growth, full and curly. In the Roman Empire beards carried a freight of meanings unimagined by contemporary hipsters in London sushi bars. A short-cropped, stubbly beard pointed to a military man and martial virtues. That style had been adopted by Caracalla and was worn by Macrinus on some coin issues. The Romans thought their distant, rural forebears, uncorrupted by cities and things like barbers, had been conspicuously hairy. So a longer, fuller beard could suggest antique, rustic virtue. But luxuriant facial hair also summoned an image of contemporary intellectuality, which inevitably held Greek connotations. And here things got more complicated. An artfully trimmed and curled big beard evoked sophists, incredibly popular high-status display orators. While a more natural, unkempt effort conjured up philosophers. And thus the beards of those philosophical seekers after eternal virtue circled back to the bucolic ancients.

Macrinus boasts a bushy beard. But looking at the sculpture, or at *any* sculpture, it is difficult to decide if the curls are the result of nature or artifice. It was a problem recognised in antiquity. The satirist Lucian wrote of the apparent disorder of hair being the result of the art of the barber. The image projected by Macrinus' beard comes into focus if we think about his gait and voice. Sophists strode about, slapping their thighs and gesticulating. Their speech aimed at sounding fluent and melodious. When some talked they sounded as if they were singing. By contrast, philosophers moved with stately self-control. Dio Chrysostom composed a work praising walking sedately. They liked to be seen as stern men of few words, and those wrung out of them after laborious deep thought. Nothing but the hard-won truth: 'few words on few occasions'. At times, some gave up words altogether. Secundus, the silent philosopher in reality, and Apollonius of Tyana in fiction, somehow taught philosophy by example and the expression on their hirsute faces.

Macrinus' beard and walk and voice, as Herodian notes, were imitations of Marcus Aurelius, the great philosopher-Emperor. Marcus Aurelius was the model Roman Emperor for Herodian, the one who embodied Greek *paideia* and the one against whom all others were measured. Macrinus had copied the externals, but came up short in every other aspect. Neglecting duty for mime shows, it did not matter how luxuriant his beard, or how slowly he walked, if he was decked out in gold and precious stones. Lacking true *paideia*, the reign of Macrinus brought only 'the semblance of freedom'.

II *Death in Apamea*

While Macrinus was cultivating his beard in Antioch, his officers in the field were trying to stamp out the revolt. After the defeat of Julianus at Raphaneae the manuscript of Cassius Dio breaks off. In the gap of some twenty lines (what scholars call a *lacuna*, plural *lacunae*) only a few letters and a couple of words can be made out. When it becomes legible again the manuscript resumes with: '... for Marcellus was dead, he put this man to death; but, lacking courage to proceed further on his own responsibility without Macrinus, he sent for the Emperor'.

Marcellus was Sextus Varius Marcellus, the father of Heliogabalus, who had died in AD213–14 and been buried in Italy. Part of another name can be read in the *lacuna*: ... cianus. Given the presence of Marcellus, the father of Heliogabalus, the ... cianus who is executed can be confidently identified as Gessius Marcianus, the father of the future Emperor Severus Alexander. Twenty lines is a long passage to record the killing of just one member of the Emesene family. As we saw in chapter 1, Gessius Marcianus had another, elder son, called Marcus Julius Gessius Bassianus. The latter had been a senator and member of the priesthood of the Arval Brethren, in AD214. He was absent from Rome in the inscription that attests his existence. Perhaps he was already in the East? Marcus Julius Gessius Bassianus is never heard of again. Quite probably his execution is hidden in the gap in the manuscript.

Where were the father and son killed? Gessius Marcianus came from Arca Caesarea. But the Emesene family had connections and properties across the province of Syria Phoenice. After the killings, the officer summoned the Emperor. And Macrinus came to Apamea.

Who put these men to death? The executions are sometimes ascribed to the praetorian prefect Julianus, and linked to his killings of the daughter of Gessius Marcianus and her unnamed husband. But these happened earlier in Cassius Dio's story, before the siege of Raphaneae. The last time we saw Julianus in the text he was on his own, fleeing for his life from the mutiny of his troops. He reappears while arriving in Apamea, depending on how you look at it, on his own or with one soldier. Either way, he was in no position to hunt down and execute local notables.

If the killings happened in Apamea, and were not the work of Julianus, the obvious candidate is the prefect of *Legio II Parthica*. This legion was created, along with two others, by Septimius Severus in AD 196. All three were commanded by equestrian prefects. The First and Second Parthian legions were stationed in the province of Mesopotamia. The permanent base of *II Parthica* was the Alban hills outside Rome. There it could both contribute to keeping order in the city, and, along with the Praetorians, form the nucleus of a central imperial field army to act as a strategic reserve. In the latter capacity, it always accompanied the Emperor on campaigns. When these were in the East, the winter quarters of the legion was Apamea. The city was a second home to the legion.

The prefect of *II Parthica* has often been identified as Publius Valerius Comazon. This introduces us to one of the most extraordinary figures of the time. When Comazon was a soldier in the province of Thrace (an auxiliary, as there were no legions in Thrace), for some unspecified misdemeanour the governor, Claudius Attalus, relegated him to the fleet. This is often assumed to mean that he was condemned to be chained to a bench as a slave rowing a war galley. Such punishments were not completely unknown – we saw one in chapter 1 – but they were extremely rare. With just the occasional exception, those who served in the Roman fleet were not slaves but free men. In fact, such demotion to a less prestigious branch of the forces was a normal punishment for relatively minor offences in the military. A legionary would be downgraded to an auxiliary, an auxiliary to a marine. That was what had happened to Comazon. But he had bounced back. Cassius Dio says that he was a prefect of the camp. At a stretch this could mean that he was commanding *II Parthica*. Comazon, however, was an early adherent to the revolt and went on to dazzlingly elevated heights under the regime. Such a career was utterly improbable if Comazon's initial actions had been to declare himself, and his legion, loyal to Macrinus and to execute both Heliogabalus' uncle and one of his cousins. Far better to credit precision to the words of Cassius Dio. Comazon, the ex-ranker, was prefect of the camp of *II Parthica*. The executions were the work of his unknown commanding officer. Then, as Cassius Dio says: 'Lacking courage to proceed further on his own responsibility without Macrinus, he sent for the Emperor.'

III *The Feast*

Macrinus came speedily to the Alban troops at Apamea.
  (Cassius Dio 79.34.2)

Emperors did not travel on their own. Events at Apamea will show that Macrinus was not accompanied by an army. But there would have been a bodyguard, at least five hundred or a thousand Praetorians and *equites singulares* (imperial horse guards), and possibly some 'Scythian' (i.e. Germanic) mercenaries. And there would have been many others – secretaries, cooks, doctors, masseurs and, given Macrinus' career and intellectual pretensions, doubtless a few jurists and philosophers: all the people who made life bearable for an autocrat.

It was just under sixty miles from Antioch to Apamea. Three days on the road. If this was a novel, it would be enjoyable to construct detailed timelines for all the characters (a messenger urging his foundering horse through the night from Apamea, Macrinus dithering for a couple of days in Antioch, before setting out…). But it would be pure speculation. Only two dates are certain. They bracket the revolt. Heliogabalus was acclaimed on 16 May, and the final battle was fought on 8 June. A lot of events were crammed into twenty-four days.

Apamea was not some recent garrison town like Raphaneae, and it was not a settlement of previously nomadic Arabs like Emesa. Founded by Alexander the Great's general Seleucus, it had a proud history stretching back half a millennium. It was prosperous, with a population of over a hundred thousand. Miles of aqueducts supplied its baths. Its theatre looked out over the green Orontes valley. For splendour it rivalled Antioch. Its colonnaded main street was longer and wider than those of either Antioch or Palmyra.

At the heart of Apamea, just by the agora, was the Temple of Zeus Belus. There the god gave oracles in not always entirely accurately quoted lines of poetry by Homer or Euripides. When Macrinus arrived, the one he received was a masterpiece of ambiguity.

> *Truly indeed, old man, young warriors sorely beset thee,*
> *Spent is thy force, and grievous old age is coming upon thee.*

At first hearing the oracle seems to be backing the revolt. But if Macrinus could not recall the context there would be those around him who could. The lines in the *Iliad* were Diomedes urging the aged Nestor to fight with him against Hector. Only Zeus himself stopped them. Nestor, of course, survived the siege of Troy, and Hector did not.

Macrinus was not yet fifty-five. Nestor lived for three generations: ninety or, as some reckoned, three hundred years. Possibly buoyed up by such reflections, Macrinus fashioned an act of political theatre. When he took the purple, his son, Diadumenianus, had been named Caesar and thus made heir to the throne. Now, in Apamea, Macrinus promoted Diadumenianus to Augustus, co-ruler of the empire. It was designed to create stability, to reassure. The revolt had no future. If Macrinus fell, his son would take his place. Except it offered no reassurance for a very long time. Diadumenianus was only nine years old.

More immediately, the elevation of Diadumenianus gave Macrinus an excuse for courting the favour of the troops in Apamea. They were promised a donative of 20,000 sesterces each. Four thousand sesterces were handed out on the spot. To further appease them, full rations and other privileges, which he had previously removed, were now restored. The citizens of Apamea also benefited. Not mentioning the revolt – so that it might seem not a bribe but just an honour to his son – Macrinus gave a lavish feast costing six hundred sesterces a head.

At that price, the food and drink would have been sumptuous, featuring local delicacies. Syria was famous for its dates and plums, and its wine was prized across the empire. When the feast was in full swing – somewhere between the eggs and the apples, as the ancients would have said – a soldier entered carrying a heavy parcel wrapped in many layers of cloth and securely tied with cords. Imagine Macrinus' delight when the soldier announced it contained the head of the rebel Heliogabalus. The bundle was indeed sealed with the signet-ring of the praetorian prefect Julianus. All anxieties were dispelled. The revolt was over.

It would have taken some time to untie all those cords, to unwrap all those coverings. Did the severed head thump down onto the floor, or was the grisly thing held aloft by the hair? Delight would have turned to horror. This was not the head of a teenage boy, but a mature man. It was the head of none other than Julianus himself.

While the hideous object was being uncovered, the soldier slipped away. He had been sent by the rebels. They had discovered Julianus hiding somewhere, presumably near Raphaneae. The praetorian prefect had been dragged out and decapitated.

As he had at the battle of Nisibis, Macrinus lost his nerve. Precipitously, he fled back to the apparent safety of his main forces at Antioch. Perhaps he hoped that *Legio II Parthica* would remain loyal. Its commander had shown his commitment by executing Gessius Marcianus. The legionaries were not Syrians, but mainly recruited in the Balkans. They did not worship a local cult controlled by the Emesene family.

Such hopes, if Macrinus entertained them, proved illusory. As soon as the Emperor was gone, *Legio II*, along with the other troops that had wintered at Apamea, declared for the rebels. Presumably the prefect of the legion either bolted after his Emperor, or, like Julianus, was hunted down and killed.

Comazon, the prefect of the camp, assumed command and oversaw the troops taking the *sacramentum*, the military oath to Heliogabalus: *idem in me* (the same for me). The citizens would have been equally keen to demonstrate their enthusiasm for the new regime. Apamea had been the hometown of Sextus Varius Marcellus, the late father of Heliogabalus. The citizens were to dedicate a statue to Maesa in the colonnade by the agora.

The rebels now had two legions, but the odds were still stacked against the uprising.

IV   *Messages*

And now each side was making its preparations against the other and sending rival messengers and letters to the provinces and the legions.

(Cassius Dio 79.34.6)

For the provincial governors who received these messages it was a moment of terror. Picking the wrong side in a revolt was likely to lead to execution. An indication of the depth of the fear, and the paranoia it induced, was the awful suspicion that any letter claiming to be from a rebel might actually be from the Emperor himself, as a perverse test of loyalty. Of course, for the messengers themselves the occasion could not be more fraught with danger. Cassius Dio tells us that 'many of the couriers on both sides lost their lives'.

A study of the provincial governors in the eastern provinces indicates looming disaster for the rebel cause. Prosopography is the name given by modern scholars to such research. From the Greek *prosopon*, meaning person, prosopography seeks to find underlying patterns by looking at such links between individuals as shared service in political office or the army, family and marriage connections, the same geographic origins or owning neighbouring properties. It flourishes for periods where we have a lot of evidence about many named individuals: for example, the last century BC, where we have the letters of Cicero, and the first two centuries AD, from which huge numbers of inscriptions survive. Incidentally, the third century AD produces less prosopography, as the number of inscriptions drops, or, as it can be described, the 'epigraphic habit' declines.

Prosopography works best for broad issues over a long time. It is good for the *longue durée*. For instance, without it we would not know how the structure of a typical equestrian career evolved under the Emperors. And we saw in the last chapter how it illuminates the changing geographic origins of membership of the Senate. It is more contentious when applied to the small scale and intimate, such as the existence of political 'factions', and the supposed allegiance of individual politicians. Roman political 'factions' by their nature were ephemeral groupings, coming together over a specific issue, and dispersing when it was resolved. Also, prosopography tends to marginalise, often completely ignore, personal emotions – friendship and love, or enmity and hatred – let alone political principles and philosophical belief.

Despite all these caveats, prosopography is useful to us here. It does involve quite a lot of names of secondary characters. But it produces results, showing us how the odds were stacked in the revolt.

Although there are gaps, we know quite a few of the governors of the eastern provinces in the early summer of AD218. We can judge their responses to these conflicting, and deeply troubling, messages from their fate after the rebellion.

Iulius Basilianus, the prefect of Egypt, remained loyal to Macrinus. The Emperor had appointed him to that post, and after the grisly unveiling of the severed head of Julianus at the feast in Apamea, Basilianus was promoted to the rank of praetorian prefect. Oddly, Basilianus remained in Egypt. Perhaps events moved too fast for him to leave to join Macrinus. After the revolt, Heliogabalus had Basilianus executed.

Also in Egypt, as we saw in chapter 1, was Marius Secundus, the governor of Syria Phoenice. An equestrian elevated into the

Senate by Macrinus, Secundus was another loyalist killed in the aftermath of the revolt.

Two more eastern governors were summarily executed by the new regime: Fabius Agrippinus of Syria Coele and Pica Caesianus of Arabia. The latter was replaced as acting governor by the procurator of the province, Caius Furius Sabinus Aquila Timesitheus, a man who would have a great future.

The governor of Cappadocia, Marcus Munatius Sulla Cerialis, seems to have prevaricated. Cerialis was not killed, but merely dismissed from his post. He returned to live in private life in Rome. But, as we will see, the regime of Heliogabalus continued to regard him with suspicion.

We can find only one eastern governor who might have responded positively to the messengers of the rebels. Later, Macrinus avoided the city of Nicomedia because he was afraid of Caecilius Aristo, the governor of Bithynia. Yet by then Macrinus was on the run and might have feared that the news of his defeat had overtaken him. Bithynia was an unarmed province, containing no legions. It would have been a brave move by Aristo to declare for Heliogabalus at the outset.

None of this boded well for Maesa's revolt. Of those governors in the East whose response to the messages we can ascertain, four remained loyal to Macrinus, one attempted to sit on the fence and just one *may* have thrown in his lot with the rebellion.

Things looked no better for the rebels if we consider the distribution of the legions. The rebels had two legions: *III Gallica* and *II Parthica*, won over respectively from Secundus in Syria Phoenice and Agrippinus in Syria Coele. They were outnumbered by those remaining loyal to Macrinus.

In Syria Coele, Agrippinus still commanded two other legions: *IV Scythica* and *XVI Flavia Firmata*. Basilianus had *II Traiana* in Egypt and Caesianus *III Cyrenaica* in Arabia. The odds, as we have them – and we do not know the allegiance of the two legions in Mesopotamia, or the two in Syria Palaestina (Judaea), but the subsequent actions of the rebels indicate that it was unlikely that either province, especially the latter, had declared for Heliogabalus – were two to one against the uprising. These odds get worse when we add in the Praetorians, roughly the strength of a double legion, with Macrinus at Antioch: three to one against.

Maesa and Heliogabalus had only one factor in their favour: geography. Raphaneae was fewer than a hundred miles from Antioch, and Apamea, which was en route, under sixty. The nearest legion loyal to Macrinus was *IV Scythica* at Zeugma, about a hundred and thirty miles from Antioch. The rest were considerably further away. If the rebels made haste to bring *III Gallica* up from Raphaneae to join *II Parthica* at Apamea, and then force-marched north, they might bring Macrinus to battle outside Antioch before overwhelming numbers could be concentrated against their small army.

v *The March*

A look at a map of ancient Syria shows the shortest route from Apamea to Antioch for those in a hurry.

This map is based on maps 67 and 68 of the *Barrington Atlas of the Greek and Roman World*, which is not only an invaluable resource, but an aesthetic pleasure to use.

There is the direct road, following the Orontes river, running almost due north. It crosses the Orontes by bridges at Seleukobelos and Derkoush, snakes between the hills and, after sixty or so miles, emerges into the plains at a village called Gephyra. From there Antioch lies just twelve miles to the west.

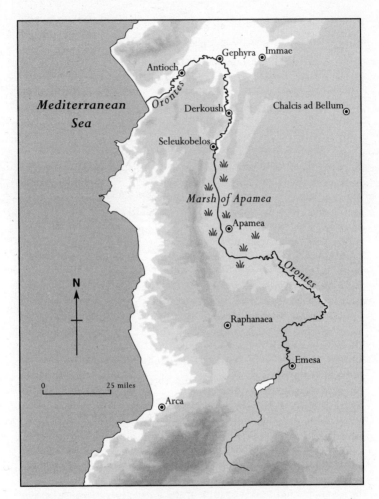

Apamea to Antioch

But the army of Maesa and Heliogabalus did not take that road. Cassius Dio says that the forces of Macrinus met them at a village in the territory of Antioch, some twenty-four miles from the city. This was identified in the last century as Immae (sometimes Imma, modern Yenisehir). The identification has since been confirmed by the discovery at Apamea of the tombstone of Atinius Ianuarius, soldier of *II Parthica*, who fell in battle at Immae. To reach Immae the rebels took the road northeast out of Apamea, that went through the town of Chalcis ad Bellum, looped back over the limestone massif of Kynegike and came down the pass in front of the village. In all it was some ninety miles from Apamea to Immae, with another twenty-four from the latter to Antioch. Time was against the rebels, so there had to be reasons for taking this circuitous route.

The first reason is found on the map. By the Orontes on the shorter route are little blue-green clumps of vegetation that indicate a swamp. It had a name: the 'Marsh (*Limne*) of Apamea'. Ancient rivers were not canalised and had wide floodplains. In early June the Orontes would still be high from the spring meltwater that ran down from the hills. The passage of an army – thousands of boots and hoofs and wagon wheels – would reduce the road to a quagmire.

A fly over the route on *Google Earth* discloses a second reason. At the narrowest point heading north there is only just over a mile for road, river and marsh between the enclosing cliffs. The rebels had to bring Macrinus to a decisive battle. A blocking force here could hold them up for months, while reinforcements reached the Emperor.

Autopsy, in the sense of going to look for yourself, is always the ideal. Second best is to look at the *Barrington Atlas* and *Google Earth* (with the tourist photos posted) together. Sometimes autopsy is not possible. At the time of writing (autumn 2020), Covid precludes a flight to Syria, and the routes discussed run either side of Idlib, the last rebel stronghold in the Syrian civil war.

Heliogabalus' army drew up for battle in the pass. The intelligence-gathering capacity of Roman armies is often doubted. In this civil war, it served both sides well enough. Cassius Dio says that the rebels advanced rapidly. Even so, Macrinus was told that the rebels were coming, and by which route, in time to head them off, albeit with difficulty, a long day's march from Antioch. Equally, Heliogabalus' men had enough warning of the approach of the Emperor to hastily assume a defensive position in the pass.

Several modern accounts claim that Heliogabalus had the larger force at Immae. This seems at odds with their deployment. The rebel army drew up with its wings protected by the pass to avoid being outflanked out on the plain. Usually, it is the outnumbered force that fears being outflanked.

The two sides were roughly equal in main combat units: two legions against the Praetorians, in campaign conditions, probably about eight thousand each. But Herodian contrasts the performance of the Praetorians to the 'great mass' of Macrinus' troops in the battle, and Cassius Dio records that, as well as *II Parthica*, 'the other troops' wintering around Apamea had gone over to Heliogabalus. These 'other troops' on both sides were auxiliaries and detachments of legions based in Europe.

The legions were heavy infantry, designed for close combat in battle. The auxiliaries were 'force multipliers', adding tactical skills to the army. They provided light troops, missile capacity and cavalry, while also being able to stand in the line of battle. The auxiliaries were either regular units or ad hoc allies or mercenaries from the tribes on the frontiers or beyond. The Moors who deserted Julianus for Heliogabalus at Raphaneae were the latter type of tribal levies. As a rule of thumb, it is thought that across the empire there were the same numbers of auxiliaries as legionaries.

At the start of the twentieth century, an Oxford don, G.L. Cheesman, undertook the mammoth task of bringing together and tabulating everything then known about the origins and location of every auxiliary unit. Subsequent research has amplified and corrected many of his findings, but his overall picture remains, and we are not seeking precise figures, but a general order of magnitude. He found twenty-nine units of auxiliaries at some point based in Syria, and estimated their normal strength in the province at 16,500 men. It is likely that there were as many auxiliaries as legionaries on either side at Immae.

There were three main army groups in the Roman Empire: those on the Rhine, the Danube and in the East. Lacking a significant strategic reserve, when there was a major campaign on one frontier it was necessary to strip troops from the other two. While whole units of auxiliaries were sent, only detachments were despatched from the legions. These detachments, usually of either five hundred or a thousand men, often brigaded together, were called vexillations (*vexillationes*, from *vexillium*, a standard). Apart from the very untypical frontier town of Dura-Europos, the garrison town in the East we know best is none other than Apamea. The numerous inscriptions, mainly tombstones, record the presence of vexillations from five legions, as well as two auxiliary units, and one of the urban cohorts from Rome. The modern insistence that Heliogabalus had more troops than Macrinus at Immae seems to stem from a misunderstanding of these vexillations at Apamea. The inscriptions, which are seldom precisely dated, are all those we know were *ever* based there: they were not *all* there in the spring of AD218.

The strategic position suggests that Macrinus had more vexillations at Immae than the rebels. As the peace negotiations with the Parthians continued into the winter of AD217–18, the field army had to remain in the East. If the diplomacy had broken down, the war would have been resumed in Mesopotamia. If a treaty were concluded in the spring, the European troops would begin the long march home. In either eventuality, it made more sense for the vexillations to winter in northern Syria, in the province of Syria Coele, rather than southerly Syria Phoenice. In Syria Coele they were closer both to where the war could resume and the roads across Cilicia, where their journey to Europe would begin. Also, in Syria Coele they could be supplied from stores assembled in the Mediterranean ports of Seleukia Pieria and Katabalos.

Probably outnumbered, the rebels made ready to face the enemy.

> *Now in the battle Gannys made haste to occupy the pass in front of the village and drew up his troops in good order for fighting, in spite of the fact that he was utterly without experience in military affairs and had spent his life in luxury.*
>
> (Cassius Dio 79.38.3)

Hang on a moment. Who is this Gannys? Cassius Dio has never mentioned him before. His sudden, unexplained appearance in the text as the military leader of the rebels has led to all sorts of confusion. Two writers, much later in antiquity, thought that Gannys was actually another name for Comazon, the prefect of the camp. Some modern scholars have followed them. The idea can be dismissed straight away. It is hard to see how the long and chequered army career of Comazon, which Cassius Dio has related, might equate with a life of luxury and a complete inexperience of military affairs. In a later passage of Cassius Dio they appear as two separate people.

In some modern works, both popular and scholarly, Gannys is a completely new character, not to be identified with anyone else that we know about. It is assumed that his introduction to the story is lost in one of the gaps in the manuscript of Cassius

Dio. But here is how Cassius Dio describes Gannys later: *the man who had brought about the uprising, who had taken him* (Heliogabalus) *to the camp, who had also caused the soldiers to revolt, who had given him the victory over Macrinus… to be sure Gannys was living rather luxuriously.* Cassius Dio has already credited the first three items to Eutychianus, the freedman of Maesa. In his last two books Cassius Dio is very fond of nicknames: Caracalla is Tarautas, Heliogabalus is Pseudo-Antoninus, or Sardanapalus, or Tiberinus, and so on. Gannys presumably is derived from either *ganao* (to shine, or be cheerful), or *ganymai* (to be delighted). Gannys is Eutychianus' nickname: something faintly belittling, like *Cheerful Boy*, or *Delightful Lad*.

All of which raises the question of why the rebels, at this desperate moment, entrusted command of their army to Eutychianus/Gannys. This *Delightful Lad*, a young freedman, who had 'given people pleasure in amusements and gymnastic exercises', might not be an obvious choice. But who else was there? As far as we can tell, not a single senator. Instead, three old women, two children, a couple of ex-rankers in Comazon and Verus, a few other freedmen and a handful of town councillors. At least Eutychianus (let's stick with that name) had shown initiative at Raphaneae. Eutychianus might lack any military experience but, and probably crucial in Maesa's view, he was loyal.

VI *The Battle*

The sun rose at 5.19 a.m. on 8 June in Syria. The legionaries of *III Gallica* hailed the risen god. Heliogabalus, as priest of Elagabal, offered libations and performed sacrifice. Rituals matter in the heightened tension before a battle. The religious ceremonies may have helped the morale of the rebels.

It was going to be hot. The average June temperature was in the mid-seventies Fahrenheit, rising to a maximum of almost ninety degrees (about 24 to 32 Celsius). Terribly hot for men in armour, wearing helmets, burdened by shields and weapons and oppressed by fear. To make them lighter in battle, Macrinus had taken away the heavy shields the Praetorians normally used and their breastplates of scale armour. Even so, it would be an exhausting day. There were fourteen and a half hours to the potential safety of darkness. A long time to survive.

A modern battlefield is often eerily empty. As the saying goes, *if you can see it, you can kill it*. By contrast, an ancient battlefield was full: wide blocks of infantry and cavalry, close-packed, several ranks deep. We should not overemphasise the uniformity of Roman troops. The third century was a period of transition. The iconic legionary equipment – the rectangular shields and banded metal body armour, so-called *lorica segmentata*, famous from Trajan's Column – was giving way to oval shields and mail coats. Each soldier's equipment was replaced as it wore out. At Immae, both sides would have presented much the same slightly ragtag appearance. The standards, and devices painted on shields, would have allowed units on the other side to be recognised. Both armies would have formed up out of effective bowshot, perhaps no more than a couple of hundred yards apart. Easily close enough to make out individuals in the enemy line. Ancient battle had a horrible intimacy.

As Emperor, Macrinus was expected to command his own army. The only senior officer we can place with certainty at his side was Julianus Nestor, the survivor of his two original praetorian prefects. Presumably the brothers Nemesianus and Apollinaris, the tribunes of the Praetorians who had been implicated in the assassination of Caracalla, were stationed with their men. As we have seen, the rebel forces were led by the freedman-tutor Eutychianus. The two legions would be commanded by the ex-rankers Comazon and Verus. The imperial women – Maesa, Soaemias and presumably Mamea – remained in carriages to the rear. Probably with them were Heliogabalus and his young cousin.

The role of a general is not a universal constant, which is the same across all times and societies. What generals do, and are expected to do, in battle is a product of their culture. Ancient generalship can be analysed via three categories: the 'physical', actually fighting; the 'practical', drawing up the troops and issuing tactical orders; and the 'symbolic', formal and off-the-cuff speeches and a range of non-verbal gestures, like picking up a standard or sending away his horse, aimed at altering morale.

Different Classical cultures put different emphases on the different categories. Unlike the Macedonians of Alexander the Great, the Romans had marginalised the physical. Fighting hand-to-hand was a last resort. When all was lost, a Roman commander should seek an honourable death at the hands of the enemy, or fall on his own sword. A Roman general was meant to stay behind the lines, acting, in modern terms, as a 'battle-manager'. Yet, after he had drawn up the battle line, once the fighting started it was difficult to get new orders implemented. The battle frequently escaped his tactical control. As such, the Romans placed a heavy emphasis on the symbolic actions of a general. And, as we will see, symbolic actions were to be all-important at Immae.

Battle narratives were central to Greek and Roman history writing. Herodotus, inventing history in the fifth century BC, wrote about the Persian Wars. At the heart of his story were big set-piece battles, like Salamis and Plataea. A generation later, Thucydides reinvented history. Out went geography and ethnography, the gods and women. History was boiled down to men doing politics and war. So battles remained, with lengthy expositions like those on Amphipolis and Mantinea. The rules of the genre were set for historians for the rest of antiquity. Anyone writing history had to include a set-piece battle.

'You can as well write the history of a ball as of a battle', the Duke of Wellington commented on an attempt to retell Waterloo. Battles are big, chaotic and terrifying events. They are utterly confusing. Every participant or observer experiences them differently. Writing battle narratives is notoriously difficult. Whose eyes to see them through, at what points in the action? What to include, what to leave out? How to give the story dramatic form, make the whole comprehensible to a reader?

Our two contemporary historians, Cassius Dio and Herodian, both give narratives of Immae. Neither were eyewitnesses. Cassius Dio was in Rome. We have no idea where Herodian was on 8 June, but he was not at the battle, which he misplaces at the border between the provinces of Coele and Syria, and thus south of Apamea. Their accounts differ, but agree on the crucial factor that decided the battle.

How Herodian tells the story. Heliogabalus' troops put up intense resistance, fearing punishment if they were defeated. Those of Macrinus, on the other hand, brought little energy to the fight and deserted to the rebels. Seeing this, towards evening Macrinus took off his imperial cloak and other insignia and fled. The story appears finished, but then, after a brief glimpse into the future, unexpectedly lurches into life again. After the flight of Macrinus, the battle continued. The Praetorians fought magnificently, but the mass (the *plethos*) of the soldiers took the side of Heliogabalus. After a time, the Praetorians, unable to see Macrinus or the imperial standards, were unsure if the Emperor was among the dead or had run away. They faced an urgent moral dilemma: being unwilling to fight for someone who was not there, but ashamed to surrender. Hearing from the deserters that Macrinus had gone, Heliogabalus sent heralds to tell the Praetorians the truth and to offer them a pardon and enrolment in his guards. Finally, the Praetorians joined the rebels.

How Cassius Dio tells the story. The unmilitary Eutychianus drew up his troops in good fighting order. *Tyche* (good fortune) bestows understanding on the ignorant, as Dio tartly observes. Despite their excellent dispositions, the rebel troops made a very weak fight. They would never have stood had Maesa and Soaemias not jumped down from their carriages, rushed among the fleeing men and rallied them by their lamentations. At the same time, the soldiers saw young Heliogabalus dashing along on horseback, brandishing a sword – the very sword he had taken at his acclamation – seemingly divinely inspired, as if he was about to charge the enemy. The words *as if* in the translation might be important. 'Even so they would have again turned their backs, had not Macrinus fled when he saw them offering resistance.' Earlier, before recounting omens of the fall of the Emperor, Dio had commented that the zeal of the Praetorians would have conquered, had not Macrinus been defeated by his own cowardice.

Which story to choose? Cassius Dio is generally the better-informed historian. Here he is proved right about the location of the battle by the tombstone of Atinius Ianuarius, a soldier of *Legio II Parthica*, who died in the fighting at Immae. Cassius Dio's story has the advantage of being coherent and relatively straightforward. There is something fishy about the second half of Herodian's story – the battle is over, then, oh no, it is not! How come the deserters know Macrinus has fled, but the Praetorians do not? Why does the mass of soldiers appear to go over to the rebels twice? Yes, the clouds of dust raised by thousands of feet could limit visibility on ancient battlefields. Yes, the Praetorians would not have surrendered on the instant Macrinus fled. But the scene is highly wrought and dramatic: abandoned by all, in the twilight, the Praetorians fight on alone. It reads like something out of a novel, and we will see in chapter 5 that Herodian was given to inventing episodes like a modern historical novelist. The episode is not only dramatic, but ironic. In Herodian's text soldiers, especially Praetorians, usually are morally bad. Yet here they are brave and loyal and better than Macrinus, the man they had sworn to protect. Herodian had read Cassius Dio. It is possible that he picked up on Cassius Dio's passing remark about the zeal of the Praetorians and worked it up into an elaborate scene.

Whichever story we pick, or if we ingeniously try to combine both, symbolic gestures are at the heart of the action: the Emesene women leaping down from their carriages, Heliogabalus brandishing his sword (Cassius Dio), Macrinus shrugging off the imperial cloak (Herodian). They precipitate what both authors see as the turning point – the flight of Macrinus. As he had when faced with the Parthians at Nisibis, as he did when confronted with the severed head of Julianus at Apamea, Macrinus lost his nerve and took to his heels. For Cassius Dio such behaviour was to be expected from a Moor.

VII *To Antioch*

Leaving the battlefield, the imperial party split up. Macrinus entrusted the safety of his son Diadumenianus to Epagathus, a resourceful imperial freedman, who had served Caracalla. The Emperor pressed on through the gathering gloom to cover the twenty-four miles to Antioch. Arriving at the city – presumably the gates were shut – Macrinus gained admittance by claiming that he had been victorious. The lie did not buy him much time. Later that night, when the news of his defeat was noised abroad, carnage ensued. 'Many were slain,' Cassius Dio tells us, 'both along the roads and in the city, on the grounds that they had favoured this side or that.'

In the dead of night, spurred on by the killings, Macrinus made a fateful decision. He had his head shaved. Off too came his bushy philosopher's beard. So much for his emulation of Marcus Aurelius. Then Macrinus either put on the clothes of an ordinary traveller (Herodian), or slung a dark garment over his robe of imperial purple (Cassius Dio). Probably the latter: as we will see in chapter 5, the Roman elite were very inept at pretending to be lower class. Disguised, with just a handful of trusted centurions, Macrinus either mounted a horse (Cassius Dio), or called for a carriage (Herodian).

Many were slain. The customary level of violence in Roman cities is hard to appreciate if you are lucky enough to live in a comparatively safe modern town like Oxford. The prevalence of *stasis* (violent unrest) is indicated by the many surviving works of philosophers praising and advocating its opposite: *homonia* (peaceful concord, literally *oneness of mind*). Even under the *Pax Romana* – always more of an ideal or mission statement than a reality – age-old rivalries between cities, although stopping short of outright war, could cause mass violence. Internally, cities were riven by fault lines: the rich against the poor, the bitter rivalries among the elite, the poor turning on one another. Although many cities in the Greek East – and we know more about them than those elsewhere – had municipal 'police' forces, self-help was the order of the day. Brought up to admire the 'man-killing hands' of Achilles in the *Iliad*, and lacking anything like the Judeo-Christian commandment 'thou shalt not kill', in a heart-beat such self-help could become very violent indeed. People were stabbed, beaten and stoned to death or burnt alive.

As well as the *stasis* in Antioch, Cassius Dio tells us of an outbreak when news of the defeat of Macrinus reached Alexandria in Egypt: 'many of the populace and not a few of the soldiers perished'. There were other incidents, which Dio omitted, 'as they are all very much alike, and their details have no particular importance'. It reminds us that Roman civil wars did not just affect the soldiers that fought them and the civilians unfortunate enough to be caught up in their path. The violence rippled out across the empire. Wherever you were, regime change provided a perfect excuse to settle old scores.

Heliogabalus' forces camped at the scene of their success. A battlefield was a horrible and unsettling place the night after combat: littered with piles of dead men and horses, echoing to the moans and screams of the wounded and alive with the eerie sounds of carrion beasts and birds. As this was a civil war, and the losers had joined the victors, the survivors should seek out all the injured. But they would not be alone. No matter how remote, a battlefield in antiquity attracted human scavengers, eager to loot and strip the dead and often willing to finish off the helpless wounded. Yet worse people were believed to be drawn to the stricken field. The body parts of corpses were ingredients for dark magic. Most efficacious were those ripped from the unburied who had died by violence. Battlefields were a rich source for the supplies of witches. They were the scene of necromancy. The dead could be made to foretell the future. While the shades of the long dead merely gibbered and squeaked like bats, the freshly slaughtered spoke in a clear voice. The incantations of witches, according to the poet Lucan, sounded like 'the bark of dogs and howl of wolves, the owl's cry of alarm, the screech-owl's night-time moan, the wild beasts' shriek and wail'. It was easy to take the noises of nocturnal predators as evidence there was unholy magic out there in the darkness. As priest of his native god, Heliogabalus was attuned to the supernatural. As Emperor he would be accused of meddling in magic, even necromancy.

A night on the battlefield of Immae might have piqued his interest in the dark arts.

On the morning of 9 June, the army of Heliogabalus began a long day's march to Antioch. The young Emperor and his advisers had a serious problem – how to stop their own forces sacking the city. It was, Cassius Dio tells us, a thing the troops 'were very anxious to do'. Roman soldiers, always contemptuous of civilians, and given to inflicting casual violence on them, had no scruples if given the chance to plunder, rape and kill in a city that had backed the wrong side in a civil war. Never mind that half the army had also supported Macrinus. The cause of Antioch was not helped by the fact that neither the Praetorians nor *III Gallica* and *II Parthica* were based there, and so had no families or dependants in the town. Attempting to restrain them would be dangerous. In similar circumstances, the Emperor Postumus in AD 268 would be lynched by his own men when he tried to prevent the sack of the city of Mogontiacum. The solution at Antioch was to promise each soldier two thousand sesterces. Later, part of the money was raised from the inhabitants of the city. As we do not know the size of the army, we cannot know how much money was involved. Yet it would have been a large sum. Perhaps the Antiochenes were sanguine about the extortion, considering the alternative.

Late in the day the rebels reached Antioch. They would have entered by the Eastern Gate, processed up the wide, colonnaded street, turned right at the Omphalos, the *navel* of the city, and taken the street that led down to a bridge to the island in the Orontes, where stood the imperial palace. Antioch was one of the three largest cities in the empire after Rome. It could be thought of as the capital of the eastern half of the imperium. Now the city was in the possession of Heliogabalus. But the rebellion was not over. There could be no victory until Macrinus was dead. And Macrinus had vanished.

CHAPTER 4   IDENTITIES AND RACISM

When Heliogabalus entered Antioch he had done nothing wrong. Indeed, his speech at Raphaneae and his sword-waving at the Battle of Immae were exemplary. But their promise was illusory. There had been little time to transgress. It was less than four weeks since he had been acclaimed by the soldiers of *III Gallica*. But by that winter in Nicomedia things had changed. The youth from Syria Phoenice was well on the way to being hated. Did his origins play a part? Was the loathing *because* he was Syrian or Phoenician? Which poses the much bigger, and more controversial, question – were the Romans racist?

I   *Classical Racism?*

In scholarship of the nineteenth and early twentieth century, race was a very big deal indeed. On the dynasty from Emesa it ran as follows. Heliogabalus and the women of his family, especially Domna and Maesa, embodied a tide of orientalism flowing into Rome. They brought eastern religion and superstition, luxury and vice, cruelty and despotism. It tainted everything: politics, morality, philosophy, art. The family were a sordid way-station on the decline of the Roman Empire: from the manly and open Republic based in the West (753–31 BC) – via the principate

(31BC–AD284): still western, but less free – to the servile decadence that had slouched off to the East as the Dominate (and later, after Rome had fallen, to Byzantium, AD284–1453).

The Second World War, but really the horror of the Holocaust, undermined racial characteristics as an explanation. Classical scholars began to marginalise race. Sometimes it is reduced to no more than geographic origins in the endless lists in prosopography: Emperors merely gave some advancement to men from the same province. Often it has ceased to exist altogether. Maesa and her kin become just a normal elite Greco-Roman family (whatever that means). Those who raise racism at all water it down to 'proto-racism' or 'ethnic prejudice'. With heightened twenty-first-century sensibilities the area has become a minefield. A scholar whom a reviewer infers *might imagine* (but not *state*) the – self-evidently true – proposition that there are (and thus perhaps were) different degrees of racism is criticised because 'that is precisely the kind of argument employed by many racists'.

The problem of wishing Roman racism out of existence is the ancient evidence. For example, we have already seen that Cassius Dio thought that Macrinus was a coward simply because he was a Moor. Similarly, the historian wrote that Caracalla 'belonged to three races and he possessed none of their virtues at all, but combined in himself all their vices; the fickleness, cowardice and recklessness of Gaul, the harshness and cruelty of Africa, and the cunning of Syria, whence he was sprung on his mother's side'. Everything like this – and there is a great deal of it under the empire – has to be dismissed as a literary commonplace, a joke or caricature, harmless satire or something else without meaning or intent. This entails believing that literature and life move in completely separate worlds. It takes some fast footwork to believe that Cassius Dio can think these things when dictating a book in his study, but when kept waiting all day for an audience while Caracalla drinks with common soldiery, such thoughts would never enter his mind.

The Romans were racist in ways unimagined by modern racists. Northern barbarians were huge, unpleasantly pale, lazy, drunken and violent. Ferocious in the first rush of battle – lacking discipline and thus true courage – they quickly became dispirited. Their sexuality was shameless: given the chance they were dedicated gang rapists, while their wives openly coupled with other men, and youths were equally flagrant in soliciting passive male–male sex. Naturally stupid, indeed lacking rational faculties, they were incapable of improvement or civilisation.

Easterners, on the other hand, talked too much and were too clever by half. It made them cunning, treacherous and avaricious. They were prone to worshipping strange gods and practising magic. Habituated to autocracy, they were naturally servile, soft, effeminate and cowardly. The Greeks created the stereotype of the easterner when defeating the Persian invasions (490–478 BC). Ironically, when the Greeks were conquered by Rome in the last two centuries BC, they found the stereotype applied to themselves.

The Roman ethnography of the world was built out of very few blocks. When the Romans looked west, they saw nothing at all, except perhaps the mythical Islands of the Blessed, inhabited by a select few of the virtuous dead. Before they were conquered by Rome, Spaniards were considered the same as simple northern barbarians. Some traits continued. In his novel *The Life of Apollonius of Tyana*, Philostratus has credulous Spanish provincials who have never heard of the Olympic Games and are terrified of a tragic actor, whom they mistake for a *daemon*. Likewise, when Romans looked south, they saw cunning easterners. The identification was encouraged by the historical settlement of

Phoenicians from the Near East on the North African coast, above all at Carthage.

Various causes underpinned these stereotypes. With different stress in different authors, it was down to climate and geography (the most popular explanation), heredity, the political systems (easterners ruled by despots), or even the alignment of the stars as revealed by astrology.

Not all Romans at all times subscribed to these stereotypes. What it meant to be Roman itself changed over time. Not all inhabitants of the empire saw their primary identity as Roman. Indeed, the whole ideological edifice could be turned on its head. (Did you notice above that Cassius Dio said Caracalla possessed all of the *vices* of Gaul, Africa and Spain, but none of their *virtues*?) Northerners could be presented as freedom-loving 'noble savages', uncorrupted by city ways. In the hands of Dio Chrysostom, the Dacians north of the Danube ended up as natural philosophers. Similarly, easterners might appear as possessors of ancient and alien wisdom.

So far there has been no mention of Roman attitudes towards black people. Among modern scholars it is axiomatic that the Romans, to use the title of a well-known book, lived *Before Color Prejudice*. This suits modern agendas, especially that racism was an invention of modern European colonialism, but does not totally square with the ancient evidence. Take an anecdote about Heliogabalus. The Emperor 'would often shut up his friends in halting places for the night with old hags from Ethiopia, and compel them to stay there until morning, saying that the most beautiful women were kept in these places'. Almost certainly the story is invented. But fiction reveals attitudes. Why are the aged women black? Presumably to tap into existing prejudices such as that expressed in the description of an old slave woman in an ancient Appendix to Virgil: she was 'African, every part of her body bearing witness to her origin, woolly-haired, thick-lipped, black, with great, pendulous breasts, pinched belly, scrawny legs, and huge feet'.

Somewhere near Hadrian's Wall, Heliogabalus' 'grandfather' Septimius Severus met a black auxiliary soldier. It was an omen of the Emperor's death. Shades of the dead were dark-skinned. Long before, the army of Brutus had a similar encounter on their march to the Battle of Philippi. They ran the black man through with their swords. If you left your house and the first person you saw was black, it signified bad luck. Just as it did if you met a eunuch or a monkey. Hard not to see this as racist.

It is true that there are not all that many anti-black statements in the ancient literature. This can be put down to there not being many black people in the Roman Empire. The Romans had no provinces in sub-Saharan Africa. But probably more significant is that the Romans had lots of other groups to demonise and dislike: all those big and pallid northerners, and those hordes of shifty easterners. And, of course, there was the immanent and almost invisible enemy. Most slaves looked just like their masters.

II *The Identity of Emesa*

Emesa in many ways looks like it was a typical Greek city under Roman rule in the lifetime of Heliogabalus: that it had adopted enough Greek culture to be considered thoroughly Hellenised. All the inscriptions found in the vicinity, more than seven hundred of them, are in Greek, as is the wording on the coins issued by the city. These were not automatic choices. At Palmyra, over eighty miles to the east, but intimately linked to Emesa by the caravan trade, many inscriptions were in the local language. To the west, Sidon and Arca minted coins in Phoenician in the third century AD. We have seen town councillors from Emesa assisting Maesa's revolt. From this we assume the settlement possessed the three institutions necessary to be counted as a Greek *Polis*: magistrates, council and assembly. Emesa had received the status of a Roman colony, either from Septimius Severus or Caracalla. From AD212, after the *Constitutio Antoniniana*, all free inhabitants were Roman citizens and thus subject to Roman law. We know from the civic coinage that Emesa held games with impeccably Greek names: the Pythian and Eleian. That the novelists Iamblichus (probably) and Heliodorus (certainly) came from Emesa indicates a developed level of *paideia* (Greek culture). The medieval and modern cities of Homs were built on the site of Emesa. Few substantial archaeological artefacts survive from its ancient incarnation. A dedication to the god Elagabal found on the *Tell*, the man-made mound in the centre of the town, probably indicates the site of the temple. We know what it looked like from coins.

The temple was set on a podium, with a flight of steps leading up. The entrance was flanked by six columns that supported a tall pediment. Whatever the cult inside, the architecture was completely Greek.

Image 6: Elagabal in the Temple at Emesa

The family of Heliogabalus, like their hometown, had many markers of Greek and Roman identity. They had held Roman citizenship for many generations, probably for two centuries. They were of equestrian or senatorial status. In imperial service they travelled the length and breadth of the empire. An inscription survives from near the headwaters of the Danube, erected by Caius Julius Avitus Alexianus, the maternal grandfather of Heliogabalus, when he was governing the province of Raetia. By law senators, like Avitus, had to own estates in Italy. Heliogabalus' father, Sextus Varius Marcellus, owned land at Velitrae in the Alban Hills. The family, which (as we will see in a moment) spent considerable periods of time in Rome, must have had property in the city itself. This has been thought to include the 'Gardens of Varius' (*Horti Variani*) and the 'Gardens of Old Hope' (*Horti Spei Veteris*), although, as we will see in the next section, both suggestions are dubious. To make a career in the service of the Emperor it was necessary to be fluent in Latin. To be accepted in the elite circles of the empire it was not enough just to speak Greek: you had to be able to hold an educated conversation. A working knowledge of literature was expected, especially the poems of Homer. A slip of the tongue in either language was more than an embarrassment: it could lead to loss of office and status.

So far so Greek and Roman. These categories, however, did not encompass the entire identity of Heliogabalus' family. And the relationship between Greek and Roman identities themselves was not entirely straightforward. Before we go any further, these need to be sorted out. The scholarly orthodoxy used to run like this: in the last two centuries BC the Roman elite became thoroughly Hellenised, and in the first two centuries AD the Greek elite became similarly Romanised, and thus the two merged into an empire-wide undifferentiated Greco-Roman elite. Except they didn't. It was all rather more nuanced, and more interesting.

The Roman elite embraced Greek culture. Apart from its evident intellectual and aesthetic attractions, they used it as a badge to mark themselves off from the non-elite. Acquiring *paideia* took money and leisure. Elite Romans could admire the Greeks of the past, say from the age of Alexander the Great or earlier. Contemporary Greeks, although there were exceptions, were often little better than the stereotype of the shifty easterner. Even when they meant to be kind, Romans tended not to call them Hellenes, but *Graeculi*, 'Little Greeks'. A Roman, no matter how Hellenised, remained a Roman.

Some of the Greek elite, but not all, sought to pursue an imperial career and to enter into the heart of the empire. They wanted to be equestrian officers and friends of senators, or perhaps even senators themselves and advisers to Emperors. But they retained their Greekness. On his monument in Athens, Philopappus, the distant kinsman of Heliogabalus, was depicted in the toga of a Roman consul as well as in the *himation* and tunic of a Greek magistrate. The iconography of the two did not merge. Different identities for different circumstances. There was a tendency among Greek writers – even those with imperial posts, like Herodian – either to disparage the Romans or to affect to know nothing about them. An individual could shift between their Greek and Roman identity, but the two never combined into the modern construction of Greco-Roman.

There was a third important element in the self-fashioning of Heliogabalus' family. It was a local Syrian or Phoenician identity. The majority of their estates remained in the region around Emesa. They married into other families from the same area: from local towns such as Apamea or Arca, or from Emesa itself. Even Domna's marriage to Septimius Severus from Africa was not a total exception. Despite much bad modern popular history, and poorly researched historical novels, Severus was not a black African. His mother's family were Italian immigrants, and on his father's side Severus was descended from Phoenician settlers. Along with their Roman first two names, the Emesene family often used Syrian *cognomina*: Soaemias, Maesa, Domna. People tended to be known by their *cognomina*. When Emesenes travelled they took their 'ancestral god' with them, and, as we will see, the rituals of Elagabal were self-consciously 'eastern'. The tomb of a member of the family, Gaius Julius Sampsigeramus – who carried not just an Emesene *cognomina* but also the alternative Syrian name of Silas – stood in Emesa until 1911, when it was dynamited to make way for the railway station. Although built in Roman materials, its design was Near Eastern, with influences from Mesopotamia. As well as Greek and Latin, the family would have spoken Aramaic, even if only to servants. Not only were Emesenes identified by others as Phoenician, as Herodian introduces Maesa, but they also did the same themselves. Heliodorus the novelist stated he was 'Phoenician from the city of Emesa, one of the clan of Descendants of the Sun'.

The categories Syrian and Phoenician overlapped. People could be referred to as Syrophoenician. They could also – with a deliberately antiquarian connotation – be called Assyrian. The geographic boundaries were vague, but Phoenicia was a part of Syria. So all Phoenicians were Syrians, but not all Syrians were Phoenician.

The Emesenes had adopted their Syrian and Phoenician identities, just as they had their Greek and Roman. The founders of Emesa in the last century BC were nomadic Arabs moving to a sedentary lifestyle. Although the label Syrian was available – to themselves, and to outside observers – from the start, in the lifetime of Heliogabalus that of Phoenician was very recent. The

Orontes valley had not been considered part of Phoenicia until AD194, when Septimius Severus divided the province of Syria into two: Syria Coele in the north and Syria Phoenice to the south. In just one generation a Roman administrative measure had allowed the Emesenes to acquire a new self-representation.

Being Syrian brought all the freight of negative connotations of the stereotype of the 'easterner'. Being Phoenician heightened these in three specific ways. Phoenicians were thought of as especially cruel because of their historical – and long since abandoned – practice of sacrificing their own children. The cemeteries in Carthage for infants burnt alive haunted the ancient imagination, as they do the modern. Two common sayings reveal the other two. 'A Phoenician story' meant a plausible lie. Among all those shifty easterners, Phoenicians were the most mendacious of the lot. In both Greek and Latin the verb *Phoinikizein*, to 'act like a Phoenician'/'play the Phoenician', meant to perform cunnilingus. In the public sexual morality of the two Classical cultures there was nothing worse. The Latin poet Martial makes endless jokes about not wanting a kiss in greeting from 'cunt-lickers'.

Given all this, what induced the Emesenes to identify themselves as Syrian or Phoenician? Perhaps it was just not as bad as being Arab? In a fable, the wagon of the god Hermes, weighted down with lies, villainy and fraud, broke down among the Arabs. They stole the lot. Being Phoenician, unlike being Arab, also plugged the Emesenes into the ancient Greek past. There were Phoenicians in Homer, already seafarers, not always depicted negatively. In myth Phoenicians invented the alphabet, and Cadmus, the founder of the Greek city of Thebes, also came from Phoenicia. In history Phoenicians had fought bravely at the naval battle of Salamis and – albeit with ingenious cruelty – against Alexander the Great.

Or was it imposed from outside, an ancient form of the 'Orientalism' Edward Said claimed the West inflicted on the Near East in the nineteenth century, which made its people see themselves as weak, corrupt and decadent? On this line, it has been suggested that Syrians, like the Emesenes, were suffering from a sort of a 'measure of ambivalence' about their ethnic identity, if not 'ethnic self-hatred'. Evidence has been found in the embarrassment of Alexander Severus, Heliogabalus' cousin, at his Syrian origins and in the self-deprecating statements of Lucian the satirist from Samosata. Except the former is fiction in the *Augustan History* and the latter are actually boasts: 'Look how much Greek culture (*paideia*) I have, even though I come from the East!'

Self-loathing is far less likely than two other and complementary strategies. First is denial: 'You are wrong. We are not like *that*, but like *this*; not cowards but courageous.' Second is adaptation, putting a positive spin on the stereotype: 'What you condemn as cunning, we value as intelligence.' An obscure work of geography from the first century AD allows us to see a Phoenician employing both strategies. Pomponius Mela was from Tingentera in southern Spain: the opposite end of the empire from Emesa. Yet his ancestry was Phoenician, and in his *De Chronographia* he exhibits a Phoenician world view.

> The Phoenicians have made Phoenicia famous. They are a clever race of men, and excel in the duties of war and peace. They invented the alphabet, as well as literature and the other arts: how to sail on the sea by ship, how to conduct naval conflict, how to rule over other peoples, dominion and battle.

III *The Making of Heliogabalus*

In May AD218, at the outbreak of the revolt, Heliogabalus was fourteen. So he was born early in AD204. In that year Septimius Severus celebrated the Saecular Games in Rome. Spread over three days and nights, these were meant to be held every one hundred and ten years after the foundation of Rome. No one in AD204 could have predicted that the rise of Christianity to become the state religion in the fourth century would mean that these would be the last games held. On 1 June (the *Kalends*), sacred banquets were given on the Capitol for one hundred and ten married matrons. An inscription tells us who attended. Domna, as empress, presided. Most of the women were the wives of senators, and eighteen were married to equestrians. The latter were headed by Soaemias, wife of Sextus Varius Marcellus. Their son would have been a few months old. The 'Syrian/Phoenician' Emperor Heliogabalus was thus born in Rome.

Sextus Varius Marcellus had been procurator of the Roman water supply in AD198. It was an equestrian post of no great eminence, with a salary of 100,000 sesterces. It is possible that Marcellus was still in office in AD204, although it has been suggested that the careers of Domna's relatives suffered while her enemy Plautianus, the praetorian prefect, had great influence over the Emperor Severus (AD200–5).

Although not a senator, and thus not legally obliged to own estates in Italy, Sextus Varius Marcellus had a property in Rome. The *Augustan History* provides the sole mention of the 'Gardens of Varius' (*Horti Variani*) as the destination of a journey from the Palatine that went past the Temple of the Sun, built by the Emperor Aurelian (AD270–5). This would place them somewhere off the *Via Flaminia*, possibly at the northern end of the Campus Martius. Unfortunately, the passage is complete fiction. The

Temple of the Sun brought Heliogabalus, priest of the sun, to the mind of the mischievous author, and he had a habit of spinning fantasies around the Emperor's family name, Varius.

A more trustworthy section of the *Augustan History* tells of Heliogabalus as Emperor retiring to the 'Gardens of Old Hope' (*ad Spem Veterem* or *Horti Spei Veteris*), which contained a circus for chariot racing. These have been identified with extensive archaeological remains off the *Via Labicana*. The problem here is that this was already an imperial property in the reign of Septimius Severus, by AD 202 at the latest, and thus cannot have been owned by Marcellus in AD 204.

There is one fixed point in the topography of Heliogabalus' infancy. His father's sarcophagus was found at Velitrae, some twenty miles south-east of Rome. The Alban Hills around Velitrae were a favoured resort for elite Romans escaping the stifling heat of summer in the city. Marcellus had been buried on his own estate.

The first four years of Heliogabalus' life, years in the charge of his mother and nurse, were spent in the unlocated house or houses in Rome, and on country estates: his father's at Velitrae and others owned by his family and their friends.

By AD 208 Plautianus was dead and the careers of Domna's relatives could resume. In that year Septimius Severus decided to remove his sons, Caracalla and Geta, from the corrupting influence of life in Rome. There was unrest among the Caledonian tribes of northern Britain, and what could instil better morality than a bracing campaign of conquest? Domna and the court accompanied the Emperor. Heliogabalus' father and maternal grandfather were part of the entourage. Maesa's husband, the ex-consul Avitus, went as a *comes*, one of the official companions of the Emperor. The role of Marcellus was more specific: procurator, financial overseer, of the province. It was an important post, especially in wartime, and brought a stipend of 200,000 sesterces. It was customary under the principate for an official to travel with his family. When Severus and Caracalla campaigned north of Hadrian's Wall, from AD208–11, Domna, Geta and the civilian administration were established in Eboracum (modern York). From the age of four to seven the future Emperor Heliogabalus was growing up in what is now Yorkshire.

Cassius Dio records a conversation between Domna and the wife of a Caledonian. When the empress teased the British woman about their habit of having sex with many men, she got the answer that they consorted openly with the best men, whereas Roman women let themselves be seduced in secret by the worst.

As a child of the elite, Heliogabalus, no matter how precocious, was sheltered from much exposure to the local culture. One event of AD211 would have impacted on his life. In February of that year the Emperor Septimius Severus died of old age and illness in Eboracum. Perhaps Heliogabalus saw him cremated, and watched the eagle released from the pyre soar into the sky, symbolising the ascent of the dead Emperor's soul to the heavens. Perhaps the rumour that Caracalla had tried to hasten his father's end came to his ears. Certainly, he would have been aware of the purge of certain courtiers that followed the death. Familiar faces about the court – the imperial freedmen Euodus and Castor and the physiotherapist Proculus (a closet Christian) – were gone. Their remains may be among the eighty skeletons, over half of them decapitated, found some years ago in York.

Caracalla and Geta ended the war, and the imperial court set off for Rome. The bitter animosity between the brothers could not have escaped Heliogabalus' attention. The two new Emperors travelled separately and took different lodgings. Subsequent events reveal Heliogabalus' father as a partisan of Caracalla. On the journey, or shortly after arriving in Rome, Marcellus received a new post: procurator of the imperial privy purse. It brought an annual salary of 300,000 sesterces. Marcellus' career was on the rise. He would go higher still.

Back in Rome the palace was divided, and the Emperors maintained separate households. In December AD211 Caracalla, pretending to want a reconciliation, arranged to meet Geta in Domna's apartment in the palace. It was a trap: the rooms were surrounded by soldiers loyal to Caracalla. Geta was murdered in the arms of their mother. In the attack, Domna herself was accidentally wounded in the hand. It was a dangerous moment for the dynasty. The soldiers had sworn their oaths to both Emperors. They might not accept the killing. Caracalla went to the Praetorian camp with a story that he had escaped a conspiracy. A pay rise, extended to the rest of the army, made the tale more acceptable. Now the Emperor took the extraordinary step of appointing Marcellus acting commander of both the Praetorians and the urban cohorts. This was a position of great trust and immense power. Heliogabalus' father became an automatic member of every council summoned by the Emperor. The only man entitled to be armed in the presence of the Emperor, he led some seventeen thousand armed men: all the frontline troops in the city of Rome.

It is notable that at this tense time Marcellus holds a far more sensitive post than his father-in-law. Soaemias' father, and husband of Maesa, the grand ex-consul Caius Julius Avitus Alexianus, is found as prefect of the *Alimenta* (AD211–13), running an imperial foundation feeding needy and deserving children in Italy.

As a child, Heliogabalus would not have been present either in Domna's chambers or the Praetorian camp, but he would have witnessed the aftermath. Caracalla launched a terrible wave of terror. Cassius Dio claims 20,000 supporters of Geta and their families – men, women and children – were killed. The troops who hunted them down were the Praetorians and the *frumentarii*, whose commander (the *princeps peregrinorum*) also answered to Marcellus as praetorian prefect. At this fraught time Marcellus, and his family, would have been quartered in the palace. Heliogabalus might not have witnessed the executions – although they might have been hard to miss – but he could not have failed to see the effect of the condemnation of Geta's memory: the men overturning his statues, chiselling his names from inscriptions, smearing shit on his portraits.

When the crisis passed, Marcellus was replaced by a regular prefect of the city and praetorian prefect, but his loyalty was rewarded. Elevated from the equestrian order to the Senate, with the status of an ex-praetor, he was put in charge of the military treasury (prefect of the *aerarium militare*). Given the troops' pay rise, this was a demanding job.

With the return of calm. Marcellus and his family moved from the palace to their own home. Outwardly Marcellus had been honoured, and he was still performing a function vital to the regime. Yet in reality he no longer commanded troops, and it was a move away from the Emperor, and thus from power. By the next year the distance would be greater.

In AD213 Marcellus was appointed governor of Numidia. This did bring with it the command of *Legio III Augusta*, the only legion in the North African provinces, but it was a long way from Rome, and governors of Numidia did not always go on to the most prestigious offices. It looks as if Marcellus was being sidelined.

In the normal run of things Heliogabalus, now nine, would have travelled to Africa with his father. But the Severan dynasty was wary of the governors of armed provinces. Their children often remained in Rome to be educated at the imperial school on the Palatine. There, of course, they acted as hostages for their absent fathers.

Numidia was to be the end of Marcellus' career. He died either in Africa or soon after returning to Italy. His sarcophagus at Velitrae lists in Latin and Greek the high offices of his career and says that this most loved husband and father was buried by Soaemias and his children (*Soaemias... cum fili(i)s marito et patri amantissimo*). At this point Heliogabalus had a brother or sister, or maybe more than one.

Heliogabalus next appears in the early spring of AD214 in the town of Thyatira, inland from Smyrna (modern Izmir) in the Roman province of Asia. A local woman, Aurelia Alcippilla Lailiana, at least four years later, during the reign of Heliogabalus, erected an inscription in honour of her father, who had presided over games during the visit of the Emperor Marcus Aurelius Antoninus (Heliogabalus) and his father the Emperor Antoninus (Caracalla), when the latter gave the town the right to be an assize centre. It is a remarkable document. Alcippilla advertises her allegiance to Heliogabalus, and the previous links of her family to the Severan dynasty, which, together with their generosity (her father would have paid for the games), she implies, won the town the advantageous status as an assize centre (a place where governors would hold court when travelling through the province, like a modern circuit judge). She also completely rewrote history. In AD214 no one had raised the possibility that Heliogabalus was the son of Caracalla. Later, in the summer of AD222, or whenever the news of the fall of Heliogabalus reached Thyatira, his name was partly mutilated. History was redacted again.

As an aside, Alcippilla reminds us of something easily forgotten by those who study inscriptions (epigraphers). The ancients did not put up inscriptions to provide us with information. They were public statements, which cost money. Far from unbiased reportage, they had their agendas and biases and could play with the truth, just like literary texts.

We do not know when Heliogabalus, and presumably Soaemias, perhaps also Mamaea and Alexander, had joined the imperial entourage in the East. Given the difficulties and dangers of travelling in the winter, most likely it would have been the previous autumn (AD213), when Caracalla was holding court in Nicomedia.

After Thyatira, Heliogabalus vanishes until the mild spring night of 15 May AD218, when he leaves Emesa for the camp at Raphaneae. When had Heliogabalus arrived in Emesa? Two late fourth-century writers, Aurelius Victor and the author of the *Augustan History*, claim that he fled for sanctuary into the priesthood or temple of Elagabal at Emesa only after the death of Caracalla. So after 17 April AD217. But the two are not independent. The *Augustan History* drew material from Aurelius Victor and both used the same earlier fourth-century source. The latter may well have invented the incident based on the return of Maesa to Emesa. Another possibility is a hypothetical visit by Caracalla to Emesa on his way back from Egypt in AD216. Whatever the answer, it is important that Heliogabalus was not born and bred in Emesa. At the time of his revolt, he had only been there for a few months, or a few years at most.

We have quite a lot of anecdotes about Heliogabalus' childhood. How he would harness four huge dogs to a chariot and drive about his country estates. How his schoolfellows called him *Varius*, because he seemed to be the product of *various* sperm, like the son of a whore. Most concern his extravagance. He was the first commoner to spread golden covers on his couches. Perfumes from India he burnt as if they were coals, and he never travelled with fewer than sixty wagons. When someone asked him if he was not worried about becoming poor, he replied that nothing could be better than being his own heir.

Unfortunately for history, all are the product of the novelistic imagination of the author of the *Augustan History*. To take just one example. The playful writer had a thing about chariots pulled by unlikely creatures. When he became Emperor, Heliogabalus put lions, tigers, stags, camels and elephants in the traces. To accommodate the elephants, some tombs in the Vatican had to be knocked down – which looks like an anti-Christian jibe. Not content with exotic animals, Heliogabalus harnessed naked women. Apart from the women, other characters in the *Augustan History* did the same. Stags also drew the chariot of the splendidly named Gothic king Canabas, or Canabaudes. Surely the name is used as a sly joke. The Goths were also known as Scyths, and in Herodotus the latter howled with pleasure when inhaling hemp.

On a more sober account, Heliogabalus had the upbringing of a conventional upper-class Roman child. Until the age of six, as an infant in Rome and Britain, his life was controlled by women: his mother Soaemias and his nurse. At seven, having returned to Rome, his elementary education began at the hands of men. Most boys were sent out to a schoolmaster (*Ludi Magister*), and some had a private tutor at home. These teachers were freeborn or freedmen, often of Greek origin. Given the wealth of the family, most likely Heliogabalus had a tutor. That may have changed when his father was posted to Numidia, and Heliogabalus probably enrolled in the imperial school on the Palatine. Another important figure in the boy's life was his *paedogogus*, a trusted slave child-minder, who accompanied him whenever he left the house. At this stage he was taught to read and write, in both Latin and Greek, with much learning by rote. Discipline was strict and unashamedly physical, and floggings commonplace. At twelve, probably not long before Heliogabalus arrived in Emesa, it was time to be handed over to a *grammaticus*. The family chose Eutychianus, the *Delightful Lad* who had been raised as a slave in Maesa's household. Heliogabalus later referred to him as his foster-father and guardian. Teaching under a *grammaticus* focused on poetry, with Homer and Virgil at the heart of the syllabus. The teaching method centred on reading aloud, followed by explanation and analysis. Long passages had to be learnt by heart. Syntax was taught by encouraging correct speech and criticising any solecisms. Every aspect of a boy's life was overseen and prescribed.

All this changed when Heliogabalus was made high priest of the conical black stone: the sun god Elagabal of Emesa.

Heliogabalus would have had some previous experience of the deity. His family took Elagabal wherever they went. Avitus, his grandfather, had erected an inscription to his 'ancestral god' when governor of Raetia. In the Transtiberim district of Rome a distant kinsman, Julius Balbillus, had been a priest of Elagabal. But, as will see in chapter 8, Elagabal had won no converts abroad. In the wider empire only Emesenes honoured the deity. Elagabal was a minor cult, confined to his family. In Emesa it was very different. Elagabal was the leading god of the city, and Heliogabalus, as his high priest, for the first time had an adult and very public role. It was a role that would dominate the rest of his life. Given that Heliogabalus had been raised in the West, and 'Syrian/Phoenician' was only one strand in the identity of his family, why did it so quickly overshadow everything else?

A modern explanation sees it as a political move, probably initiated by Maesa, designed to appeal to the army. We know that some of the legionaries of *III Gallica* attended the ceremonies in the temple at Emesa before the revolt. No doubt the god aided the initial acclamation at Raphaneae. But after that its utility was at an end. Elagabal, unlike some other eastern gods, notably Jupiter Dolichenus and Mithras, was not worshipped throughout the army. Indeed, the 'barbaric' rituals performed by Heliogabalus as high priest when Emperor seem to have been part of the reason the soldiers turned against him. If it was a piece of realpolitik on the part of Maesa, it ran out of control. Her grandson had taken it as something else.

A recent commentator interprets the religious zeal of Heliogabalus as an act of adolescent rebellion. After all those years of being told what to do, he would now do as he liked. It is possible. But the Classical world had no mental category identical to our 'adolescent'. Neither the Greek *ephebes* nor the Roman *iuvenes* were the same as a modern monosyllabic, awkward teenager. Can adolescent rebellion exist in a culture that has no concept of adolescence?

The life of a younger contemporary of Heliogabalus suggests another interpretation. In AD228, six years after the death of Heliogabalus, a twelve-year-old boy in Mesopotamia received a divine revelation. His heavenly twin told the boy the truth of his paternity (divine, not human), and his future role in spreading the true religion. With admirable prudence, in view of his youth, his twin told him to keep quiet until he had reached maturity. Further visions and signs followed, 'which were short and brief, such as I could bear, for sometimes he came like lightning'. Understandably, even when he was twenty-four, the youth had doubts. 'My enemies are great in number, but I am alone. They are rich, but I am poor. How, then, will I who am alone against all be able to reveal this mystery among the great numbers caught in error? How will I go to kings and governors?' The heavenly twin was reassuring on that score. 'If you ever summon me when you are oppressed, I shall be found standing by you, and shall be your protector in oppression and danger.' So the prophet Mani, pulling on his red and green striped trousers, throwing a multi-coloured cloak over his shoulders and hefting a stout ebony staff, set off to found the religion that bears his name. Manichaeism demanded a great deal of renunciation on the part of its founder – no meat, wine, hunting or sex – and a lot of praying, hymn singing and novel rituals. And, of course, it led to his death.

The parallels are very far from exact. Heliogabalus was rich and not at all alone. His god was not new. But the life of Mani shows that in the third century, in the same part of the world (the predominantly Aramaic-speaking Near East), a boy of the same age could experience a genuine religious conversion. And there are similarities: the exotic priestly dress, special dietary requirements, elaborate ceremonials, leadership of the cult (combined with newly revealed paternity): and above all there was the mission. As Mani wrote to the Persian king, 'my religion is of the kind that will be manifest in every country and in all languages, and it will be taught in faraway countries too'.

At the age of fourteen the young Emperor Heliogabalus had learnt all about the fear and uncertainty of the imperial court, of the fragility of family, even of life itself. Over the last few years there had been so many deaths. The executioner or disease had cut a swathe through his family: Geta his second cousin, Marcellus the man he had thought was his father, Avitus his grandfather, a sibling (maybe more than one), a female cousin and her husband, Gessius Marcianus his uncle, and Marcianus' son, as well as the man he now knew had been his natural father, the Emperor Caracalla. In such a dangerous world, it was good to be close to an invincible deity, to have Elagabal beside you in oppression and danger.

And Heliogabalus needed divine protection when he rode into Antioch. Until Macrinus was dead, there was no safety.

CHAPTER 5 THE JOURNEY

The East, Summer to Winter AD218

I *Where was Macrinus?*

Where was Macrinus? As they settled into the palace in Antioch on the evening of 9 June, the question was on the lips of all Heliogabalus' advisers. For the women, Maesa and Soaemias, for the freedman Eutychianus and for the soldiers, Verus and Comazon, it was a matter of life and death. Unless the fugitive Emperor was captured and killed the rebellion was not over, and their own lives were at risk. A terrible uncertainty: *Where was Macrinus?*

There were four paths Macrinus could have taken. One way was south. Basilianus, the prefect of Egypt, was loyal. Macrinus had recently appointed him one of his two praetorian prefects. Marius Secundus, the governor of Syria Phoenice, was with him. The governor of Arabia, Pica Caesianus, was another loyalist. Egypt and Arabia each contained one legion. But there were another two legions in Syria Palaestina (Judaea), and we do not know the identity, or the allegiance, of the governor. Anyway, four legions were not enough. South was unlikely.

Macrinus could have headed east (north-east to be precise – Heliogabalus had entered Antioch from the east). Fabius

Agrippinus of Syria Coele still had two legions and had not joined the revolt. But Sulla, commanding the two legions in Cappadocia, had prevaricated and we have no information on the attitude of whoever led two more legions in Mesopotamia. Even should all six legions remain true to their oaths to Macrinus, most likely they would be outnumbered by the Praetorians and two legions, augmented by the detachments from the west, that now made up the rebel army.

The East offered another possibility. In the reign of Commodus, Heliogabalus' kinsman Julius Alexander had attempted to flee to the Parthians. Delayed by affection for a favourite, the Emesene had killed his young male lover and himself rather than be caught. Mulling over Macrinus' whereabouts, Maesa would have remembered a more recent example from her family history. Defeated by her brother-in-law, Septimius Severus, in the civil war of AD 193–4, Niger was said to have also tried and failed to reach Parthia. In the third century AD the Parthian king was the only barbarian ruler who might dare to refuse a Roman demand to return a fugitive. But like Julius Alexander and Niger, many were apprehended en route. We can assume a correlation between the status of the fugitive and the urgency of the pursuit. Even those who escaped across the eastern frontier were not safe. Caracalla demanded the return of a Cynic philosopher called Antiochus. The Parthian king declined. When Caracalla prepared for war, Antiochus was handed over. For Macrinus, flight to Parthia might be unappealing: an admission of defeat that would put his life at the whim of an oriental despot.

The final path lay to the west. For Cassius Dio the obvious destination for Macrinus was Rome, 'in the expectation that he could gain some assistance from the Senate and people'. The historian went on, 'he would certainly have accomplished something… so that even the soldiers either would have voluntarily changed their minds, or, refusing to do so, would have been overpowered'. This judgement seems unlikely. If the soldiers did not change their minds (and there was no particular reason to think they would), how exactly were the Senate and people going to 'overpower' them? It is an extraordinary statement of Cassius Dio's senatorial wishful thinking. Civil wars were not decided by senators (let alone by the urban populace of Rome, for whom Cassius Dio usually had nothing but contempt), but by armies.

Under the Emperors Rome had been remarkably successful, for a pre-industrial empire, in avoiding civil wars: just two serious outbreaks in two and a half centuries. In AD69–70 the eastern army may have first declared Vespasian Emperor, but it was the army of the Danube that had won him the throne. In the wars of AD193–7 the Danubian army under Septimius Severus had first taken Rome, then beaten the eastern army, before defeating that of the Rhine and Britain. The lesson was clear. It was not a matter of numbers (ten legions on the Danube, nine in Germany and Britain, no fewer than twelve in the East). Instead, it was a combination of geography (the central position, and relative closeness to Rome, of the forces on the Danube) and perceived martial spirit. The soldiers along the Danube were, as Herodian put it, 'tall men of fine physique, natural and fierce fighters, although intellectually dull and slow-witted'. Herodian expanded on the theme of their prowess (tactfully drawing a veil over their stupidity) in a speech addressed to them that he puts in the mouth of Septimius Severus. 'You are highly trained in battle by constant wars against the barbarians; you are used to enduring all kinds of hardship, ignoring heat and cold, crossing frozen rivers… you are so magnificently equipped to demonstrate your courage that no one, even if they wanted to, could withstand you.'

Contemporary military thinking argued that Macrinus should go to the legionary camps along the Danube. As we will see, two of his staunchest supporters were governors there. But Macrinus, like Cassius Dio, was not a military man. Where was Macrinus?

II *The Object of Reproach*

Macrinus was in a boat. Having sailed from Chalcedon, he was crossing the narrow straights of the Propontis between Asia and Europe. Byzantium was almost within reach. 'So near was Macrinus to escaping', when a contrary wind got up. The fugitive Emperor was blown back to his fate.

An exciting story, it reads like fiction. For that is what it is. Herodian was given to inventing dramatic scenes, both to enliven his story and to emphasise what was important ('so near, but so far': but for this slight chance the war would have continued).

Cassius Dio has a more likely boat trip. Leaving Antioch on the night of 8 June, disguised as a courier (*frumentarius*), with a few companions, Macrinus had reached Aegae in Cilicia. Securing a carriage, he drove through the provinces of Cappadocia, Galatia and Bithynia, until he reached Eribolon, the port of the city of Nicomedia. He did not dare enter Nicomedia for fear of Caecilius Aristo, the governor of Bithynia. As the road ran through Nicomedia, he took a boat along the coast to Chalcedon. There he broke his cover, sending to an imperial procurator, asking for money. It was a fatal mistake. The procurator had him arrested. Then Macrinus was handed over to a centurion called Aurelius Celsus, one of those sent out by Heliogabalus.

The elite of the Roman Empire had trouble travelling or living incognito. Ingrained habit made it difficult to pretend to be one of the *humiliores*, the *humble* lower classes. They were bad at fending for themselves. If you needed money, you sent someone to ask for it from either a subordinate or one of the *honestiores*, the *honest men* of your own status. It was not just money. They were betrayed by their accent and manners. In the murderous political turmoil of the Late Republic, Marcus Licinius Crassus went to Spain to hide in a cave. He took with him three companions and ten servants. When the problem of food reared its head, he sent to a local landowner, who arranged for substantial meals to be left on the path down to the cave. After a time, it occurred to the landowner that a young man like Crassus needed sex. So he sent two slave girls, telling them they would find a master in the cave. Even in hiding, a member of the Roman elite needed lots of company, plentiful food and a varied sex life. There was no need to tell the girls which of the fourteen men in the cave was Crassus. Accent and manners would out. Extraordinary to our way of thinking, as an old woman one of the slave girls spoke of the whole experience with 'the greatest pleasure'.

Both Cassius Dio and Herodian agree – Macrinus had been making for Rome. A bad choice. We may doubt the judgement of Cassius Dio that it would have 'accomplished something', unless the legions on the Danube had remained loyal. Herodian hedges his bets: Macrinus was travelling in the 'expectation' of popular support.

Herodian has Macrinus decapitated at once in a suburb of Chalcedon. Again Cassius Dio has a fuller, and more convincing, story. The centurion Aurelius Celsus put the Emperor in a cart 'like the commonest criminal', and set off to take him all the way back to Antioch.

Macrinus can have had no hopes for himself. Much later, in Christian times, a deposed Emperor might be mutilated – have his eyes put out or his nose lopped off – and confined in a monastery. Although there was already a prejudice against a cripple taking the throne, in the pagan empire that was not an option. Macrinus knew that he could not be allowed to live. Heliogabalus would want revenge for the assassination of his 'father' Caracalla. Yet Macrinus still had one hope – that his son had got away.

Leaving the battlefield at Immae, Macrinus had entrusted Diadumenianus to an imperial freedman, Epagathus, and some other attendants, with orders to take him to the Parthian king. Macrinus had made a peace treaty with the Parthian, which included a large payment of money. That, and his usefulness as a counter in the diplomatic game, meant the boy might expect a good welcome. Diadumenianus' party went to cross the Euphrates at Zeugma (the name means *The Bridge*). A strange decision by Epagathus. The town had a major Roman garrison: *Legio IV Scythica*, commanded by Gellius Maximus. Also, it was where Diadumenianus had been proclaimed Caesar the previous year. There was a high likelihood of the boy being recognised. Sure enough, Diadumenianus was arrested: not by Gellius, but by Claudius Aelius Pollio, a centurion, possibly the *primus pilus* (first centurion) of the legion. The ex-slave Epagathus was a survivor. A favourite of Caracalla, and trusted by Macrinus, he went on to hold high office under the regime dominated by Maesa in the early years of Alexander Severus. To remain close to the throne through the violent deaths of three Emperors called for guile and unscrupulousness. It suggests the trust of Macrinus was misplaced. Epagathus betrayed Diadumenianus. That the child was handed over to Pollio, not to Gellius, was to have repercussions (keep their names in mind), although not for the agile freedman Epagathus.

The news of the arrest of his son reached Macrinus somewhere on the long road across Asia Minor. There was no longer any point in living. The captive Emperor was not bound. He tried to take his own life by hurling himself out of the moving cart.

All he did was break his shoulder. The end came not long after in Cappadocia. A later tradition named the town of Archelais. Perhaps his attempt to escape brought forward his execution. Macrinus was beheaded. The killing was not carried out by his captor, Aurelius Celsus, but by another centurion, Marcianus Taurus. After the killing (because of the gaps in the text of Cassius Dio?) both centurions vanish from history. Macrinus' head may have been taken to Antioch. His corpse was left by the roadside.

Cassius Dio implies Diadumenianus was executed after his father. We do not know when or where. Likewise, we know nothing real about his character. The *Augustan History* depicts him as a precocious and bloodthirsty monster, but it is complete fiction, a memory traduced. We do know that when he was killed Diadumenianus was just nine years old.

Cassius Dio, having previously damned Macrinus with faint praise, changed tack when summing up the old man (Macrinus was not yet fifty-four!). He might have been praised above all men had he elevated some senator to the throne. Instead, taking the throne himself, 'he brought discredit and destruction alike upon himself, so that he became the object of reproach and fell a victim to a disaster that was richly deserved'.

III   *Securing the East*

In Antioch, unbridled joy greeted the news of Macrinus' capture, relief that of his death. Maybe the latter brought a tinge of disappointment. The intention had been to bring the fallen Emperor to Antioch. Never mind, now his memory could be damned. It was time to break out the hammers and chisels and start defacing his statues and inscriptions. Soon it would be as if he had never existed. But his creatures still held office across the East, and posed a threat.

Herodian describes the functioning of the new regime of Heliogabalus. 'The immediate business in the East was dealt with by his grandmother and his circle of advisers because he was young and without administrative experience or education.' We will go into the influence of the imperial women later (chapter 11), but for now Herodian's statement seems plausible. Heliogabalus was only fourteen, and, as we will soon see, he had other things on his mind.

Maesa had spent a quarter of a century with her sister at the imperial court. She had witnessed her brother-in-law emerge victorious from the civil wars of AD 193–7. She knew the importance of provincial governors and military commanders. Now she conducted a purge in the East.

Macrinus' remaining praetorian prefect in Syria, Iulianus Nestor, was executed. An unsavoury character of lowly origins – Nestor had started his career as a *frumentarius* (imperial spy) – few of the elite would have mourned him. With him presumably died the two tribunes of the Praetorians, the brothers Nemesianus and Apollinaris, implicated in the assassination of Caracalla. The first senator to die was Fabius Agrippinus, the governor of Syria Coele: another who had been in the plot against Heliogabalus' 'father'. The governor of Cappadocia, Marcus Minatius Sulla Cerialis, was luckier, at least for now. Dismissed from his post, he made his way back to Rome.

Cassius Dio ascribes a different motive to the killing of Claudius Attalus, the senatorial governor of the unimportant and unarmed province of Cyprus. Many years earlier, as governor of Thrace, Attalus had demoted Comazon to the fleet. There may have been more to it. A year or two before the revolt, when Heliogabalus' maternal grandfather, the ex-consul Caius Julius

Avitus Alexianus, died of old age and sickness, he had been serving as a special adviser to Attalus on Cyprus. Perhaps there was a falling out, and a lingering family resentment. Anyway, the link did not save Attalus.

Death warrants were sent to the south. The prefect of Egypt, Basilianus, whom Macrinus had promoted to praetorian prefect, could not be found. The wanted man had fled by sea. But Marius Secundus, the governor of Syria Phoenice, was apprehended and despatched. The final known victim of the purge of the East was Pica Caerianus, governor of Arabia.

Seven dead, one man on the run and another relieved of command. Nothing out of the ordinary after a violent change of regime. Nothing that would necessarily cause widespread resentment among the governing class. All the victims had either been close to Macrinus, or had not changed sides with sufficient alacrity. The stakes were always high in imperial politics.

The vacant places were filled by loyalists. Comazon became praetorian prefect. The ex-ranker would go yet higher. The centurion Verus was made a senator, and appointed governor of Syria Phoenice, thus remaining commander of *Legio III Gallica*. Subsequent events suggest Verus had been hoping for more. In Arabia the equestrian procurator (financial officer), Timesitheus, took over as acting governor (*agens vice praesidis*). The same in Egypt, where a judge (*iuridicus*) called Callistianus oversaw the province.

At first glance a motley crew – it appears the new regime was still short of high-status supporters. Not a senator in sight. But the prefects of the Praetorians and of Egypt were always equestrians. As for Arabia, over the previous century it had become common for equestrians to be appointed temporary governors of senatorial provinces. By the end of the year Timesitheus would be replaced by the established senator, Flavius Iulianus. In Egypt by AD219, Callistianus would give way to a regular equestrian prefect in Geminius Chrestus. The latter would prove loyal and useful to Maesa in the final crisis of the reign.

To judge the normality or otherwise of the appointments, and so form an estimate of the new regime, we need to make another venture into prosopography, and look at some second-ary characters in the story. Everything would come into better focus if we could be sure who succeeded to the vital provinces of Cappadocia and Syria Coele (two and three legions respec-tively), and who governed the other two armed provinces in the East: Syria Palaestina and Mesopotamia (both with two legions).

In AD219, Theodorus was governing Cappadocia. Theodorus had been an equestrian imperial secretary answering petitions for Caracalla (AD212–13) and thus had been promoted into the Senate. The appointment of this 'new man' – an easterner, judging by his name – might seem to support an argument that Heliogabalus' regime was desperately short of high-status fol-lowers and forced to rely on locals from non-senatorial back-grounds. However, Theodorus may already have been elevated to the Senate by Caracalla and may well not have been the first to succeed Sulla in AD218.

Syria Coele might point the other way, towards followers from a traditional political elite background. At some point before AD221, Heliogabalus appointed the Italian senator Quintus Atrius Clonius, who had previously governed Thrace and been consul, to the province. Normality personified, except Clonius might not have gone to Syria Coele until three years after the revolt.

Syria Palaestina reveals only one of its governors under Heliogabalus. A mutilated inscription has C. Iul(ius) Titi(anus). We do not know what years he spent in the province, or anything else about him, except that the mutilation shows him condemned for treason. Mesopotamia reveals no evidence at all.

For certain, one thing would have caught the eye of the traditional elite – and been unwelcome to senators like Cassius Dio – the lowly origins of Comazon and Verus. Such prejudice would have been well known to Maesa. But early adherents of the revolt had to be rewarded. There was a fond hope they would prove loyal. With the East seemingly secure, it was time to turn to the West.

IV *Securing the West*

From Antioch letters in the name of Heliogabalus were sent to the Senate and people of Rome. Cassius Dio, who was present when they were read in the Senate House, said the first one contained just what one would expect, 'attacking Macrinus in various ways, in particular for his low birth and for the plot against Antoninus (Caracalla)'.

The *Augustan History* claimed 'all classes were filled with enthusiasm'. Conversely, Herodian said there was 'general gloom'. In reality, the reaction of the senators would have been mixed. Some Severan hard-line loyalists, and those particularly hostile to Macrinus, were gleeful. One such was the ex-consul Fulvius. During the revolt Fulvius had dared to exclaim in open session of the Senate that all were praying for Macrinus' death. Cassius Dio thought such temerity insane. Not all agreed. Fulvius would prosper under Heliogabalus. Other senators were evidently less positive. To get him out of Rome, where he might have swayed the Senate against the new regime, the resolutely outspoken Silius Messalla was summoned to Syria, on the pretence that his advice was needed by Heliogabalus. No doubt most, like Cassius Dio, kept their views to themselves and acquiesced.

The senators overall had not much to cheer. They had disliked Macrinus, but they had hated Caracalla. And Heliogabalus was presented as Caracalla's son. Cassius Dio says they were consumed by fear. Many had good reason. The Emperor was the ultimate source of patronage. You could not enter the Senate, or ascend through the magistracies (the *cursus honorum*), without his approval. Friendship (*amicitia*) with the Emperor brought status. As the poet Ovid said, 'what acquaintance of the Caesars fails to claim their friendship'. The opposite, enmity (*inamicitia*), at best brought retirement (a sort of social death), but more likely exile, suicide or execution. When they were not with the Emperor, senators wrote him letters. Their content was not crucial. Judging by those preserved between Pliny and Trajan, and Fronto and Marcus Aurelius, it could often be mundane or trivial. The point was to write to the Emperor and for him (hopefully) to reply. Each exchange re-established and publicised the friendship. It was not necessary to actually publish the correspondence, as did the *littérateurs* Pliny and Fronto, to make the connection widely known.

It is easy to imagine what was in the letters senators had sent to Macrinus: the elegant flatteries of the Emperor, dressed up as frank advice, which had found their ultimate expression in Pliny's *Panegyric* to Trajan; denigration of Caracalla; and, after the revolt, disparagement and abuse of Heliogabalus and the women of his family. More than enough reason for their authors to be afraid.

Cassius Dio tells us Heliogabalus wrote offering reassurance. He would take as role models good Emperors: 'he would do every single thing in imitation of Augustus, whose age was not unlike his own, and in imitation of Marcus Antoninus (Marcus Aurelius)'. The latter was well chosen. The philosopher-Emperor had left the best of reputations. The former, with its reference to youth – Augustus had been seventeen when named heir to

Julius Caesar, while Heliogabalus was fourteen, perhaps only thirteen – was less comforting. By the end of his long sole reign (31BC–AD14) Augustus had constructed an image of a kindly father of the country (*Pater Patriae*), but when young his career had reeked with bloodshed: the proscriptions (mass judicial murders) of 43BC, and the massacre of senators after the siege of Perusia in 40BC.

Heliogabalus tried to allay the fears of the senators. Only the notebooks of Macrinus and the Emperor's letters to the prefect of the city (*praefectus urbi*), Marius Maximus, would be made public. In his own letters, Heliogabalus complained that Macrinus had ridiculed his age, while appointing his own son Emperor aged just five. That Diadumenianus had actually been nine was irrelevant. The complaint showed that all the imperial correspondence had been captured in Antioch. It was not being used for now, but there was nothing about it being destroyed. Even then copies might have been made, as they once had by Caligula, to be used as incriminating evidence later. Their letters still hung over the heads of the senators.

The charm offensive did not work. In part it was undermined by senatorial etiquette. Heliogabalus had written to the Senate as Imperator Caesar Marcus Aurelius Antoninus Augustus, son of Caracalla and grandson of Septimius Severus. He gave himself the titles Pius and Felix (Fortunate), the power of a tribune of the plebs (*tribunicia potestas*) and the overriding military authority (*maius imperium*) of a proconsul (we will look at these powers, the twin legal basis of an Emperor's position, in the next chapter). In a letter to the troops remaining in Italy he seems – the passage in Cassius Dio is fragmentary – to have added that he was consul and Pontifex Maximus (chief priest of Rome). In theory, the titles and powers could only be awarded by the Senate. Of course, the vote was a formality, especially after a civil war. Nevertheless,

Cassius Dio took offence with such presumption, just as he had with that of Macrinus. It is hard for us to sympathise with this touchy adherence to convention (obviously, when I say *us* here, I really mean *me*!), but it meant something to senators like Cassius Dio.

Letters were not enough. Someone had to be sent to oversee the establishment of the new regime in Rome. The man chosen was Claudius Aelius Pollio, the centurion who had captured Diadumenianus at Zeugma. By imperial authority, Pollio was given the status of a senator with the rank of an ex-consul. Some advisers in Antioch, say Eutychianus or Comazon, may not have realised the offence this would cause the Senate. Maesa would have been aware. Pollio was a military man, who had demonstrated that he could take decisive action. He travelled with instructions to appeal to the soldiers – the rump of the Praetorians in Rome, and that of *Legio II* in the Alban Hills – in the event of trouble. The regime was not sanguine about its acceptance in Rome.

On the way to Italy, Pollio was also tasked with dealing with trouble in Bithynia. We do not know the nature of the unrest. This was the province where Macrinus had avoided the capital Nicomedia for fear of the governor, Caecilius Aristo. Perhaps Aristo had to be removed. Whatever the problem, Cassius Dio says Pollio 'subdued Bithynia' quickly.

In Rome, if the Emperor and the prefects of the Praetorians and *Legio II* were away, along with the majority of the soldiers, the men that most mattered were the consuls, as the senior magistrates, and the prefect of the city, who commanded the six thousand men of the urban cohorts. Macrinus had been one of the consuls, his place now taken by Heliogabalus. The remaining consul, Marcus Oclatinius Adventus, was resident in Rome. Of low birth and no education – it was said he was illiterate – Adventus had advanced through the ranks from common soldier via *frumentarius* and procurator to become praetorian prefect under Caracalla. Now old and blind, he had renounced any interest in aiming for the throne when Macrinus was acclaimed. In reward, he had been briefly prefect of the city in AD217 and then consul with Macrinus in AD218. Unable to hold a respectable conversation (according to Cassius Dio), he pretended to be ill to avoid public ceremonies and had no influence in the Senate. Adventus posed no problems.

The man who had replaced Adventus as prefect of the city was another proposition. Marius Maximus was an educated senator who had governed provinces and commanded armies under Septimius Severus. He would go on to write biographies of the Emperors. His work is lost, but, as far as we can see, refracted through the unreliable prism of the *Augustan History*, his life of Heliogabalus was thoroughly hostile. Despite this, as a previously reliable supporter of the Severan dynasty, it is usually assumed that he remained in office for these crucial early months of the reign. That might be to overlook something. The new regime had broadcast Macrinus' letters to Marius Maximus. They were read out in the Senate. The intention was to blacken the memory of Macrinus. But they also undermined Marius Maximus by revealing him as a close confidant of the disgraced Emperor. Most likely Marius Maximus was dismissed straightaway. He held no further office under Heliogabalus. The biographer had a personal reason to loath his subject from the start.

When he arrived in Rome, Pollio addressed the Senate. A mutilated passage of Cassius Dio shows that was not the original intention. Losing his nerve, a man called Censorinus handed the task to Pollio. Although he cannot be identified with certainty, Censorinus obviously was a high-ranking senator. Quite possibly he replaced Marius Maximus as prefect of the city. The trepidation of Censorinus implies a continuing level of opposition to the new regime in the Senate, and probably in the city as a whole.

In the event, things passed off smoothly. Pollio did not need to call on the troops. With Marius Maximus sacked, and probably replaced by Censorinus, and the bold Silias Messalla on his way to Syria, Rome was quiet. Now to deal with the armies on the northern frontier.

Cassius Dio tells us that Pollio was sent to Germany. An inscription records him as governor of Germania Superior, an important province with two legions along the upper Rhine. And there the trail goes cold. After a year of meteoric success (centurion – capturer of Diadumenianus – senator with rank of ex-consul – governor of Bithynia – spokesperson of the regime in the Senate – governor of Germania Superior) we hear no more of Pollio. The inscription is not defaced. Pollio did not suffer *damnatio memoriae*. Perhaps he enjoyed a quiet retirement, living off the million sesterces that had come with his senatorial status.

The allegiance of the Danubian army, as we have seen, was essential to the security of an Emperor's reign. Maesa may have dealt with this area before Rome itself. Macrinus had sent two of his henchmen to the Danube, both implicated in the assassination of Caracalla. Marcus Claudius Agrippa had started life as a slave, a beautician or hairdresser. Under Septimius Severus, somehow Agrippa had become an agent of the imperial treasury. This was an equestrian post, not to be held by a freedman. When Severus discovered his servile origins, he ordered Agrippa into exile. Caracalla brought him back, placing him in the imperial secretariat, before adlecting him into the Senate, with the rank of an ex-praetor. At the death of Caracalla, Agrippa was commanding the fleet. Immediately afterwards, Macrinus promoted Agrippa to the status of an ex-consul, and sent him to govern Pannonia Inferior.

Macrinus had soon transferred Agrippa to the province of Dacia. From there he was appointed governor of Moesia Inferior. It has been plausibly argued that while in Moesia he retained control of Dacia.

Aelius Decius Triccianus replaced Agrippa in Pannonia Inferior. For Triccianus it was a triumphant return to where his career had begun. As a soldier in *Legio II Adiutrix*, he had been a doorman to the then governor of Pannonia Inferior. Caracalla appointed him prefect of *II Parthica*, where he acquired a reputation as a strict disciplinarian. In that position, he had joined the conspiracy against his benefactor. Like Agrippa, on governing Pannonia Inferior Triccianus had been granted the status of an ex-consul by Macrinus.

Between them Agrippa and Triccianus commanded no fewer than six legions. Cassius Dio claims that the legionaries of *II Parthica* demanded the death of their old commander, Triccianus. It made a convenient excuse. Both men were dangerous and were thought to have played a part in the murder of Caracalla, now acknowledged as Heliogabalus' father. Both men were executed. Given their humble origins, traditional-minded senators like Cassius Dio will not have shed any tears.

The vacant provinces gave the new regime an opportunity to exercise its patronage and to send a message to the traditional senatorial elite. Although an equestrian, Ulpius Victor was put in charge of Dacia as acting governor. As we saw in Arabia, there was nothing unusual or offensive to conservative sentiment in this. The other two replacements were more telling. The new governor of Pannonia Inferior was Pontius Pontianus. Three, possibly four, men of this name are known. Any of them could be the new governor. If not, they are close relatives. This was a reputable senatorial family, with at least one consul in its ancestry, and thus part of the nobility. The man entrusted with

Moesia Inferior, Novius Rufus, was an Italian from the heart of the establishment. He had been consul, as had his father and grandfather before him. These men were no hairdressers or doormen. After the elevation of Comazon, Verus and, at this point in the forefront of people's minds, Pollio, the regime now was demonstrating to the Senate the normal functioning of the *cursus honorum*: men from old, noble families would be held in honour and continue to be advanced.

Interestingly, the message seems to have worked. Although it may be a trick of our surviving evidence, we hear of no revolts in the western half of the empire until the end of the reign of Heliogabalus. The East, as we will see in a few pages, was another story.

V *Heliogabalus' Face* – 1

Power was personal in Rome. People needed to put a face to their Emperor. As in a modern dictatorship, subjects exhibited his image everywhere as a public expression of loyalty. A new regime had to get his picture out as fast as possible. Even while Heliogabalus was in Antioch, portrait busts were sent to the provinces and thousands of coins minted. We have no direct evidence of how the imperial portrait busts were commissioned, made or distributed. That the process existed at all is an inference from the often striking similarity of the busts of some Emperors found across the empire. We are better informed about coin portraits, but will defer our discussion until it becomes vital: when Heliogabalus is in Rome and 'talking' to the rest of the empire. It is enough for now, as it was with Maesa's Face, to say that both coins and busts were official images that bore a resemblance to the Emperor.

Image 7: Type One Portrait of Heliogabalus

All portraits of Heliogabalus fall into two versions. This is an example from early in his reign. Only four unaltered and unmutilated Type One busts survive. They are identified as Heliogabalus because of their similarity to each other and to portraits on his early coinage (AD218–19).

Heliogabalus has short hair, a high forehead, arched brows and large eyes, and a full mouth, with the lower lip fuller than the upper. His face is symmetrical and slightly plump (perhaps a hint of puppy fat?). His cheeks are smooth: either clean-shaven, or he has not yet reached puberty. All in all, an unremarkable looking youth. No hint of eastern origins, and he is depicted wearing a conventional toga.

The one distinctive thing about the early portraits of Heliogabalus, on which almost all scholars agree, is that they are consciously crafted to look very much like those of his 'father' Caracalla at a similar age. The resemblance is so close numismatists have difficulty telling some of their coins apart. This could not be less surprising. Unless you came from the city of Emesa, or somewhere nearby, as did the legionaries of *III Gallica*, and you happened to worship the god Elagabal, there was absolutely no reason for his high priest Heliogabalus to be Emperor except that Caracalla was claimed as his father.

This was far from reassuring to the Senate. But that was not the point. The majority of state expenditure was on the army. Most imperial coins were destined for the troops. The soldiers had loved Caracalla. In these early months of the reign the loyalty of the army to Heliogabalus was still uncertain.

VI *The Journey*

Heliogabalus remained in Antioch for some months of the summer of AD218. Why the delay in setting out? The new Emperor needed to travel to Nicomedia, and cross to Europe, to show himself to the troops on the Danube, and then to the Senate and people in Rome.

Various explanations have been offered.

First: if Macrinus was on the run for a long time, might it have been unsafe to leave until the fugitive was apprehended? Nothing supports this modern suggestion. Both Cassius Dio and Herodian have a headlong flight to Nicomedia, where Macrinus is arrested almost at once. Even after the capture, Heliogabalus remains in Antioch and orders the fallen Emperor brought to him.

Second: was Heliogabalus detained at Antioch by unrest in Syria? The idea cannot be dismissed out of hand. There was soon to be trouble, and not everything was peaceful in Antioch. The eminent senator Silius Messalla arrived from Rome expecting to take his place on the Emperor's council. Instead, he was executed.

Yet, although his chronology is vague, Cassius Dio places the eastern unrest after Heliogabalus had reached Nicomedia.

There is a third possible reason. Heliogabalus took the god Elagabal with him from Emesa to Rome. Coins show the black stone in a chariot drawn by four horses and shaded by parasols. Herodian tells us about the elaborate rituals later in Rome when the god processed from one temple to another. Such ceremonies take time to organise. In addition, with both the high priest and the main cult object leaving, arrangements had to be made for the continuation of religious worship in the temple of Emesa. It is an argument from silence, but if this was the cause of the extended stay in Antioch, it shows that from the very start of his reign Heliogabalus neglected the expected duties of an Emperor of Rome for those of a high priest of Elagabal.

Finally, in the autumn, not before September, the Emperor left Antioch bound for Nicomedia. The route across Asia Minor was reconstructed on the assumption that civic coinage featuring Elagabal on the reverse side celebrated the arrival of the god in the issuing town. Subsequently, it has been pointed out that many of these coins are dated later in the reign, that they all depict Heliogabalus as mature on the obverse side, and so none can have been issued in AD218; and that some were minted in cities, like Alexandria in Egypt, that could not have been on the route. Interpretation has moved to the coins commemorating the introduction of the cult of Elagabal in each town. This might be to throw the baby out with the bathwater. Actually, the two interpretations are compatible. Each town had its own specific reasons for introducing the cult of Elagabal (as we will see in chapter 9). For some, these may well have been that the god had honoured the town with its presence on its way to Rome. Like the procession of Elagabal itself, a civic cult was not arranged overnight. Temples had to be built, or at least rededicated, images

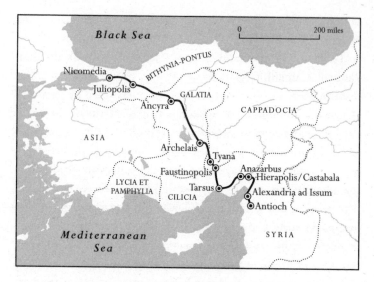

Antioch to Nicomedia

made, priests appointed, festivals established and funding for everything allocated.

If we put those towns in Asia Minor which later instituted cult for Elagabal together with where the Emperor viewed the corpse of Macrinus, and fill in the gaps from the *Barrington Atlas*, it gives us a plausible route that runs Antioch – Alexandria ad Issum – Hierapolis/Castabla – Anazarbus – Tarsus – Faustinopolis – Tyana – Archelais – Ancyra – Juilopolis – Nicomedia.

The arrival of the imperial entourage was a time of opportunity for any town. Contacts could be made and a (hopefully) enduring line of communication opened: with the Emperor himself, as well as those close to him. Favours could be solicited. These might be titles – Colony, Metropolis, First, Greatest, Most Beautiful, Temple Warden – all useful in the ceaseless struggle for status between neighbouring cities, or they might be more material benefits: the right to be an assize centre (which boosted revenues, as it brought to the town litigants and others, apparently including droves of prostitutes), or to expand the city council (councillors paid fees), or, best of all, freedom from taxation.

On the downside, the appearance of the Emperor brought expense and potential suffering. All those courtiers, functionaries, servants and soldiers had to be lodged and provisioned, and the more important among them entertained. Billeted troops were always trouble: indulging in theft, violence and rape. And, if displeased, instead of rewards the Emperor could dish out punishments: loss of status and fines for the city, exile or death for individuals. At the very worst he might unleash the soldiery on the citizens and initiate a massacre, as Caracalla had in Alexandria. The arrival of an Emperor was a time of extreme tension.

The tone of the visit was set by the ceremony of arrival (*Adventus*), where a civic dignitary made a formal speech of welcome at the gates of the town. A handbook on how to write such speeches survives from the third century, under the name of Menander Rhetor. If we read it while putting ourselves into the tunic and *himation* of an anxious local worthy of a Greek city of Asia Minor preparing to address Heliogabalus, some of the difficulties become very apparent.

The handbook instructs us to amplify the good things and allow no mention of any ambivalent or disputed features. That will not prove easy. The oration should begin with the ancient distinction of the Emperor's native country. A tricky task when that is the relatively recently founded Emesa, which lacks almost any mention in history. Failing that, the speaker should dwell on the character of his countrymen: are they brave, like Gauls or Pannonians, famed for culture, like the Greeks or renowned for law, like the Romans? Unfortunately not. They are Syrians, and we saw their unsavoury reputation in the last chapter. If neither city nor people are famous, turn to his family. Again, something of a problem, as – if our orator knows anything about them at all – they are a bunch of Arabs with ridiculous names like Sampsigeramus. Here perhaps best to talk at great length about Caracalla and his father Septimius Severus, and go back to their supposed ancestors: Marcus Aurelius, Antoninus Pius, perhaps all the way to Trajan.

In the middle of the speech things get a bit less taxing. Omens at the birth of the Emperor; 'if it is possible to invent, and to do this convincingly, do not hesitate'. Then nature: extol his beauty. Safer ground here, as Herodian claims it was his beauty that first attracted the soldiers to Heliogabalus. Next, nurture: was he raised in the palace? Indeed he was. Time to praise 'his love of learning, quickness, enthusiasm for study, his easy grasp of what is taught'. That can all be rattled off, true or not. As can his virtues, his temperance and humanity: after all, he has not had time to demonstrate the reverse.

Things take another nasty turn towards the end of the speech, when it comes to his deeds. War might seem promising. Heliogabalus performed creditably at the Battle of Immae. But that was a civil war. It was awkward trying to produce an encomium on slaughtering fellow citizens. His actions in peacetime are equally problematic: just government (well possibly, if we ignore the growing reputation of Eutychianus for taking bribes); wise laws (as far as we know Heliogabalus has promulgated none); style of life (is the Emperor wearing the barbarian robes of his priesthood?); and as for the qualities of his wife and the promise of his children, let alone comparing his reign to other rulers, like Alexander the Great… !

The epilogue can't come too soon.

> *What greater blessing must one ask from the gods than the Emperor's safety? Rains in season, abundance from the sea, unstinting harvests come happily to us because of the Emperor's justice. In return, cities, nations, races, and tribes, all of us, garland him, sing of him, write of him. Full of his images are the cities, some of painted tablets, some maybe of more precious metal. After this, you must utter a prayer.*

Or, on the other hand, you might hurl the handbook at a slave and hire a professional rhetorician.

VII *In Nicomedia*

Nicomedia was used to Emperors. It was on the main route between the Danube and the East. Caracalla had held court there in AD213–14. Heliogabalus perhaps had been with him, in the days when everyone still thought the boy was the son of a recently deceased senator from Syria. Now returning as Emperor, and son of the deified Caracalla, Heliogabalus was forced by the lateness of the year to stay in Nicomedia. The sailing season ended sometime between 14 September and 10 November. It did not reopen until 10 March at the earliest. During the winter of AD218–19 in Nicomedia things began to go badly wrong.

Cassius Dio records a wave of revolts in the East. Verus had been left in Syria Phoenice in command of *Legio III Gallica*. To govern the province, he had been made a senator with the status of an ex-praetor. It seems not to have been enough. Comazon had held the same rank, prefect of the camp, and had joined the revolt to make Heliogabalus Emperor later than him. Appointed praetorian prefect, Comazon was at the centre of the imperial court, with the status of an ex-consul, the second most powerful man in the empire. Frustrated ambition and jealousy may have prompted Verus' revolt. Whatever the motive, it was crushed and Verus executed. That was not the end of the matter. An unnamed son of a centurion 'undertook to stir up the same Gallic legion'. This might be connected to a notice in Herodian that the legion was to be transferred to a new base. The second revolt was also quelled, and this time the regime took the unusual step of disbanding the legion. Inscriptions record some of its soldiers stationed in distant Africa.

There was also revolt in Syria Coele. Gellius Maximus had been commanding *Legio IV Scythica* at Zeugma when Diadumenianus was captured. Pollio, the centurion who had made the arrest, had been made a senator with the status of an ex-consul, had governed Bithynia, been the regime's spokesperson in the Senate and now was governing Germania Superior. Gellius Maximus was still at Zeugma with the Scythian legion, serving under a new governor of the province. He had received no reward. Again, we can suspect frustration and jealousy. After the execution of Gellius Maximus, 'another, a worker in wool, tampered with the Fourth'. He too was killed. Unlike *III Gallica*, the Fourth Legion was not disbanded. Instead, it was given a new and unusual commander. Known from two inscriptions found in Rome, both deliberately mutilated, only part of his name survives: …ATVS. He is going to have a spectacular career under Heliogabalus, although, given the damage to the inscriptions, you already know how it will end. He was an equestrian imperial secretary. As *a studiis*, his job was to guide the young Emperor's reading. Now he was sent to Zeugma, instead of a senator of Praetorian status, to bring *Legio IV Scythica* back to its allegiance. When it came to a crisis, as it had with Pollio, the regime flouted convention and turned to the perceived loyalty of those close to the court.

It is significant that *Legio II Parthica*, with its eastern base at Apamea, between the two rebellious legions, was granted new honorific titles by Heliogabalus: *pia fidelis felix aeterna* (pious, faithful, fortunate, eternal).

'Yet another, a private citizen,' Cassius Dio continued, 'tried to rouse the fleet while it was in harbour at Cyzicus, while Pseudantoninus (Heliogabalus) was passing the winter in Nicomedia.' An unwise venture. The fleet never produced an Emperor. This man too would have paid the ultimate price.

Cassius Dio claims 'there were many others elsewhere'. One might have been 'that prefect' we saw mentioned on a papyrus from Egypt, leading a failed revolt (see above, chapter 1).

There is something odd, almost counter-intuitive, about these uprisings. We would assume that an armed revolt would have most chance of success if led by a senior military figure commanding troops a long way from the Emperor. But all these insurrections are in the East at no great distance from Nicomedia. It is as if imperial power, like electricity, could only jump a certain distance. Had familiarity already bred contempt? Observing Heliogabalus, did these men think they would make a better Emperor? Did they genuinely believe that Heliogabalus would be a bad ruler? If the latter was their assumption, of course, they were right.

Cassius Dio stresses the lowly origins of all the rebels. We should be wary. The father of Gellius Maximus was not just any doctor, but a physician at the imperial court, an equestrian procurator and a member of the prestigious Museum of Alexandria. His son was a senator who had been praetor. Centurions like Verus could come from wealthy equestrian families, as, of course, could their sons. The individual who tried to rouse the fleet may have been a private citizen, but that does not show he was one of the *humiliores* (the humble). His background might have been elite. Given Cassius Dio's love of nicknames (remember Eutychianus as Gannys), the 'worker in wool' may have been nothing of the sort. Cassius Dio's snobbish line here is that if Macrinus and Heliogabalus could become Emperors, almost anyone can bid for the throne.

We hear of no military actions against these usurpers. All were speedily executed. There are no revolts known from later in the reign. The regime had weathered these insurrections of troops in the provinces. But all was not well in the imperial court in Nicomedia.

Basilianus, the praetorian prefect of Macrinus, who had fled by sea from Egypt, had been arrested in Brundisium in Italy. The fugitive had been betrayed by a friend in Rome, to whom he had sent secretly asking for food. The elite were never good at travelling incognito. Now Basilianus was transported to Nicomedia and executed.

Sulla, who had been dismissed as governor of Cappadocia, was summoned from Rome to Nicomedia. Perhaps suspecting the same fate that had befallen Silias Messalla when he arrived in Antioch from Rome, Sulla contrived to meet the troops heading back from the East to Germany. Such meddling ensured his execution.

The eminent Caius Julius Septimius Castinus, consul and governor of Dacia under Caracalla, had been banished from Rome by Macrinus. The exile was living near Nicomedia in his home province of Bithynia. Heliogabalus wrote to the Senate announcing the restoration of Castinus. Something happened. 'Castinus perished because he was energetic and was known to many soldiers, in consequence of the commands he had held.'

Cassius Dio says the same fate had already befallen Caius Julius Asper. Twice consul and prefect of the city, Asper had been passed over for the governorship of Asia by Macrinus. Heliogabalus wrote to the Senate about Asper, then had him executed.

Three distinguished consulars and a senior equestrian dead. The body count was rising. But there was a more unsettling killing that winter in Nicomedia.

Eutychianus, the Emperor's tutor, had engineered his initial acclamation by *III Gallica*, giving him victory at the Battle of Immae. He was thoroughly satisfactory to the imperial women, having been raised by Maesa, and was living virtually as Soaemias' husband. This *Delightful Lad* or *Cheerful Boy* (as he was known by his nickname, Gannys) was devoted to the young Emperor, who regarded him as a foster-father and guardian. Heliogabalus was even thinking about appointing Eutychianus as Caesar, thus making him heir to the throne. To strengthen the link there was talk of a marriage contract. Presumably with Soaemias. Not, as some modern scholars think, with Heliogabalus himself. Cassius Dio would neither have missed the opportunity to fulminate against that nor have judged Eutychianus so favourably. 'To be sure, Gannys was living rather luxuriously, and was fond of accepting bribes, but for all that he did no one any harm, and bestowed many benefits upon many people.'

Over that winter in Nicomedia, Eutychianus overstepped himself. No doubt encouraged by Maesa, he tried to compel Heliogabalus to live temperately and prudently. The damaged manuscript of Cassius Dio does not tell us what was wrong with the Emperor's lifestyle. The *Augustan History* makes it all about sex: 'living in a depraved manner, and indulging in unnatural vice with men'. That is likely to be true, but the rest of the passage is fiction. Better to follow Herodian – the bone of contention was religion: the ceremonies Heliogabalus performed as high priest of Elagabal.

The dispute came to a head. Heliogabalus ordered the soldiers to kill Eutychianus. Cassius Dio says they hung back: 'not one of the soldiers had the hardihood to take the lead in murdering him'. The young Emperor 'himself was the first to give Gannys a mortal blow with his own hand'.

Did he use the sword he had girded himself with at Raphaneae? Once there was blood on the Emperor's blade, the troops joined in the stabbing and hacking. Were Maesa and Soaemias present? What was the reaction of Soaemias? Her son had just killed her lover.

Heliogabalus might have justified his action with family history. His 'father' had arranged the killing in the palace of his hated father-in-law Plautianus, another over-mighty subject. Caracalla was not thought to have struck the blow himself, but later dedicated the weapon in a temple as if to claim the deed.

Whatever the justification, Cassius Dio wrote that because of the killing Heliogabalus 'was regarded as the most impious of men'.

As one would expect, the story has been rejected by some modern scholars. It is 'too much like a topos, a literary commonplace, meant to make Elagabalus (Heliogabalus) look bad, to be credible'. One wonders what they would have made of the death of the Iraqi minister for health in March 1982. Riyadh Ibrahim Hussein suggested that Saddam Hussein step down as president to enable a ceasefire to be negotiated in the Iran–Iraq War. 'Saddam showed no outward sign of irritation. He merely interrupted the cabinet meeting and asked the minister to escort him outside. "Let us go to the other room and discuss the matter further," said Saddam. The minister agreed and the two left the room. A moment later a shot was heard and Saddam returned alone to the cabinet as though nothing had happened.' Autocrats have a distressing tendency not to behave like western academics.

Eutychianus was dead, killed by Heliogabalus. But Maesa was not going to give up. She was deeply worried about the effect

Heliogabalus' religion would have on his subjects in Rome. Her fears were well grounded. She had lived most of her life in the West and knew the prejudices against Syrians and Phoenicians. She continuously tried to persuade her grandson to tone it down, or at least abandon eastern clothing. That took courage, considering the fate of Eutychianus. The young Emperor ignored her advice. Indeed, it had the opposite effect. Heliogabalus commissioned a huge painting of himself in his priestly robes, sacrificing to his god, which he had sent ahead to Rome, with instructions that it be displayed in a prominent place in the Senate House. Herodian tells us, 'He was anxious that the Senate and people of Rome should get used to his dress, and to test out their reactions to the sight before he arrived.' Certainly, they were warned.

CHAPTER 6 POWER

Wintering in Nicomedia (AD218–19), Heliogabalus was already neglecting the duties of a Roman Emperor. Instead, according to Herodian, he devoted himself to the ceremonies of his god. The *Augustan History* has him 'living in a depraved manner, and indulging in unnatural sex with men'. While Cassius Dio has him turning murderous when Eutychianus tried to make him live 'temperately and prudently'. Of course, these lifestyle choices were not incompatible. But neither was it the way an Emperor was meant to behave. Before we turn to what was expected, and that turns out to be a bone of contention among modern scholars, we need to look at the basis of his power: by what legal right did an Emperor rule at all? Were his actions constrained by law?

I *The Legitimate Emperor: Above the Law*

In 31BC Octavian defeated Antony and Cleopatra at the Battle of Actium. The following year he hounded them to suicide in Egypt. As the last man standing of the military dynasts, whose civil wars had brought down the Republic, Octavian faced a dilemma: how to continue his rule without suffering the fate of his adoptive father, Julius Caesar. A mob of knife-wielding senators had murdered Julius Caesar in the name of Liberty.

To be sure *Libertas* had a particular meaning for those senators: the liberty to compete among themselves for magistracies and commands, to ascend the *cursus honorum* and to reap the benefits of empire. Somehow, Octavian had to find a way that allowed such proud *nobiles* to serve his regime. Overt monarchy would not be acceptable to the *dignitas* of senators. Becoming Perpetual Dictator, like Julius Caesar, let alone a king, was not an option.

After almost a decade of experimentation with combinations of titles and powers, a formula was achieved. It rested on an act of renunciation. On 1 July 23BC Augustus, as he had been renamed four years earlier, resigned as consul, an office he had held every year since Actium. The Senate, well primed, promptly voted to give him back what he needed: overriding military authority (*maius imperium*) and the powers of a tribune of the plebs (*tribunicia potestas*). The *maius imperium* left him in undisputed control of the army. Not only did Augustus govern, through deputies, those provinces where the overwhelming majority of the legions were stationed, but he also had the right to supreme command anywhere in the empire. Unlike other holders of *imperium*, Augustus' did not lapse even within the sacred boundaries of the city of Rome itself. Every New Year all the soldiers, wherever they were serving, reaffirmed their military oath (*sacramentum*) to Augustus and his family.

The *maius imperium* took care of the army. It is important never to forget that the office of Emperor was in origin a military autocracy. The *tribunicia potestas* dealt with civilian affairs. With it came the sacrosanctity of a tribune of the plebs. It was sacrilege to harm the person of the Emperor. Not that that ever held back a fanatic with a blade. The *tribunicia potestas* brought two more important powers. An Emperor, as if he were a tribune in the old free Republic, could veto or stop any action of any magistrate: a negative form of political control. Nothing could happen against the will of the Emperor. On the positive side, an Emperor could propose laws, again as if he were a tribune of the plebs. Given his control of the army, and his overwhelming *auctoritas* (the English word authority is not strong enough for this distinctively Roman concept), unsurprisingly anything he put forward became law. By the time of Heliogabalus the best legal minds stated that the will of the Emperor was law and that he was above the law.

Augustus proclaimed that the Republic had been restored (*Res Publica Restituta*). In the Roman mindset every reform, no matter how novel or even revolutionary, always had to be a 'restoration'. The political statement was not entirely without substance. The machinery of the Republic functioned: elections were held and magistracies filled, the Senate met and passed decrees. But this was a new Republic, where the Emperor had supreme military authority and where his will was law.

What was the purpose of Augustus' elaborate 'Restitution of the Republic'? It was not, as Theodore Mommsen held in the nineteenth century, a 'Diarchy', where Emperor and Senate shared power. Nor was it an attempt to 'hide' the rule of the Emperor. In a papyrus of 30/29 BC, the lamplighters of Oxyrhynchus took an oath to supply oil for lamps in the temples as they had 'up to the 22nd year which was also the 7th'. As perspicaciously pointed out by Fergus Millar, the lamplighters believed that one monarch (Cleopatra) had been replaced by another (Augustus). If these lamplighters, half of whom were illiterate, in an out-of-the-way corner of Egypt, knew Augustus was a monarch, it is impossible that the fact had escaped the political elite of Rome. The 'Restitution of the Republic' was a formula designed to mollify the pride, or *dignitas*, of the senators. The Emperor might be a sole ruler, and be above the law, but the legal basis of his power, his very legitimacy, rested on a vote of the senators themselves. That their vote was a formality, and that subsequently it was rubber-stamped by a vote of the people, mattered little. The Senate was embedded in the 'Restored Republic', and its members could serve the new order without the humiliating loss of their precious *dignitas*.

Augustus' 'Constitutional Settlement' (as it is often known in modern textbooks: the 'Settlement' rather playing down its revolutionary nature) was one of the most successful political experiments in history. For three centuries the *maius imperium* and *tribunicia potestas* voted by the Senate remained the twin bases of the authority of every Emperor. Of course, there was next to never any choice, but the formality mattered to senators: remember how Cassius Dio complained about both Macrinus and Heliogabalus using the imperial titles before their formal vote by the Senate.

Heliogabalus' successor said that although the Emperor was freed from the laws it befitted him to live by them. Far from being provocative, Alexander Severus was making a conciliatory ideological statement. An Emperor was above the law and could quite legally do whatever he wished. Apart from his own character, all that might hold him back were the expectations of his subjects.

II *The Passive Emperor: 'Petition and Response'*

Very, very occasionally a book changes the way we think about a whole period of history. One of those was *The Emperor in the Roman World (31 BC–AD 337)* by Fergus Millar (1977). It is a monumental work: 657 pages, including Appendices, with well over 4,000 footnotes, most including multiple references. The breadth and depth of knowledge are staggering. Millar set out his methods in the Preface: no 'contamination' from 'societies other than those of Greece and Rome', but 'the proper objective of a historian, to subordinate himself to the evidence'. The book starts with the physical location of the Emperor, his entourage and wealth. It ends with the relationship between the Emperor and the Church after the adoption of Christianity. The meat in the middle is its enduring legacy: an exhaustive survey of the Emperor's responses to endless communications from his subjects, both spoken and in writing, almost always asking for things such as money, status, friendship and justice. From innumerable examples the conclusion was reached that 'the Emperor was what the Emperor did'. And that was a daunting amount of bureaucratic work, reacting to the stimulus of others. There were no policies or strategies: indeed, no real initiative at all. The Emperor was essentially 'passive'.

Millar's many followers soon elevated this to the 'Petition and Response Model'. In interminable research conferences the phrase was parroted by graduate students, as if repetition proved its truth and precluded any need for other views. In an Afterword to the second edition (1991), Millar announced that he had actually not been writing evidence-led history (as any reader might have thought), but a more sophisticated hypothesis-led type, as he had been inspired by a model all along; although, oddly, the Preface with its subordination to the evidence remained unchanged.

Very, very occasionally a book changes the way we think about a whole period of history – not always totally for the better. After the last couple of paragraphs, it must be obvious that I am not a fan of the 'Petition and Response Model' (*exhaustive*, *innumerable* and *parroted* did not end up in the text by chance). Its appeal is evident: it makes the role of the Emperor very easy to grasp, and it spares its adherents the challenge of thinking about the Emperor in any other way. And not thinking about other ways is one of its main problems.

Before we get to those other ways of thinking about the Emperor, we need to realise that the evidence deployed to support the 'Petition and Response Model' is skewed towards those who communicated with the Emperor and then commemorated those communications. They were the literate elite of the empire, especially the Greek half of its domain. Millar acknowledged this: 'If we follow our evidence, we might almost come to believe that the primary role of the Emperor was to listen to speeches in Greek.' *Almost*, but not quite. Millar did not come to believe the primary role of the Emperor was to listen to speeches in Greek, without seeming to notice how that undermined his own methodology – you subordinate yourself to the evidence only when it fits your argument. And, of course, ancient historians can never avoid 'contamination' from 'societies other than those of Greece and Rome'. They live in one.

Another problem was not addressed. The Emperor was not just 'what the Emperor did'. He was also what his subjects thought he did or thought he was. As the Emperor could only directly interact with an infinitesimally small percentage of his subjects, far more important in maintaining his rule was his image in popular consciousness.

Even if we stick to Millar's own limited and pragmatic terms, an awful lot gets left out. The Emperor did a great deal more in life than he is observed doing in *The Emperor in the Roman World*. Very little of what is deliberately omitted from the book fits its central contention that the Emperor was 'essentially passive'.

Let's start with the Emperor as the supreme commander of the army, a topic avoided by Millar. An Emperor could raise new legions and disband others. We saw Heliogabalus cashiering *Legio III Gallica*. He could give units new titles, or remove ones previously granted. After the revolts in AD218–19 Heliogabalus dubbed *II Parthica* pious, faithful, fortunate, eternal. The troops could be given new weaponry. Caracalla created a Macedonian-style phalanx armed with long pikes. As it is not heard of again, presumably Macrinus rearmed them. The Emperor could raise the soldiers' pay and grant privileges (as did Septimius Severus and Caracalla), or hand out cash bonuses. Conversely, he could try to remove existing grants (which contributed to Macrinus' death). He could move units from garrisons at one end of the empire to the other. He might appear in front of his soldiers and make speeches; not only to those based in Rome, as many Emperors went to make themselves known to the armies on the frontiers. Finally, and crucially, not all Roman wars were defensive. An Emperor could decide to start a campaign and lead the troops in battle.

The troops might request things from their Emperor. The concept of the Emperor as 'fellow-soldier' gave them particular freedom of speech. An anecdote records 1,500 soldiers making the long journey from Britain to Rome to denounce an imperial favourite in the reign of Commodus. Yet this was an extraordinary exception. Almost all interaction between ruler and soldiery was initiated by the former. The Emperor in the world of the Roman military was active and dynamic, next to nothing like the 'passive' figure of the 'Petition and Response Model'.

Religion appears in *The Emperor in the Roman World* only as communications from subjects. This does not tell half the story. The Emperor was worshipped as a god across the empire. In the East, the imperial cult is considered to have been 'bottom up'. That is, the Greek elite asked permission to worship the Emperor. This fits snugly into the 'Petition and Response Model'. However, in the West the cult was introduced by the imperial government to act as a focus for provincial loyalty. Which, like the Emperor's relations with the army, does not fit at all.

As the ultimate mediator between mankind and the gods, the Emperor could innovate in religion. Usually, this amounted to no more than establishing the occasional new festival, or altering the membership of a college of priests. But some Emperors set about altering the entire religion of Rome. Constantine was successful in introducing his crucified god. Heliogabalus, as we will see in chapters 8 and 9, ultimately failed to establish his Emesene deity as the head of the state pantheon. No one can suggest that either Emperor was responding passively to a petition: 'Please, *Domine*, overturn the traditional religion, which has secured the safety of Rome for centuries, and in which the vast majority of us believe.'

In the Roman world there was no rigid line between public and private, and thus no clear division between the political and social life of the Emperor. The council of the Emperor, his *Consilium*, was where the big decisions were made. It had no fixed membership. The Emperor invited whom he wished, where and when he wished. Domitian summoned them in the middle of the night for advice on how to cook an especially fine fish (at least he did in a *Satire* by Juvenal). The outlines of the council could become blurred. If food was served in the *Consilium*, it became a dinner party. If talk turned to politics over dinner, it became a *Consilium*. As in any autocracy, who the Emperor talked to, and in what contexts, was the most important factor in politics. The Senate very much thought the Emperor should spend his time with members of their order. But they were often disappointed. Needless to say, this crucial and proactive social-political role of the Emperor does not square in the least with him being 'essentially passive'.

The Emperor was expected to partake in intellectual life: not just as a passive consumer, but also as an active participant. We will explore this in the next chapter. For now, it is enough to point out that Marcus Aurelius was not responding to a petition when he wrote the *Meditations*.

One area of politics where no one could argue that the Emperor was ever passive (unsurprisingly) finds no mention in *The Emperor in the Roman World*. Every autocracy intends to perpetuate itself. There are few universal rules in history, but this seems to be an exception. Every Emperor made plans for his succession. As far as I am aware, no Emperor pondered restoring the Republic, like Marcus Aurelius in the film *Gladiator*. Even if he had male children, there were proactive choices the Emperor had to make. If he had two sons, what should he do: promote both, select one? If just the sole heir, when grant him the *maius imperium* and the *tribunicia potestas*, and when elevate him from Caesar (heir-apparent) to Augustus (co-Emperor)? If he had no natural sons, whom should he adopt? Of course, influence might be brought to bear by those around the Emperor, but the choice was his alone.

It might seem unfair to criticise a book for what it does not cover. But not in this case. *The Emperor in the Roman World* scrutinises in isolation one aspect of the role of the ruler – responding to requests – and then generalises its unavoidable passivity to every other area of the Emperor's life.

Two substantial problems remain. All Emperors are homogenised into one rather dull bureaucrat, endlessly replying to his subjects. This does not do justice to the rich variety in our evidence and fails to understand the nature of autocracy. As Mary Beard nicely put it, 'over the half millennium of one-man rule in the western part of the Roman Empire, there were libertines as well as hard workers… even those most devoted to duty must have let their hair down sometime… casual sadism is not incompatible with bureaucratic efficiency'. Not all Emperors were the same.

There is a final problem with *The Emperor in the Roman World*. Its relentless accumulation of detail makes few allowances for its reader. Subordinating oneself under a mass of evidence is no substitute for a methodology which attempts to engage the reader's imagination. As Keith Hopkins put it in a hostile review: 'Aesthetic and intellectual pleasures are compatible with high scholarship.'

The 'Petition and Response Model' is not the only, and certainly not the most enjoyable, way of thinking about the role of the Roman Emperor. Let's try another: one that tells us more about the experiences of Heliogabalus.

III   *The Active Emperor: 'Four Constituencies'*

Far from attempting the impossible task of avoiding outside 'contamination', we can frame a question in deliberately anachronistic terms: what were the 'constituencies' whose support an Emperor had to cultivate? There were four that really mattered: the Senate, the plebs of the city of Rome, the army and the *Familia Caesaris* (the staff of the imperial palace). These were the groups that could destabilise his rule, even overthrow him. This posed an acute problem for the Emperor. All four wanted the Emperor to do different things: indeed, to be a different kind of ruler. To incline to one group risked alienating the other three. Being Emperor was a delicate balancing act.

The Emperor and the Senate at a structural level were opposed institutions. The Senate had been the focus of politics in the free Republic and the memory remained strong. But the senatorial order was not a closed caste. To maintain its numbers each generation needed a significant influx of new men. One of the most striking phenomena of the cultural history of the principate was that every generation of senators took on the attitudes of their predecessors. They accepted the necessity of the rule of the

Emperors, otherwise the empire would relapse into civil wars, but hankered for the freedom of the past. The Emperor was in essence a military autocrat. His role was forged in civil war and underpinned by the army. The Marxist interpretation that Senate and Emperor combined to maintain their position at the top of the social pyramid is not incompatible with them being at odds with each other. Senate and Emperor were bound together. The Emperor needed the Senate to vote him his powers, to endow him with legitimacy. He needed the senators to govern his provinces and command his armies. The Senate needed the Emperor to maintain its status as the most prestigious body in the empire, and its members now had to look to the Emperor to advance their careers up the *cursus honorum*.

Augustus' 'Constitutional Settlement' created a formula that largely salved the prickly *dignitas* of the senators and allowed them to serve the new regime. The senators responded by redefining the concept of their own freedom. *Libertas* now primarily meant freedom of speech and freedom from unjust condemnation. But this refashioned *Libertas* led on to other desires.

The Senate wanted the Emperor to be a first among equals, a *primus inter pares* among senators, or as they also put it a *Civilis Princeps*: perhaps best translated as a 'civilian prince'. They expected the Emperor to respect the Senate, attend its meetings, and, when he did, exhibit the right demeanour. They wanted free access to the Emperor, for him to spend the majority of his time with senators and to take advice only from them. This desire for him to step down to their level is encapsulated in a passage of fiction from the *Augustan History* about Heliogabalus' successor.

> *He forbad men to call him Dominus, and he gave orders that people should write to him as if he was a commoner, retaining only the title Imperator. He removed from the imperial footwear and garments*

all the jewels that had been used by Heliogabalus, and he wore a plain white robe without any gold, just as he is always depicted, and ordinary cloaks and togas. He associated with his friends on such familiar terms that he would sit with them as equals, attend their banquets, have some of them as his daily guests, even when they were not formally summoned, and held a morning levee like any Senator, with open curtains and without the presence of ushers, or, at least, with none but those who acted as attendants at the doors.

Of course, the senators could not enforce such behaviour on the Emperor. So each time the Emperor voluntarily chose to step down to the level of the senators, it actually symbolised and reinforced his dominance. But at the same time it bolstered the position of the Senate by exhibiting imperial respect.

Senators also wanted money. The conspicuous consumption and gift giving necessary to maintain their status was ruinous. In the days of the free Republic, a senatorial family could hope to replenish its coffers with windfall capital from commanding in warfare and the (more or less corrupt) governing of provinces. Under the principate the former had almost completely disappeared (plunder was reserved for the Emperor), and the latter was much curtailed by imperial surveillance. Instead, a senator fallen on hard times, through no fault of his own (at least in contemporary terms), asked the Emperor for a handout. The issue was not would the Emperor give – he does in every anecdote that survives – but how graciously he gave: did he behave like a *Civilis Princeps*?

What the Senate did not want was to be treated with contempt – Tiberius muttering 'men fit to be slaves' – or humiliated – seeing an elderly senator kissing Caligula's foot – or terrorised: Commodus waving the freshly severed head of an ostrich at them. The ideology of the *Civilis Princeps* only extended to the senators themselves. They despised an Emperor fawning on the plebs of Rome, or rubbing shoulders with common soldiers, and they loathed the idea of an Emperor aloof in the palace, hedged round with ceremonies orchestrated by the *Familia Caesaris*.

The populace of Rome (the *Plebs Urbana*) was in one way the least significant of the four 'constituencies' the Emperor had to consider. The plebs could riot and often did. Twenty-nine popular outbursts are recorded in the half century to AD238. These riots could resemble full-scale urban warfare and might leave large areas of the city devastated. The plebs might bring about the death of an imperial favourite. To calm them Commodus had the head of his praetorian prefect Cleander displayed on a pike. But Rome had a large garrison of soldiers, and if the troops were united and there was enough political will the mob could always be crushed. The *Plebs Urbana* never actually overthrew an Emperor. They could destabilise, but not end, a regime.

History dictated the privileged position of the Roman plebs. Under the Republic their votes had been necessary to pass laws and for senators to gain office as magistrates. Which is not to say that Republican Rome was a democracy. The senatorial elite employed the plebs as a pressure valve: an external arbitrator to prevent even more vicious infighting among themselves. For several centuries the strategy had been successful: until Julius Caesar and the other military dynasts became too powerful for the collective elite to contain. Under Augustus the plebs had exchanged their political powers for what Juvenal contemptuously called 'Bread and Circuses'. Food and entertainments should not be despised, given the grinding poverty and appalling conditions in which the vast majority of the urban population of Rome lived.

The plebs wanted more than the regular shows and the corn dole. The latter only reached the 200,000 or so on the register, who were not necessarily the poorest in a city of a million.

These things were expected, and won the Emperor no credit for generosity. Extra gifts and spectacles were looked for, no matter what the occasion. Yet, as with the Senate, it was not just the giving, but the way things were given. They wanted the Emperor to enter into the spirit of the events, to be seen taking evident enjoyment in their pleasures. They loved Claudius bantering with them and calling them 'My lords' at the games. Neither Julius Caesar nor Marcus Aurelius endeared themselves by doing administration or reading in the imperial box. The plebs enjoyed the scrambling free-for-all when Emperors threw tokens for gifts. They wanted an Emperor who was a man of the people: a man of levity (*levitas*), not stiff senatorial *dignitas*. They had no time for a ruler off hobnobbing with the soldiers, or secluded with the *Familia Caesaris* in the palace. The plebs approved of stories of Emperors in disguise (surely transparent: remember how bad the Roman elite were at pretending to be lower class) slipping out of the palace at night to roister in the streets and inns and brothels.

The lower orders, as Herodian complained, had a distressing habit of taking pleasure in the suffering of their betters, like Caligula making senators run alongside his chariot. Better still was the Emperor humiliating the elite by forcing them to appear on the stage in the theatre, or drive chariots in the circus. Best of all was making them fight in the amphitheatre. Class hatred, or at least hatred between rich and poor, was alive in ancient Rome.

In the film *Gladiator*, a tattoo is the mark of a Roman soldier. The evidence for that is very thin before the late empire. But after Augustus instituted a professional army, joining involved assuming a new identity: that of soldier replaced what had gone before. Sometimes, for those in auxiliary units, it involved actually taking a new name. Soldiers were set apart from civilian society. They lived under different laws: harsh discipline was compensated by particular benefits. Even off duty they were recognisable. They spoke their own vernacular 'Latin of the camp', and they dressed and walked differently. You could hear them coming: the clatter of their hobnails and the thrumming of the long ends of their military belts as they twirled them through the air.

It was best to get out of their way. They had a reputation for casual violence. In Apuleius' novel *The Golden Ass* a soldier asks a Greek gardener a question in Latin. When he gets no response, the soldier beats up the gardener, before asking the question again in Greek. Not just violence, but rape and theft. Civilians feared soldiers, and soldiers despised civilians.

The soldiers wanted an Emperor who was a 'fellow-soldier' (*Commilito* in Latin). This was more than just inspecting their manoeuvres and making formal speeches from a tribunal. It was more than just raising their pay and handing out donatives. To be a true *commilito* he should dress like them, march on foot with them, take a turn carrying a heavy standard, sit on the ground and share their rations. Nothing was better than Caracalla keeping senators like Cassius Dio waiting all day while the Emperor drank and joked with his guards.

When someone in the Roman Empire mentioned the *Familia Caesaris* they did not mean the Emperor's relatives, but his family in the extended sense of the slaves and freedmen in his household. Over four thousand surviving inscriptions show the sheer size of the *Familia Caesaris*. It grew over time and not only because imperial wealth increased. With each new dynasty the *familia* of another elite family was added, and when that dynasty fell its members remained in the imperial household. A bewildering number of posts proliferated. The Emperor had doctors and masseurs and astrologers, cooks and wine stewards and waiters, gardeners and jewellers and a range of wardrobe masters for different types of clothing (private, military, legal, triumphal, hunting, 'Kingly and Greek', and so on). As we have seen, he had a functionary to guide his studies (*a studiis*) and even a *procurator voluptatum* to facilitate his pleasures (presumably a busier post under Heliogabalus than Marcus Aurelius). With no strict divide between public and private, from the start the *Familia Caesaris* had a 'governmental' role. The *a rationibus* oversaw imperial finances, the *ab epistulis* dealt with correspondence, the *a legationibus* with embassies, the *a libellis* and the *a cognitionibus* with legal affairs (written and in court), the *ab admissionibus* controlled access to the Emperor and the *a cubiculo* ran his bed chamber.

There was a dissonance between status and power. The vast majority of these men were slaves and ex-slaves, predominantly drawn from that great arc of the Greek world that ran from Asia Minor to Egypt. For the traditional elite they were the lowest of the low, despised both for their social and their ethnic origins. Yet they were close to the Emperor, and that meant power. When two embassies disputed before Caligula, the *a cubiculo* Helikon could ensure which received a favourable hearing, as the Jewish writer Philo tells us: 'For, when Gaius [Caligula] was playing ball, taking exercise, at his bath and at his breakfast, and retiring for the night, he was with him; so that he had the ear of the Emperor at his leisure, and on all occasions more than any other man.' Proximity to the Emperor also meant wealth. The largest known private fortune – 400 million sesterces, equivalent to the property qualification of two thirds of all members of the Senate – was amassed by Narcissus, the *ab epistulis* of Claudius. Ambitious, or frightened, members of the elite paid good money to freedmen to whisper to the Emperor, or even to know what he was saying or doing or perhaps thinking.

By the end of the first century AD freedman had been replaced by equestrians, the second order of the elite, as the great high imperial secretaries. And by the time of Heliogabalus it was usual for the *ab epistulis* to be a man of letters, and the *a libellis* a leading jurist. The elite, including Emperors, boasted that imperial freedmen were kept in their place. From these not unbiased statements, modern scholars have concluded that the heyday of influence of the *Familia Caesaris* was brief. But this overstates the case. A freedman *a rationibus* still ran the imperial finances, another still acted as chamberlain (*a cubiculo*), while a third continued to control access to the Emperor (*ab admissionibus*).

In any autocracy, closeness to the ruler always trumps formal status. A modern example. One of the more influential men in the court of Haile Selassie looked after the Emperor's small Japanese dog. During the ceremonies Lulu 'would run away from the Emperor's lap and pee on the dignitaries' shoes. The august gentlemen were not allowed to flinch or make the slightest gesture when they felt their feet getting wet.' Another example, Roman, from the philosopher Epictetus, thinking about the reign of Domitian. 'How should a man become wise all of a sudden when Caesar puts him in charge of his chamber-pot? How is it that all at once we are saying, "With what wisdom has Felicio spoken to me"?'

Did the *Familia Caesaris* have a group outlook? As the great German scholar Ludwig Friedländer exclaimed in the nineteenth century: 'if they had only told their tale!' Instead, it was their enemies, literary men of the social elite, who made disparaging comments. Yet we get the occasional hint. The *Augustan History* writes about Hadrian: 'The imperial pomp he reduced to the utmost simplicity, and thereby gained the greater esteem, though the palace attendants opposed this course, for they found that since he made no use of go-betweens, they could in no way terrorize men, or take money for decisions about which there was no concealment.' What the *Familia Caesaris* wanted was what the other 'constituencies' wanted: power, wealth and the Emperor to themselves. For the *Familia Caesaris* this meant the Emperor as a hierarchical figure screened by 'imperial pomp' orchestrated by themselves. Definitely not a *Civilis Princeps*, or a 'fellow-soldier', or a man of the people roaming the streets at night.

The four 'constituencies' – Senate, urban plebs, soldiers and *Familia Caesaris* – were hostile to each other and their expectations of the Emperor mutually exclusive. Being Emperor was a juggling act. The 'constituencies' competing for his time and favour, trying to mould his identity, meant that the Emperor continually had to make choices. The choices he made were proactive. To incline to one 'constituency' was likely to alienate the other three. That was potentially fatal. The Emperor Tiberius described his role as 'holding a wolf by the ears'.

When he reached Rome, Heliogabalus proved very bad indeed at holding that wolf by the ears.

CHAPTER 7   IN ROME

AD219–21

I   *Adventus*

Having spent the winter in Nicomedia (AD219–20), Heliogabalus 'made his way into Italy through Thrace, Moesia, and each Pannonia, and he stayed there until the end of his life'. A late third-century document known as the *Antonine Itinerary*, which set out halting places and became a road map for later Emperors, might have its origins in the journey to the East of Caracalla in AD213. It is possible that Heliogabalus retraced the route of his 'father' when heading west. The one certainty is that Maesa ensured that her grandson toured many of the garrisons in the provinces through which they passed. An Emperor needed to show himself to his troops.

Artefacts in two locations might record the visit of the young Emperor. A pair of statues found at Carnuntum, the base of *Legio XIV Gemina* on the Danube in Pannonia Superior, have been identified as Heliogabalus. Both have been deliberately damaged, and one is very unusual. We will look at them when we discuss his sexuality (chapter 10). Although it might be doubted that the imperial party travelled so far north as Carnuntum – although, as we will see, there was plenty of time – one town through which they definitely went was Aquileia, the gateway to Italy from the East. A relief sculpture has been argued to commemorate the arrival in the town of Heliogabalus and his cousin Alexianus.

Preceded by three attendants, two young males ride in a carriage pulled by donkeys. Behind them four porters carry a litter, on which might be a small shrine containing a conical object, which is about the size of one of the human heads. The young males have short hair, and the one in the foreground wears a toga, and has a chubby face.

The style of the relief points to the third century. The procession may well be religious. Alexianus could have been with Heliogabalus. But then the doubts start to mount up. Nothing in the iconography clearly distinguishes the main figure as an Emperor. One of the attendants carries something over his shoulder, but not necessarily the axe bound by rods of the *fasces* which were carried in front of an Emperor. Would an Emperor arrive for a ceremony of *Adventus* in a carriage pulled by donkeys? The two main figures are the same size – in art relative stature often was a sign of status – and in AD 219 Alexianus had no official role.

Image 8: Relief Sculpture from Trieste

Alexianus was five years younger than Heliogabalus, but these boys appear to be the same age. The object in the litter – although vaguely the right shape – is far smaller than any depiction of the black stone of Elagabal, which usually was conveyed in a chariot drawn by four horses. And the relief was not found in Aquileia, but round the gulf at the north of the Adriatic in Trieste. Once again, we must remember the factors nudging art historians to identify every ancient portrait with a famous individual.

An Emperor travelled in style, and his entourage was large. We know a few individuals who accompanied Heliogabalus. There was his family: Maesa, Soaemias, his aunt Mamaea and his cousin Alexianus (if he is on the relief from Aquileia or not). The praetorian prefect Comazon was in attendance. By the time they reached Moesia an inscription reveals that Comazon had a colleague commanding the Praetorians, Julius Flavianus. Another companion and most faithful friend (*comiti amico fidissimo*) on the journey was the ex-imperial secretary, who had brought *Legio IV Scythica* back into line, whose name only survives as …ATVS. The Emesene Aurelius Eubulus, who was there at the start of the revolt, if he had not been sent ahead, would have been in the party. It is tempting to see factions already in the court. In AD 222 Comazon and Julius Flavianus would support Maesa, and …ATVS and Aurelius Eubulus remain loyal to Heliogabalus. But that was in the future, and three years was a long time in Roman politics.

There was another *most faithful companion*, most important of all to the Emperor. Shaded by parasols, trundling along in its chariot was the Invincible Sun God Elagabal. Although none of our sources mention them, we can be certain that other priests from Emesa, apart from the Emperor, accompanied the black stone. The *Augustan History* and Zosimus, a much later Greek historian, have Heliogabalus surrounded by every kind of magician, although that might just be an elaboration on stories of necromancy.

Heliogabalus took his time getting to Rome. In the fourth century, Eutropius stated that the young Emperor was in Rome for two years and eight months, thus placing his arrival in July AD219. The date seems to be supported by coins from Alexandria issued before 29 August of that year, which celebrate Heliogabalus' marriage to Julia Paula (his first of many wives). Allowing time for the news to reach Egypt, that can place the Emperor in Rome by July at the latest.

Except Eutropius is notoriously inaccurate, especially about times and dates. And Heliogabalus need not have been in Rome to marry Julia Paula. She could have been summoned from Rome – the Emperor's will was law – for a ceremony at some point along his route. Or maybe the coins could celebrate a betrothal before the wedding, which would take place when Heliogabalus eventually reached Rome.

Does the last paragraph smack of special pleading? Maybe, but it is necessary. Another piece of evidence yields a different, later date. Once arrived, Heliogabalus never left Rome again. The *equites singulares*, the imperial horse guards, put up an inscription giving thanks to their favoured god for the safe return to Rome of Heliogabalus on 29 October. (Ideologically, Emperors always *returned* to Rome, even if they had never set foot in the city before.) The horse guards should have got the date right – they were with the Emperor.

July or late October, either thirteen or almost seventeen months since the battle at Immae on 8 June. So much for Herodian's literary cliché of the successful pretender Heliogabalus *rushing* to Rome. Maesa knew better than the Greek historian. There had not been an Emperor in Rome for five years. Pollio and Censorinus had secured the city the previous year. There was time to tour the army along the Danube and raise support among its all-important soldiery. Trajan, the *Optimus Princeps* ('Best of Emperors', AD98–117), had done exactly the same after his accession, not reaching Rome for more than eighteen months.

The Senate and people of Rome had had ample opportunity to prepare. They would have waited for the new Emperor outside the gates, perhaps at a designated milestone. The arrival of an Emperor was a grand occasion: 'Altars were lit, incense thrown on, libations poured, sacrificial victims slain' and there were speeches, lots of speeches. Inside 'the whole city had been decked with garlands of flowers and branches of laurel and richly coloured materials; and it was ablaze with torches and burning incense; the citizens, wearing white robes and with radiant faces, uttered many shouts of good omen; the soldiers too stood out conspicuous in their armour, as they moved like participants in some festival; finally the Senators walked in state.'

The Emperor Constantius, entering Rome for the first time in AD357, was amazed. 'Wherever he turned he was dazzled by the concentration of wonderful sights': the baths as big as provinces, the top of the Colosseum 'almost beyond the reach of human vision', the Pantheon, the Columns, the Temple of Rome. The list went on and on, but when he reached the Forum of Trajan he 'stood transfixed with amazement'. The Eternal City would have had less of an impact on Heliogabalus. He had been born and bred there. But what effect did the new Emperor have on his subjects? Given that he had refused to wear the traditional toga earlier in the year at the Day of Vows, perhaps it was to be expected that he was wearing his eastern priestly robes. More surprisingly, Herodian tells us that the picture of him worshipping Elagabal, which he had sent ahead from Nicomedia, had had the desired effect: 'the Romans, conditioned by the painting, found nothing strange in the sight'.

We do not know Heliogabalus' route through the city. Perhaps, like his 'grandfather' Septimius Severus, he ascended the Capitol, before proceeding to the Palatine. Perhaps, like Constantius later, 'after addressing the nobility in the Senate House, and the people from the Rostra, he entered the Palace'. Either way, by that evening the fifteen-year-old Emperor and his ancestral god were established in the sprawling imperial compound on the Palatine. It was time for Heliogabalus to start making the choices available to an Emperor.

II *Choices: Those Heliogabalus Rejected*

The Emperor was not only what he did, but what he chose not to do. Heliogabalus begins to come into focus if we look at a couple of paths he did not take.

On his deathbed Septimius Severus advised his sons to enrich the soldiers and despise everyone else. Caracalla took the words to heart, raising their pay, marching and eating with his troops and keeping senators like Cassius Dio waiting at his door all day while he drank with the common soldiery. In the revolt, Heliogabalus had spoken to the soldiers at Raphaneae and rallied them from flight at Immae. Later, as Emperor, in a letter to his provincial subjects he wrote of his 'most valiant and loyal soldiers, including the Praetorian guard'. A fragment of Cassius Dio preserves Heliogabalus speaking to the Senate: 'Yes, you love me, and so by Jupiter, does the populace, and also the legions, but I do not please the Praetorians, to whom I keep giving so much.' In another isolated passage, the historian writes that the Emperor was 'most attached' to the soldiers, but they – like everyone else – hated him because of his debauchery. Perhaps Heliogabalus did believe in the loyalty and love of soldiers; even at times the Praetorians. Autocrats are known for self-deception. Yet, once in Rome, he chose not to follow the example of the man he claimed as his father. Heliogabalus did nothing to foster his relationship with his troops, neither raising their pay nor spending time with them by touring their camps and acting as a fellow-soldier (*commilito*).

Septimius Severus had come to power in a series of civil wars. On the throne he campaigned on every frontier of the empire. Caracalla led armies along the Rhine and Danube and died in the East in the midst of a war against the Parthians. Just one source records Heliogabalus preparing for a war. It is a strange story. Certain persons had told the Emperor that 'Marcus Antoninus', with the help of astrologers and magicians, had made the Marcomanni, a confederation of German tribes, permanent subjects and friends of the Roman people by arcane rites and a hidden dedication. Wanting to stir up a conflict, Heliogabalus failed to find and destroy the dedication. There is no point in modern speculation about whether 'Marcus Antoninus' was Marcus Aurelius or Caracalla. The entire thing was invented by the author of the *Augustan History*, who gives the game away, probably intentionally, when he writes that the tale was spread by men who were marginalised at court because of their small penises (don't worry, we will come back to the importance of cock size in politics).

Better to ignore the sly fiction and listen to Heliogabalus' words given by Cassius Dio: 'I do not want titles derived from war and bloodshed; it is enough for me that you call me *Pius* and *Felix*.' The statement was not recorded for commendation. Pacifism was not an attribute looked for in a Roman Emperor. Heliogabalus chose not to fulfil the role of Emperor as war leader. He was lucky. The role was not thrust upon him. The northern frontier was quiet after the campaigns of Caracalla. In the East the

Parthians were distracted, both by a civil war and by the rebellion of their client kings in Persia.

The second thing Heliogabalus chose not to do involved a very different sector of society and was usually less violent. The Roman Emperor was expected to be a man of culture (*paideia*). In large part that consisted of listening to long speeches made by heavily bearded, self-important Greeks. The Emperor Trajan teased the philosopher Dio Chrysostom: 'What you are saying I do not understand, but I love you as I love myself.' Quite a good putdown. It was not enough to be a passive consumer of culture: the Emperor should be a participant. Caracalla could quote Euripides to Cassius Dio at a dinner party. Septimius Severus could recognise, and punish, the treasonous context of a line of Virgil. Both Severus and Caracalla wrote autobiographies. Other Emperors went further: Tiberius composed verse in Latin and Greek; Claudius wrote books on the alphabet and dicing; Domitian one on haircare; and Marcus Aurelius, of course, wrote Stoic philosophy.

Only scraps survive. That might be just as well for the posthumous reputation of their imperial authors. There is a paradox about modern dictators. By definition, they have led interesting lives. Yet without exception they have published some of the dullest books ever written. Those of the Emperors would not have been as bad. Rome was a highly literate culture. Acceptance as a member of the elite demanded a level of cultural attainment. Yet what remains, with the exception of the *Commentaries* of Julius Caesar – and, of course, it is debatable if he was the first Emperor – is far from the highest quality literature. If the lost autobiography of Augustus was anything like his surviving *Res Gestae* it would have been turgid. The *Res Gestae* (*Things Achieved*) was inscribed in bronze outside his tomb and copied in marble across the empire. It hammers away at its two themes – 'the wars

I have won' (actually, all won by other people) and 'the gifts I have given' (with no mention of proscriptions and confiscations) – in an almost literally leaden piece of propaganda. It might be unfair to criticise the *Meditations* of Marcus Aurelius. They were notebooks written 'To Himself' and never intended for publication. Yet their subsequent reputation is mystifying. In plodding prose they reveal an autocrat struggling with self-control and a martyr to duty who possessed no originality of thought and had a joyless loathing of the human body and pleasure.

The entourage of an Emperor was always rammed with purveyors of culture. Heliogabalus had his most faithful companion: his former *a studiis* ...ATVS. A replacement director of literary studies would have been appointed. The biographer and belle-lettrist Philostratus had been a favourite of Domna, who had asked him to compose a biography of Apollonius of Tyana, which he finished after her death, probably at court under the patronage of her sister Maesa. His sparring partner the Sophist Aelian quite likely was there too. Not just biographers and sophists, but philosophers, historians and poets, as well as more practical writers: doctors, jurists, astrologers, all kinds of intellectuals paced the corridors of the palace, hoping for imperial favour.

Despite all the opportunities of the imperial court, nothing links Heliogabalus to this world of culture – no apt quotations from the Classics, no dinner parties with intellectuals, certainly no literary endeavours – except two anecdotes from the *Augustan History*. (By now, you know where this is going!) First, Heliogabalus forced certain writers to relate unspeakable details in their biographies of Macrinus' son Diadumenianus. You have to think that it is extremely improbable that anyone was writing biographies of the nine-year-old in the next reign. Second, after being anally penetrated, Heliogabalus would ask 'philosophers and even men of the greatest dignity' if they, in their youth, had experienced such things.

It is worth pausing to think about something the *Augustan History* chose not to do in its portrait of Heliogabalus. (Generations of students have endured such digressions: several said they were the most enjoyable bits of my teaching – a backhanded compliment!) Visitors to the Hadrian exhibition at the British Museum back in 2008 were first confronted by a mocked-up Roman inscription of a poem.

> *Animula vagula blandula,*
> *hospes comesque corporis,*
> *quo nunc abides? In loca*
> *pallidula rigida nubile –*
> *nec ut soles dabis iocos.*

> Little soul, little wanderer, little charmer,
> Body's guest and companion,
> To what places will you set out for now?
> To darkling, cold and gloomy ones –
> And you won't make your usual jokes.

The label, and the exhibition catalogue, confidently attributed it to Hadrian. To be fair, so do most scholars. The poem, however, is from the *Augustan History*. The mischievous author enjoyed writing doggerel and putting it in the mouths of Emperors, good and tyrannical, often adding something on the lines of 'originally written in Greek, but someone has made a poor translation into Latin': which is not a bad parody of literary criticism. They are all recognised for what they are: except this poem, on the grounds of its superior quality. Try reading it aloud in the original. You don't need to know anything about the expectations of ancient readers of poetry, and you don't need to know a word of Latin. Then think about its imagery and ideas. How did it sound? And what about its content? I assume the answers are repetitive and jangly, and shallow and trite.

The *Augustan History* gives no poetry to Heliogabalus, as it pictures the Emperor as the antithesis of a man of culture. Herodian, nearer in time and better informed, had more insight. Heliogabalus deliberately rejected Greek and Roman culture. He would persecute those teachers who tried to instil *paideia* in his cousin Alexianus. Instead, he turned to an alien culture: the Phoenician/Syrian cult of Elagabal.

III Choices: Those Heliogabalus Accepted

Religion, sex and social life were the three big life choices of Heliogabalus. Religion and sex deserve chapters of their own. We will return to his energetic social life in a few moments.

Not all aspects of the role of an Emperor could be totally avoided. The choices in these areas were about time and diligence.

Heliogabalus could not always avoid acting as a judge. Cassius Dio damns the Emperor with faint praise: 'When trying someone in court he really had more or less the appearance of a man, but everywhere else he showed affectation in his actions and in the quality of his voice.' An Emperor was not only hounded by Greeks making speeches, but also by endless numbers of letters seeking judicial rulings. Two examples of Heliogabalus enmeshed in the so-called 'petition-response' system survive in the Byzantine collection known as the *Codex of Justinian*. One, issued on 19 February AD222 by Heliogabalus and his cousin Alexianus – now adopted Caesar, or heir – was addressed to a soldier called Aurelius Maro. It is worth quoting in full.

If your father, compelled by force, sold his house, it will not be held to be valid because it was not done in good faith; for a sale based in bad faith is void. Therefore the provincial governor, when approached in your name, will interpose his authority, especially since you submit that you are ready to refund to the buyer what was paid as the price.

Sensible, measured and informed, it very much has the 'appearance of a man'. The other, issued sixteen days earlier – on legal procedure, sureties and costs – is drier still. Are these the actual words of Heliogabalus, not filtered through a literary source, but talking to us directly, and showing a completely unexpected side to his character: a serious and dutiful young man with a legal mind? Probably not. Antipater, a secretary of Septimius Severus, won praise for composing imperial letters with just the right tone of majesty.

An Emperor *could* compose his own written replies (rescripts) to requests for a legal ruling. An Emperor could do anything. But there was a specialist secretary for writing these communications, the *a libellis*. In a slightly mad project, an Oxford professor devoted half a lifetime to analysing the literary style of the almost two thousand five hundred items in the *Codex of Justinian* to identify each *a libellis* in the third century. The one for Heliogabalus is Number Six. Or perhaps he isn't. Several scholars have doubted the whole methodological underpinning of the stylistic analysis.

Heliogabalus should have read these rescripts, or at least had their contents explained. But was he paying attention? The one thing he had to do, before they went out in his name, was sign them, probably in a fancy imperial purple ink. A later Emperor, Justin, was illiterate. So a stencil was cut with the letters LEGI (I have read). The Emperor held a pen while his hand was guided along the outline.

Diplomacy was another role that could not be ducked altogether. Foreign embassies were expected to appear before the Emperor. Actually, the whole process was wider and vaguer than just receiving those from beyond the frontiers. In keeping with the legal fiction that many communities within the empire were allies not subjects, they were treated in accordance with diplomatic protocol. Conversely, many peoples, on any objective view outside the empire, were regarded as having submitted to Rome merely by having sent an embassy in the first place. Individuals proclaiming orations – philosophers to instruct and improve, sophists to entertain – could merge into 'public' ambassadors when they asked for imperial benefactions for their hometowns. Speech after speech, each flowing like a river, expansive like the winter snows.

Heliogabalus had to listen to some embassies. But he could choose the location, and no one could force him to concentrate. The Alexandrian Jew Philo records a delegation from his own community trailing after Caligula as the Emperor arranged the interior décor of a villa, occasionally pausing to fire off offensive questions: 'Why do you not eat pork?'

We have evidence of perhaps three of the many embassies that appeared before Heliogabalus. An inscription records that he granted Thyatira – the town in Asia Minor that he had visited with his 'father' Caracalla – the right to hold Pythian Games, in response to an embassy headed by a famous athlete. And a very damaged inscription from Delphi contained a letter from the Emperor, with Alexander as Caesar (so between June AD221 and March AD222), that was almost certainly in reply to an embassy. Both can be considered routine. The third is more unusual.

When the village of Eummaus in Palestine was devastated by an earthquake, a delegation headed by the Christian scholar Julius Africanus was despatched to the imperial court. The

Emperor presumably granted money and allowed Eummaus to be refounded as the city of Nicopolis. Two later Christian writers – Eusebius and Jerome – date the embassy to AD221.

It is an intriguing idea: the Christian addressing the high priest of Elagabal in Rome. Modern scholarship has tried to bolster the historicity of the encounter in two ways. First, it is claimed that an inscription from Eummaus names the god Elagabal. It was perhaps erected in gratitude to the munificence of his devotee the Emperor. But on the damaged stone only the letters LAGA survive. There is a gap between the G and the A, suggesting they belong to different words. The second support focuses on the *Chronographiae*, written by Julius Africanus. Now only extant in fragments, this was a monumental chronicle of almost six thousand years of history from the creation to AD221. Perhaps the *Chronographiae* was presented as a gift to the Emperor on the occasion of the embassy and was maybe even dedicated to him? Certainly, the year – 5723 to the Christians; 974 since the foundation of the city to the Romans – contained nothing obvious to provide the climactic finale of a book. But this could be to look at it the wrong way round. The end date of the *Chronographiae* might have suggested the date of the embassy to Christian writers.

There are further problems. Two other later writers – Syncellus and the anonymous *Chronicon Paschale* – date the embassy to Alexander Severus. Julius Africanus dedicated another work, the *Cesti*, to Alexander and was appointed by him to supervise the imperial library in the Pantheon. Either the embassy or the dedication might have won him imperial favour. Alexander's mother, Mamaea, was remembered as having an interest in Christianity. Outside the luxuriant fiction of the *Augustan History* (as we will see in the next chapter), nothing suggests Heliogabalus had any interest in, let alone sympathy for, the illegal cult that Tacitus had described as a 'deadly superstition'.

As so often, just when we think we have got near Heliogabalus, discovered something definite about him, the Emperor again slips away, tantalisingly out of reach.

The empire had to be governed, and the Emperor had to appoint men for the task. The ancient sources' ridicule of Heliogabalus' choices builds to a crescendo. Herodian had read Cassius Dio, and the *Augustan History* used both Cassius Dio and Herodian. Each link in the literary chain ramped up the terrible impropriety of the men chosen.

Cassius Dio singled out the career of the ex-soldier Comazon, with his 'name derived from mimes and buffoonery', who advanced from praetorian prefect to be prefect of the city no fewer than three times, as 'one of the greatest violations of precedent'. Certain others were 'often honoured by him and became men of influence, some because they had joined in his rebellion, others because they were his adulterous sexual partners'. Aurelius Eubulus, the equestrian city councillor from Emesa, combined both roles. A participant in the 'lewdness and debauchery' of Heliogabalus, Eubulus was rewarded with control of the imperial treasury (*procurator summarum rationum*, or *a rationibus*), in which post he was a monster of rapacity: 'there was nothing he did not confiscate'. Cassius Dio was appalled by two ex-slaves from the East. The Carian Hierocles, who had been the lover of one Gordius, who had taught him to be a charioteer, became the 'husband' of the Emperor. Heliogabalus wanted to appoint him Caesar, and thus make him his heir. Then there was Zoticus, a slave from Smyrna, nicknamed *Cook*, after his father's job, who fleetingly held the post of imperial chamberlain (*a cubiculo*) because of the enormous size of his penis, before his failure to get an erection saw him exiled. There is much more to say about these men when we look at sex (see chapter 10).

When it came to senators, Cassius Dio was happier to record those executed by Heliogabalus, rather than those who held office and survived. Mention of the latter would have been an embarrassment to the individuals and their families: also to the historian himself, who was implicated in the regime.

Herodian's account, which gives no names, is marked by repetition, exaggeration and misrepresentation. The 'madness' of the Emperor led him to 'take men from the stage and public theatres and put them in charge of the most important public business'. A dancer from Rome was made praetorian prefect. This must be a misreading, probably deliberate, of Comazon in Cassius Dio. 'Similarly another was raised from the stage and put in charge of the training and morals of the youth and the census qualifications of the senatorial and equestrian orders.' The post existed (*procurator*, or *praepositus*, *a censibus*) and was sometimes twinned with that of secretary in charge of legal responses (*a libellis*), but it only extended to revising the lists of equestrians. We would expect Cassius Dio to have mentioned any such new indignity inflicted by Heliogabalus on the Senate. Again, the theatrical origins of such a procurator can be doubted: *another* from the stage, when there had not been a first.

Herodian continues: positions of the highest responsibility were given to 'charioteers and comedy actors and mimes'. The first looks like a reference to Hierocles, both of the latter to Comazon again. Finally, 'slaves and freedmen, who perhaps excelled in some foul activity, he appointed as governors of consular provinces'. If such appointments were made in reality, Cassius Dio, that stickler for tradition and respectability, would not have found the career of Comazon 'one of the greatest violations of precedent'.

With the *Augustan History* we reach a realm of mischievous fiction. The dancer who was praetorian prefect reappears from

Herodian. Zoticus and his big dick is elevated to a starring role, with no hint of erectile dysfunction. Now it is Zoticus who becomes husband to the Emperor and has to perform even when feeling unwell. When not servicing the Emperor, we are told Zoticus' exact words when shamelessly soliciting bribes: 'in regard to you this action will be taken'. This ties in with a general accusation – not found in Cassius Dio or Herodian – that Heliogabalus sold positions, either himself or via his slaves and those who satisfied his lust. All this means Hierocles has to take a backseat in this text: reduced to being kissed by the Emperor 'in a place it is indecent to mention', his dismissal being demanded by the soldiers and Heliogabalus pleading that he be allowed to stay at court. Perhaps Hierocles' role is given to Zoticus for the sake of a joke. Having sex, the Emperor is said to exclaim, 'Get to work, Cook!'

The *Augustan History* fills in the generalisations of Herodian with names, lots of names. Gordius, who gets a passing mention in Cassius Dio as the former lover who taught Hierocles to drive, becomes Cordius, a charioteer, who is made prefect of the watch (*praefectus vigilum*), but the troops insist on his removal. It could be true, although …ATVS held that post before becoming praetorian prefect. Another charioteer, Protogenes, becomes an associate in the Emperor's daily life and actions. He has been identified with a charioteer called Protogenes by the contemporary Christian writer Tertullian. Yet it is a common name, and we can find a possible source of inspiration in none other than Cassius Dio, who records a sinister freedman of Caligula called Protogenes.

The *Augustan History* has more. A barber called Claudius is made prefect of the grain supply of Rome (*praefectus annonae*). It is possible. But the individual is unattested elsewhere, and the author uses the name in several fictions in other biographies.

Best to regard the crimper as another invention. Then there is Mirissimus. As far as we know, no one else ever had this name in the Roman Empire. The *Augustan History* likes to play with names. Soaemias becomes a more barbaric and eastern sounding Symiamira. Possibly the invented female name was the inspiration for Mirissimus: take the ending ...*mira* and make it male and superlative? Mirissimus sounds vaguely oriental and certainly sinister. You have to think that the author might have underused his creation, only once deploying this favourite of Heliogabalus. Mirissimus would have been a great character to watch the petals fall, and snigger as the dinner guests start to suffocate.

Finally, we find a mule-driver, a courier, a cook (another one!) and a locksmith: all appointed to collect the five percent tax on inheritances because of the enormous size of their cocks. The *Augustan History* does love a list. Heliogabalus 'got himself up as a confectioner, a perfumer, a cook (yet again!), a shopkeeper, and a procurer'. If only the mule-driver and his companions were real, Heliogabalus would have headed the only regime in history that could be called a *macrophallocracy*.

Although often readier to believe in the reality of some of the characters above – Claudius and Protogenes are frequently accepted – modern scholars paint a very different picture of Heliogabalus' appointments from the ancient sources: one of continuity and traditionalism. It is pointed out that members of established elite families continue to hold office. Men like the impeccably upper class Quintus Tineius Sacerdos, a patrician from Italy and the son of Tineius Sacerdos Clemens, who had been consul in AD158. Quintus had been consul in AD192 and had governed Bithynia-Pontus in AD198–9, and Asia at some point between AD209 and 211. He was granted the rare honour of a second term as consul, as *ordinarius*, taking up office in January AD219 as a colleague of Heliogabalus himself. Examples are found of conventional careers spanning the reign. One Quintus Atrius Clonius had been praetor under Severus and Caracalla, was appointed governor of Thrace by Heliogabalus and went on to be consul (*suffect*, replacement, consul under Heliogabalus or his successor?), and govern Cappadocia, Syria Coele and Hispania Citerior in the reign of Alexander.

Although the numbers are tiny, they are crunched and statistics pressed into service. The results show no flood of new men. Of the twelve governors under Heliogabalus whose social origins are known, eight belonged to old senatorial families. This was actually an increase over previous reigns in the Severan dynasty. Nor was there a great influx of easterners. The geographic origins of seventeen governors can be identified. Eight are from the East, seven from Italy and two from elsewhere in the West. This is a fraction lower than the fifty-seven percent of easterners found in the Senate in general in the reigns of Severus and Caracalla. Playing with the four known consuls who are neither Heliogabalus nor his cousin, yields similar results: two from the East, two from the West and only one (Comazon) not from a senatorial background. The latter is 3:1 to the advantage of senatorial families: better than the 2.33:1 under Caracalla.

All of which is held to *prove* the 'traditionalism' of Heliogabalus' personnel policy: nothing but uncontroversial stability. But that misreads the evidence, seeking discontinuity and novelty where they can never be found, and it ignores the mindset of contemporaries.

No matter how badly they got on with the Senate – often spectacularly badly – neither Heliogabalus nor any other Emperor could ever embark on a programme of radical social engineering to marginalise it, let alone abolish it. Until after the great military crisis in the second half of the third century, all Emperors needed the established senatorial elite. They needed the Senate as a body to vote them their powers, thus giving them legitimacy, and they needed its members to govern the empire.

But all Emperors promoted their favourites. Those Heliogabalus chose outraged conservative sentiment. He considered appointing the two ex-slaves Eutychianus and Hierocles as Caesar. That he did not do so, and, as far as we know, they held no official post, made no difference. As we saw in the last chapter, power did not come from high office or status, but from intimacy with the Emperor. The menial who held the imperial piss-pot wielded far more influence than a patrician, twice consul, who governed Asia. Two soldiers, raised from the ranks, were given senior official posts. Claudius Aelius Pollio, between governing Bithynia-Pontus and Germania Superior, stood before the Senate, and, in the place of the prefect of the city, addressed the house as the mouthpiece of the regime. Worse still, Comazon actually became prefect of the city not once but twice under Heliogabalus. It was these high-profile individuals that caused men like Cassius Dio to believe their world had been turned upside down. The perception of contemporaries is a historical fact, as real as underlying statistics and considerably more significant.

It was a truth universally acknowledged that an Emperor must possess a wife. The imperial house made a marriage alliance with a family of the Roman nobility. Far more important, it should produce an heir. Remember Macrinus at Apamea desperately promoting his nine-year-old son Diadumenianus to co-Emperor. It was hoped that a son promised the continuation of the dynasty and thus promoted present stability by discouraging conspiracy.

Heliogabalus' first wife was Julia Cornelia Paula. The marriage was sometime before 29 August AD219, probably while the Emperor was still travelling from the East. Herodian says that Paula was from the most aristocratic family in Rome. Whichever branch of the *gens Cornelia* she belonged to – the *Cethegi* or the *Scipiones* – her ancestry stretched back to the Republic. If it was her first marriage, she should have been fourteen or fifteen: about the same age as the Emperor. When Heliogabalus was in Rome there were lavish celebrations. A largesse was given to the senators and equestrians, and also – this was a novelty – to the wives of senators. Wearing not his priestly robes but a purple-bordered toga, the Emperor presided over gladiatorial games and a beast hunt. Among the slaughtered animals was an elephant and more tigers (fifty-one) than on any previous occasion. The plebs (probably the 200,000 or so registered for free grain) were banqueted at a cost of 600 sesterces a head. The soldiers, at least those stationed in the city (in the region of 30,000), also got a feast, but at the lower cost of 400 sesterces each: an indication of Heliogabalus rejecting the model of his father and not adopting the role of fellow-soldier (*commilito*).

Paula, like the Emperor's other wives, is little more than a name and a face to us. Their portraits appear on the imperial coinage, but it takes faith to discern character from these generic images of respectable upper-class women. Their virtues proclaimed on the coins could not be more traditional: *Concordia*, sometimes specified as eternal, or between the Augustus and Augusta (*Augg.*), Modesty or Chastity (*Pudicitia*), Justice (*Iustitia*), Public Fairness (*Aequitas Publica*), Delightfulness or Beauty (*Laetitia*). It is the same with the other numismatic messages – the happiness of the times (*Felicitas Temporum*), or of fortune (*Fortuna Felicitas*), and again with the featured female deities: Venus, Juno and Vesta.

The marriage ended in AD 220, when Paula was divorced. The reason given was a blemish on her body. That will have displeased her aristocratic family. Heliogabalus' next choice of a bride more than displeased *all* traditional Roman society. Julia Aquilia Severa also came from a noble family: probably either the *gens Aquilia* or the *Iulii Severi*. Her aristocratic birth is certain: only girls from such origins became Vestal Virgins. In a letter to the Senate, Heliogabalus justified his extraordinary decision: 'I did it in order that godlike children might spring from me, the high-priest, and from her, the high-priestess.' This has unleashed an avalanche of modern speculation about 'Eastern Sacred Marriages', which we will cut through in the next chapter. Herodian adds another excuse: the Emperor wrote that he was a victim of manly passion, and smitten with love, but it was a pretence to provide a 'semblance of virility'.

The Vestals were vital to the good relationship between the Romans and their gods, and thus to the safety of Rome. As a college of six priestesses they tended the sacred hearth of Rome, and guarded other ancient and secret items of cult, in their sanctuary off the Forum. They were dedicated to the goddess and had to remain virgins: not for life, as Herodian claimed, but for thirty years. The penalty for breaking their vow was to be buried alive. Their lover was to be scourged in the Forum, thrown into gaol, then also executed.

The marriages of the Emperor can be dated, with no great precision, by the appearance of his wives on coins minted in Alexandria in Egypt, which also are stamped with the year of his reign. The new regnal year began on these coins at the end of August. So Year One of Heliogabalus ran from his accession on 8 June to 29 August AD218; Year Two from the next day to 29 August AD219; and so on, until Year Five ends with his death in March AD222. From this data it has been calculated that between 29 August AD220 and 28 August AD221 Heliogabalus divorced Paula, married then divorced Aquilia and married his third wife.

The marriage to the Vestal Aquilia was short-lived. Although our literary sources are not explicit, we can assume public outrage hastened the divorce. A damaged and blackened papyrus found in the tax archive of a minor official in Egypt indicates the soldiers were unhappy. It is a letter of Heliogabalus, probably initially to the Senate, but then sent out to the provinces to be displayed in public. In the letter, brilliantly reconstructed by papyrologists, the Emperor explains in Latin the reasons for the divorce. Lines four to eight can be translated like this:

> *She, who wished to give you a son of mine as princeps, and to win favour herself through her honourable character, and through whom, as it behoves me to pass over the rest in silence, my most valiant and loyal soldiers, including the Praetorian guards... (have found?) me (able to refuse nothing that they asked?), shall not remain in my bedchamber.*

The following fragmentary line appears to mention the god Elagabal.

So the Emperor claims that he has divorced Aquilia, at the demand of the troops, because she has failed to produce an heir. Quite possibly he went on to announce that Elagabal had endorsed this decision and had instructed him to marry someone else.

Here is a very different Heliogabalus from the irresponsible or mad youth of our literary sources. Talking to his subjects, the Emperor is concerned with the succession, listens to his loyal soldiers and piously heeds the command of the divine. He is discreet and fond of his ex-wife.

Yet are these his words, or those of an imperial secretary? Unlike the legal rescripts, or the reply to Delphi, this letter was an important public statement, to be posted on walls across the empire. There was far more reason for the Emperor to read and approve this document – maybe even dictate it himself? – before he added his signature and let it go out to 'talk' to his subjects about a crucial aspect of dynastic policy.

Heliogabalus' third marriage, sometime before September AD221, was to Annia Aurelia Faustina. Another aristocrat, both her parents were descended from the Emperor Marcus Aurelius. Unfortunately, she was already married. Her husband, Pomponius Basus, a well-connected *nobilis* from Italy, had been consul and governed Moesia. Tragedy stalked the family. The adult son of Basus had been falsely accused and executed under Caracalla. Now it was the turn of the father. The charge was that he disapproved of the actions of the Emperor. Heliogabalus wrote to the Senate to secure a posthumous conviction: 'the proofs of the plots I have not sent you, because it would be useless to read them, as the men are already dead'. According to Cassius Dio, Basus died because his wife was 'fair to look upon and of noble rank'. Faustina was not allowed to mourn her loss before her imperial remarriage.

Pomponius Basus was not the only high-status senatorial victim. Seius Carus, the grandson of a prefect of the city, was executed for attempting to subvert the loyalty of *Legio II Parthica* at its base in the Alban Hills. Valerianus Paetus met the same fate for stamping his likeness on gold coins, intending to begin a revolt in Cappadocia, next to his home province of Galatia. There were two legions in Cappadocia: perhaps Paetus had been nominated to succeed Theodorus, the governor in AD219. For Cassius Dio, both charges were mere pretexts. Carus was killed because he was rich, influential and prudent, while Paetus had done no more than have some ornaments made for his mistress. That was always the way. Emperors you disliked killed on trumped-up charges; those of whom you approved reluctantly executed the treacherous.

The marriage of Heliogabalus and Faustina was brief. Only one Alexandrian coin of hers survives from Year Five, September AD221 onwards. Cassius Dio has two or three more marriages (his language is obscure) to unnamed women before the Emperor weds his final wife. Perhaps the historian's rhetoric has carried him away. There does not seem time in Year Five (September AD221 to March AD222) before Heliogabalus again shocked public opinion by remarrying the ex-Vestal Aquilia.

All of those women – at least four weddings, just possibly as many as seven – do not exhaust the nuptials of Heliogabalus. As we will explore (see chapter 10), it was also claimed that he married at least one, just possibly two, men.

The marriages can be arranged into factional politics in the imperial court. On one side Maesa and Mamaea back Paula and Faustina to conciliate the nobility in general and bind some specific aristocratic families to the regime. On the other side, Heliogabalus and Soaemias promote Aquilia to break free of the control of the Emperor's grandmother, and perhaps also advance a radical new theocratic justification for the imperial position. This brilliant scheme was created over a century ago and recently has been rehashed several times (sometimes without acknowledgement of the originator). If this were a novel (and if it fitted the plot), I would happily employ this elegant explanation. In a biography, however, it has to be admitted that it is underpinned by not a single shred of evidence.

At least four imperial marriages in four years. A far higher number than any other Emperor, and, in many ways, disastrous for the regime. The marriages were consummated. Heliogabalus confidently looked forward to a son with Faustina. Cassius Dio says that Heliogabalus wed as both groom and bride, 'and in both conducted himself in the most licentious fashion'. The passage breaks off before recounting the salacious details. Later, the historian claims that the Emperor married many women and had sex with many others, so that he could improve his technique with his male lovers. All this sex, marital and otherwise, with lots of women produced no heir.

As at the court of Henry VIII, a marriage alliance with one family would have alienated those not chosen. Their animosity would have been as nothing compared with those whose women were divorced, especially if humiliated like the *gens Cornelia* ('a blemish on her body'), and those connected to Pomponius Basus, executed to facilitate a royal marriage.

The extraordinary turnover of wives not only created an impression of instability but also cost vast sums of money: largesse to the elite, banquets for the plebs and soldiers, gladiators and exotic beasts. All this had to be paid for. The banquets for the plebs and soldiers at the first wedding alone came to some 132 million sesterces. On each occasion wedding gifts were collected 'from all his subjects'. That Heliogabalus' letter explaining his divorce from Aquilia and marriage to Faustina was filed in the tax archives suggests a special impost was enforced. At least four weddings in as many years – it is as if the British taxpayer had to fund a royal wedding once every twelve months.

Instability at court, alienated aristocratic families, staggering expense and exactions, all much worse when combined with the sacrilege of violating a Vestal Virgin: not once, but twice, endangering the safety of Rome by threatening relations with the traditional gods.

A Roman Emperor was expected to give money to the plebs of Rome (the 200,000 or so registered for the corn dole) on significant occasions, like his accession, birthdays or victories. They were known as *congiaria*, but advertised on coins as *Liberalitas*. Subsequent gifts were numbered on the coinage: *Liberalitas II* and so on. The first *congiarium* of Heliogabalus was in AD218 on his accession and was distributed while he was still in the East. The second was in the following year, to celebrate either his arrival in the city, or his first marriage or perhaps a combination of both. Two further donations are recorded on the coinage. It has been suggested they marked the second and third times he was consul: AD 220 and 221. Four donations in four years: the most frequent distributions of any Emperor. Intended to win the affection of the plebs, they provided ammunition for elite criticism of the young Emperor's reckless extravagance.

Another expectation was that an Emperor would commission buildings in Rome. In part this was to provide paid work for the poor. When an engineer offered Vespasian a device to move huge columns at almost no cost, Vespasian rewarded the man, but declined the invention, saying, 'I must be allowed to feed my little plebs (*plebesculam meum*).' Imperial constructions were judged less by aesthetics than for whom they were built. Those to be used by the populace were approved, those reserved for the Emperor were denigrated. Nero was condemned for creating a series of palaces and parks known as the Golden House for his private use, and Vespasian praised for opening them to the public and building the Colosseum in part of their grounds.

Judged by these criteria, Heliogabalus is found wanting. Some construction was for the public. The Colosseum was repaired – a lightning strike had caused a fire which had destroyed the upper levels in the reign of Caracalla – but he got little credit, as the work was completed by his successor. Similarly, Heliogabalus began work to add a portico to the Baths of Caracalla, but again it was finished by Alexander. That he made a public bath in the palace, and that he threw open to all the Baths of Plautinus, is best dismissed. They feature in a passage of the *Augustan History* about the Emperor's relentless search for men with big cocks. The otherwise unattested Plautinus most likely was inspired by Severus' praetorian prefect, Plautianus.

At the other end of the spectrum, Heliogabalus put up a golden statue of himself, 'adorned with great and many coloured ornaments'. Herodian claims he constructed many circuses for chariot racing and theatres. The reality appears to be that he modified, and added towers to, the existing circus in the Gardens of Old Hope (*Horti Spei Veteris/ad Spem Veterem*), and reserved this for his private use. There is no need to entertain the baths in the *Augustan History* which the Emperor had built for himself, used once, then had pulled down. We are assured that he did the same with houses, military headquarters and summerhouses. Equally fictitious is the paving in the palace – green and red porphyry, imported from Greece and Egypt – which was torn up 'within our memory'. The *Augustan History* puts the dramatic date of 'our memory' in the reign of Constantine, although writing almost a century later.

We will explore in the next chapter Heliogabalus' main building programme, the two temples of Elagabal: one on the Palatine, the other in the Gardens of Old Hope. How we think they were received depends on our assessment of contemporary reaction to the Emperor's god. Not much of a spoiler – I argue that it was not positive.

'Bread and Circuses', although sneered at by the disdainful elite, were imperial munificences no Emperor could ignore. Although our ancient sources are on the look out for anything to blacken Heliogabalus, we hear of no riots inspired by grain shortages. In the fiction of the *Augustan History*, an amount of public grain equivalent to a year's tribute was given to all the whores, pimps and catamites within the city walls and an equal amount promised to those outside. In reality, the corn dole functioned smoothly under the *praefectus annonae*: Claudius the barber (should you believe the *Augustan History*), certainly ...ATVS and, maybe at the end of the reign, Ulpian, the famous jurist.

Heliogabalus did not skimp on the 'Circuses' side of things. He was a devotee of all the entertainments that constituted the 'Spectacles'. We have just seen the gladiatorial combats and beast-fights at the Emperor's first wedding (Fifty-one tigers slain! More than ever before!). We can assume similar events at subsequent nuptials and other occasions – this was not a parsimonious regime. As the Colosseum was under repair, the Stadium of Domitian served as the arena (the modern Piazza Navona follows its ground plan). In passing, you could note that none of our hostile sources say the Emperor himself trained or fought as a gladiator – it might be important.

Chariot racing was a passion of Heliogabalus. A fan of the Green faction –rather than following his 'father' Caracalla in supporting the Blues – he drove in races himself in front of a select audience at his circus in the Gardens of Old Hope and paid close attention to the professionals in the Circus Maximus. Hierocles crashed in front of the imperial box, his helmet was dislodged, revealing his tousled blond hair, and the Emperor was smitten.

The reign witnessed a prodigy in athletics. At the Capitoline Games in Rome, presided over by Heliogabalus, Aurelius Helix of Phoenicia won both the wrestling and the *pankration* (a kind of martial art). His attempt to repeat the feat at the Olympics was thwarted by the ill will of the organisers. After he had won the *pankration*, the wrestling was cancelled at the last moment. Helix was a superstar, mentioned in three contemporary works of literature and pictured on a mosaic surviving from Ostia. Nothing, apart from his Phoenician origins, supports the modern assertion that he was an intimate of the Emperor. Athletics never really caught on in Rome, and the association of Heliogabalus with athletes can be overstated. Zoticus, briefly chamberlain and unsatisfactory lover, was an athlete, but his appeal was the beauty of his body and the size of his penis. The athlete Protogenes was an invention of the *Augustan History*. The athlete who appeared as an ambassador of Thyatira did so because he was a rare notable from an obscure town.

The Emperor, according to Herodian, 'imagined that if he provided chariot races and all kinds of spectacles and entertainments, and if he feasted the people all night long, he would be popular'. Drawing on this passage, the *Augustan History* removed the implication that the strategy failed: 'all this so pleased the populace that after each occasion they rejoiced that he was Emperor'. As so often, the unknown biographer was mistaken. Although it is dubious if he cared. In fact, he may have done it on purpose: *Look at how greedy, shallow and fickle are the plebs!*

The Emperor threw gifts to the audience. Gold and silver cups, linen garments and domestic animals (all sorts, except pigs), from the towers of the suburban temple of Elagabal at midsummer, says Herodian. It happened in January, when he became consul, says the *Augustan History*, and not mere pieces of gold and silver, or confectionery or little animals, but fatted cattle and camels and asses and slaves (well, they were animals with voices). Far from the Emperor entering into the merriment with his subjects, elite commentators always try to spin such actions to drive an ideological wedge between princeps and plebs – the tyrant does it to watch the little people fight. Herodian takes this one stage further with Heliogabalus: he did it to gloat over them trampling each other to death, or die impaled on the spears of soldiers.

Both authors, quite deliberately, fail to mention that what are being thrown to the crowd are tokens. The actual gifts were to be claimed later. It leaves open a darkly humorous (mis-)reading: spectators, torn between greed and fear, cowering as heavy animals plummet down.

The topic was congenial and the *Augustan History* returned to it, adding characteristic lists. At the games, the Emperor distributed tokens, or 'Chances' (*sortes*) inscribed with 'ten bears or ten dormice, ten lettuces or ten pounds of gold'. A good job the tokens were mentioned this time: any reader might have

struggled with the logistics of throwing bears. Now the perform-
ers also get tokens. They might receive a dead dog, or a pound of
beef, or a hundred coins of varying worth. The passage reveals
its fictionality (slyly or inadvertently?). One of the denomina-
tions of coins was not introduced until the reign of Diocletian
(AD284–305). Again, it is asserted that Heliogabalus was the first
to introduce 'Chances'. Any well-informed contemporary at the
time of writing (*c.*AD400) – say a reader of Suetonius – would
have known the practice was established back in the first century.

The *Augustan History* has many stories of Heliogabalus' social
life. Most concern luxurious dinners. The awning shifted and
the flowers began to fall. That was the only one that was fatal.
Some were terrifying. Dangerous beasts were released without
warning. The guests did not know they were tame. Some were
humiliating. Apart from the Emperor, everyone invited shared
a physical peculiarity: one eye, gout, deafness, swarthiness, tall-
ness or obesity. Since the latter could not fit on the couches,
it caused 'general laughter'. Some were merely embarrassing:
when the couches were deflated and the occupants dumped on
the floor. Many were unsatisfying. While Heliogabalus ate real
food, his companions were served copies in wax, wood, ivory,
earthenware, marble, stone; sometimes they got glass, or images
embroidered on napkins or paintings. When the food was real,
as much was thrown out of the window as was consumed. Often
the food was extraordinarily exotic and out of season (camel heels
and nightingale tongues and snow in the summer) or bizarre:
just one ingredient (every course pheasant, or chicken, or ostrich
and so on), or all of one colour (green or blue: this one really
caught the imagination of later writers), or mixed with inedible
but expensive objects (lentils with onyx, beans with amber).
The latter hint at opportunities (provided you did not choke on
the pearls in your rice). If a guest could invent a new sauce, he

was splendidly rewarded. If it displeased, the unfortunate was forced to eat nothing else until he concocted a better one. Of course, there were 'Chances' – ten camels, ten flies, ten pounds of gold, always ten of something – and gifts: eunuchs, four-horse chariots, horses, mules, litters, carriages and cash. The cost was staggering; never less than 100,000 sesterces. If not deformed, the company was disreputable. The places of honour by the Emperor went to perverts and the presence of the elite is only explicitly recorded on two occasions. Senior senators are compelled to drive chariots around the banqueting rooms, and men of the highest rank are served with saffron: suitable 'hay' for their rank. The whole thing could be exhausting. Twenty-two courses and sex with a woman between each. Or one course in each of the guests' homes – a dash from the Capitoline to the Palatine to the Caelian: there should be nine venues. No wonder 'it was difficult to finish the banquet within a day, especially as between courses they bathed and dallied with women'. Perhaps it was as well elderly senators were seldom invited.

After dinner, the *Augustan History* assures us, the Emperor frequently would send an imperial functionary to compel the prefect of the city, and the praetorian prefects, to attend a drinking bout (which indicates they had not been invited to the meal). On one occasion he admitted the vulgar plebs. His consumption was so great, they thought it was as if he was drinking from one of his swimming pools. Once he summoned the nobles of the court (*amicos nobiles*) to a vintage-festival and quizzed the more venerable men if they still had sex. When they blushed, he settled down to swap dirty stories with the younger guests.

Only once in the *Augustan History* is he found in the theatre, where he laughed so loud that no one else could be heard by the audience. His late-night visits to prostitutes we will leave until we get to his sex life.

It is not impossible that some of the above has an origin in fact. Yet it is hard to know what to make of all this entertainment (*convivium*) from the *Augustan History*. Probably not, as one modern scholar has it, that the 'semiotics of *convivium*... allow us to parse Elagabalus' [the Emperor's] banquets and distribution of food or *apophoreta* [banquet-gifts] as operatic displays of *liberalitas* and solidarity with the lower orders, and as a systematic inversion of traditional hierarchies'. In all these stories from the *Augustan History* the vulgar plebs only get over the threshold once, and chucking food out of the window is an example of conspicuous waste, not an affectation of class solidarity. The younger men at the vintage-festival are *nobiles*, as are those who own houses in prime locations like the Caelian. Everyone seems to be at the same risk of mockery: the high and the low, even the perverts.

Heliogabalus held banquets, lots of them, and they would have been lavish. That much is uncontroversial. Yet, apart from the food-obsessed fictions of the *Augustan History*, all we hear is of the Emperor reclining, like a beloved mistress, on the breast of Zoticus during dinner. Cassius Dio and Herodian have their eyes on other things: respectively, senators and religion. Of all the Emperor's social life, only chariot racing made it into the accounts of the two historians. The passage of Cassius Dio is worth quoting in full.

> He also used to drive a chariot, wearing the uniform of the Greens – privately and at home, if one can call that place home where the judges were the foremost men of his suite, both knights and imperial freedmen [i.e. the Familia Caesaris], and the very Prefects [i.e. of the Praetorians], together with his grandmother, his mother and the women, and likewise various members of the Senate, including Leo, the Prefect of the City [we will discuss him in chapter 11] – and where they watched him playing charioteer, and begging gold

> *coins like any ordinary contestant, and saluting the presidents of the*
> *games and the members of the factions.*

Chariot driving and sex seem to be the two main choices of Heliogabalus (apart from religion). The young Emperor brought them together, according to the *Augustan History*, by harnessing beautiful naked women to his chariot, and driving about while naked himself. We will look at this closely, maybe pruriently, in chapter 10. Here, against all probability, the *Augustan History* might be telling the truth. For once there might, just might, be external corroboration of this unlikely anecdote.

IV   *Heliogabalus' Face – 2*

Image 9: Type Two Portrait of Heliogabalus

Heliogabalus was making choices. No longer a boy, he was becoming a man. In AD 221 he was seventeen, and his coins begin showing him with facial hair: always sideboards, sometimes also a wispy moustache, and sometimes they join into a short beard (see chapter 8, Image 13). Only two unaltered and undamaged Type Two portrait busts survive. The best-known image of the Emperor is in the Capitoline Museum.

Although the basic physiognomy remains the same as his earlier Type One portraits (see chapter 5, Image 7), the Emperor's face is thinner and his eyes slightly larger. As well as the thick sideboards and feathery moustache, his hair is longer and more tousled.

Heliogabalus looks less like Caracalla than before: certainly, very little like the mature image of that Emperor scowling so much the creases make an X across his face. The longer hair has been thought to look back to the Antonine Emperors; the fringe across the forehead to Augustus.

Some scholars see a new ethnic, Syrian, element in Heliogabalus' face. Others are unconvinced. Oscar Wilde thought the portrait was 'rather like a young Oxonian of a very charming kind'. We have to remember that originally the portrait was painted. If the hair and skin tones were dark, it could look Syrian. If the Emperor was depicted with pale skin and fair hair, he would not look Near Eastern at all.

This bust was designed to be slotted into a full-length statue. This would have moulded the reactions of contemporary viewers. The statue either could have represented the Emperor in a conventional Roman toga, or in the costume of the priest of Elagabal. Now we should turn to the latter, the most significant of all his choices – religion.

CHAPTER 8 RELIGION

I *Seeing the Gods*

Roman paganism was on its last legs. All those hundreds of gods, perhaps thousands, tottering with senile steps to their end, or already decomposing on some divine rubbish tip. That was the view in the middle of the twentieth century. An easy to grasp and seductively simple line, which rested on three main supports. First, elite belief in the gods had been gradually undermined, since the second century BC, by the rationality and logic of Greek philosophy. Next, the influx of eastern deities, especially 'mystery cults' like Mithras, in the first three centuries AD, demonstrated that traditional paganism was not satisfying the emotional and spiritual needs of its adherents. All that was left were empty rituals orchestrated and paid for by the non-believing elite in the hope that they would instil nameless dread and acquiescent behaviour in the superstitious masses. Paganism was in terminal decline, making it easier to explain the triumph of Christianity in the fourth century AD. Of course, turned round the other way, that was the final proof – Christianity triumphed because something had been fatally wrong with paganism.

Except that in antiquity Roman paganism took an awfully long time to die, and in the modern world, like Lazarus, it has come back from the dead. Two books were published in the 1980s which changed, especially in the English-speaking world, how paganism is seen: Ramsay McMullen's *Paganism in the Roman Empire* (1981), and Robin Lane Fox's *Pagans and Christians* (1986). It is always difficult to move from the specific to the general when talking about trends in the study of history, as it is in history itself. Perhaps I should have remained at the level of the specific and demonstrable: those two books changed *my* mind. McMullen and Lane Fox elegantly showed that it was never credible that generations of the elite devoted so much time, effort and money to something in which they did not believe. If the elite had not believed, it would have been simple enough to create other ways to maintain their social dominance. Nor did Greek philosophy undermine faith in the gods. Yes, there was Epicureanism, which sometimes held the gods did not exist. But it was one sect among many, and a minority one. Indeed, Epicureans could believe that the gods were real: it was just that they had no interest in humanity. In the centuries leading up to the reign of Heliogabalus, the most influential philosophical school was Stoicism. For the Stoics, the cosmos was run by a divine intelligence (*logos*). Every mortal contained a spark of the *logos*, and the individual gods were aspects of that divine reason. Far from destroying faith, Stoicism invested the ceremonies of traditional religion with a deeper resonance. Again, two explanations can be made for the spread of eastern cults, without recourse to hypothetical inadequacies in other gods. The *Pax Romana* made travel easier and somewhat safer. All sorts of people were on the move – administrators and soldiers, pilgrims and students, traders and slaves – and they all took their gods with them. We will see this in action in a few pages (section III). Augustus, the first Emperor, established a standing professional army. Becoming a soldier entailed a recruit taking on a new identity. Two of the most significant eastern cults mainly spread through the army: Jupiter Dolichenus (certainly) and Mithras (arguably). Something about these new divine arrivals appealed to the new group in society (although our evidence does not allow us to say what). Finally, McMullen and Lane Fox gathered many compelling examples of belief which testified to the continuing vitality of paganism. Let us set out a couple of their examples.

The Apostles Paul and Barnabas came to the backwater Asian town of Lystra, or Colonia Iulia Felix Gemina to give its formal title. There Paul healed a man crippled since birth. The townsfolk lifted up their voices, saying in the local language, 'the gods have come down to us in the likeness of men'. Barnabas they took to be Zeus, and Paul, as he had done most of the talking, the messenger god Hermes. The priest of Zeus, whose temple was in front of the city, brought oxen and garlands to the gates to offer sacrifice to them. Until Paul, still doing the talking, put him right. Of course, the whole story may be fiction. Never mind the miracle: how did the Apostles understand Lycaonian, the language spoken in this region? But it illuminates a world where pagans thought their gods were real and might, whenever they wished, walk among mortals.

Votive offerings are often called the 'touchstones of piety'. You do not publicly thank a deity for a benefit – say restored health, or rescue from a storm at sea – if you doubt that god's reality. Such inscriptions are found across the empire. The most extraordinary, and thus the most vivid, come from two areas of Asia (Lydia and Phrygia). These involve confessing a sin against the god for which the speaker has been punished and then, having been informed of their error, been spared by making the dedication. 'Stratonicos, son of Euangelos, in ignorance cut down an oak of Zeus of the Twin Oak Trees, and because of Stratonicos' lack of faith, Zeus summoned up his power.' The offender, having almost died, 'recovered from great danger, and made this dedication by way of thanks', and proclaimed 'let nobody ever belittle Zeus'.

As the Christians were to find, a generation after Heliogabalus, during the first empire-wide persecutions, the pagans very much believed in their traditional gods.

II   *Emperors: Between Men and Gods*

The Emperors were the ultimate mediators between humanity and the divine. They took over from the Senate, which had held that role under the Republic. In religion, as in everything else, now the Emperors had the final say.

Take the Sibylline Books. These were a collection of oracles of the god Apollo, spoken in Greek hexameters by a succession of prophetesses known as Sibyls (hence the name). In the Republic they were looked after in the Temple of Jupiter on the Capitoline Hill by a college of priests called the *Quindecemviri Sacris Faciundis*. In a crisis, or in the light of a particularly threatening portent, the Senate instructed the *Quindecemviri* to consult these secret books and draw up rites of propitiation, so the gods would again favour Rome. With the imposition of monarchy, Augustus moved the books to the Temple of Apollo, which was linked to his own house on the Palatine. Private possession of a Sibylline Oracle was illegal, and Augustus removed and burnt numerous 'spurious' prophesies from the official collection. Henceforth, although the *Quindecemviri* continued, the Emperors controlled these divine verses. When the Tiber flooded much of Rome in AD 15, one of the priests suggested consulting the books, but this was forbidden by the Emperor Tiberius.

The religious authority of the Emperor rested in part on his being *Pontifex Maximus*, chief priest of Rome, and his membership of various other priestly colleges. It was also supported by his links to the divine. The Emperor was the gods' vice-regent on earth, and it was commonly thought that a specific deity acted as his companion and protector. Caligula's whispered conversations with the statue of Jupiter were ridiculed. Other Emperors were more subtle and thus their relationship was more credible, as was that of Domitian with Minerva.

The Emperors were not only the friends and subordinates of the gods, but they also partook of their nature. In Rome, Italy and the 'more civilised' western provinces (Spain and southern Gaul), the *Genius* of the Emperor was worshipped. The *Genius* was understood either as something external, much like a guardian angel, or as a divine element internal to the Emperor. After an Emperor was dead, his successor might instruct the Senate to formally recognise his ascension to heaven as a *Divus*. Throughout the East, and in the 'less civilised' western provinces (Britain, Germany and the rest of Gaul), the Emperor was straightforwardly worshipped as a god (*Theos* in Greek).

All of this raises a question: did anyone actually believe in the divinity of the Emperors? Certainly, it did not prevent their assassination. In a very influential book, *Rituals and Power: The Roman Imperial Cult in Asia Minor* (1984), Simon Price argued this was the wrong question to ask, as private *belief* is a fundamentally Christian concept. Instead, we should study the religious evocations of public ceremonies of the imperial cult. This seems unsatisfactory. Writing that feels like a minor act of betrayal. Simon Price was one of the supervisors of my doctorate. We got on well, and I proofread *Rituals and Power*. It is another reminder that historians do not work in a vacuum, solely engaging with sources and modern scholarship. Often, they know those whose arguments they endorse or criticise. Had he not died tragically young, I believe Simon would have welcomed the debate.

The approach advocated in *Rituals and Power* can be thought to privilege the public over the private. It puts the modern historian in a not dissimilar position to an ancient Christian critic, such as Lactantius, who claimed paganism was 'no more than worship by the finger-tips', requiring nothing but 'the blood of one's flocks, and smoke, and foolish libations'. It does not fit with some ancient literary evidence. The philosopher Dio Chrysostom advised the Emperor Trajan that externals were not enough: it was necessary to 'believe in his heart that there were gods'. If we leave out particularly Christian elements, such as salvation and the immortality of the soul, to ask if pagans privately believed in the divinity of Emperors remains a valid question.

The answer we get depends on the type of evidence we study. There are lots of inscriptions recording the imperial cult. Those from the Greek East explicitly recognise the Emperor as a god. But it was never likely that a public inscription would add a clause doubting his divinity and thus undercutting the sincerity of whoever commissioned the piece. If votive offerings are the 'touchstones of piety', it is telling that we find none to an Emperor. Turning to literary evidence, we get a very different picture. Ancient writers seldom talk about the imperial cult. When mentioned, it tends not to be with approval. In his guide to Greece, Pausanias, almost without exception, carefully avoids discussing its monuments. Thinking of Herakles, he says that in ancient times men might become gods, but now they only do so in flattery to authority.

The imperial cult served many useful purposes. It demarked the elite, who paid for its ceremonies, from the non-elite, who enjoyed the roast dinners and wine and gladiatorial shows at its festivals. Within a city, it provided an arena for elite families to compete with each other for the status of the greater benefactor. Similarly, it allowed cities and whole provinces to rival each other. Its embassies to court, requesting imperial permission to build temples or found festivals, or to congratulate the Emperor on this or that, provided a way for subjects to advertise their loyalty. They opened a channel of communication to the Emperor, back down which it was hoped would flow open-handed imperial munificence.

There were good reasons to comprehend the Emperor in terms of the divine. In the East he had taken over the role of the Hellenistic kings. For centuries these successors to the empire of Alexander had been worshipped as gods. The power of the Roman Emperor, stretching across the known world, able to intervene at any moment wherever it wished, could only be compared to that of the gods.

But that does not necessarily mean that a subject had to 'believe in his heart' that an Emperor was a god. Perhaps some were fervent believers. Others were not. The Roman senator Tacitus dismissed the imperial cult as 'Greek adulation'. Putting advice for contemporary Severan Emperors in the mouth of Augustus' friend Maecenas, the Greek Cassius Dio recommended getting rid of the whole thing.

III *The Black Stone of Elagabal*

To form a picture of the religion of Elagabal, first we need to leave aside, as far as we can, the accretions of modern scholarship and concentrate on what we can see in the ancient sources. The results will tell us a lot about the externals of the cult – ceremonies and visual images – and very little about its internals, such as beliefs, theology or cosmography.

Let's start with a coin minted in Emesa in the reign of Caracalla.

Image 10: Elagabal in the Temple at Emesa

The god in his temple is a large conical stone. An eagle with outstretched wings stands in front. In other images the eagle is perched on top of the stone. Herodian tells us that the stone was black and had projections and markings which the faithful 'would like to believe are a rough picture of the sun'. Some coins depict stars on the surface of the stone. Behind the god stand two tall objects that look like parasols or standards. Below the god on the coin is a rectangular object. This could be a base under the stone, an altar in front or a screen around it. Sometimes, as here, the artefact is decorated, sometimes it is plain and sometimes it is not depicted. The temple itself is of a completely conventional Classical design. It rests on a podium. A flight of tapering steps leads up to an entrance flanked on each side by three columns. Another coin of Caracalla displays a three-quarter view, which shows columns down the side of the temple, just as we would expect. There is a triangular pediment with a star and a box-like object on its face. The latter has been interpreted as an altar, but as in some examples it is replaced by a crescent (see the coin illustrated in Image 6), it is more likely to be a window. The star is not always shown. The roof has projections from the corners and is decorated with small upright shapes.

Another coin from Emesa, this one with Domna on the obverse, shows the altar of Elagabal.

Image 11: Domna and the Altar of Elagabal

Two steps support a massive base, with a pilaster at either end and a cornice on top. The base is divided into two rows of three niches, each of which contains a statue, seemingly in human form. We have no clue who these figures represent: priests, worshippers, other gods connected to Elagabal, or the deity himself in anthropomorphic form? A fire smokes on a small altar resting on the base.

Lots of coins show Elagabal on his journeys.

Image 12: Heliogabalus and his God

The black stone travels in a chariot drawn by four horses. Herodian says there were six horses, all pure white. Maybe that number was a challenge to a die-cutter working on a small scale?

The coin has the eagle and the parasols/standards along for the ride and the Emperor sacrificing in front. Heliogabalus wears fancy boots, but we need to look at a better image of him performing his priestly duties.

Image 13: The 'Horn' of Heliogabalus

Look at the reverse, on the right. The first thing to note is that his pose is normal for a Roman priest. He stands still, his right hand holding a dish (*patera*) from which he pours a libation of wine onto a fire on a small freestanding altar. The attitude of his left hand is traditional, but what he holds is perhaps less so: a branch, or a club? In other coins it is more like a bunch of twigs. His costume, however, is far from conventional: not a toga, but trousers, a loose garment elaborately belted at the waist and a cloak thrown back from his shoulders. Herodian says his costume was gold and purple: 'the effect was something between the sacred garb of the Phoenicians and the luxurious apparel of the Medes'.

Herodian twice tells us the Emperor 'wore a crown in the shape of a tiara glittering with gold and precious stones'. Look at the portrait on the obverse, on the left. No tiara, but a very Roman wreath, tied with a ribbon at the back. Now look again, this time at the top of his head. Some tubular thing curling forward from the wreath. This is the infamous 'horn' of

Heliogabalus. No other Emperor is ever depicted sporting such an accoutrement. Presumably it is connected to Heliogabalus' role as priest of Elagabal. It has been variously interpreted as a solar ray, an amulet, an index finger or the dried penis of a bull. The latter can be dismissed. The hostile contemporaries Cassius Dio and Herodian would not have passed up the opportunities for mockery.

The coins show us the appearance of the cult. Herodian, with a little help from Cassius Dio, tells us about its ceremonies. Animals were sacrificed: many cattle and sheep, but never pigs. Incense was burnt and libations of wine poured. Blood and wine flowed in streams and the air was perfumed. All entirely normal, except for the participants. The entrails were not carried by servants or the lower classes but by military prefects and important officials. These wore Phoenician costume, including linen shoes. Although the Emperor considered he was imparting an honour, these members of the elite would have seen it very differently. To complete their humiliation, the bowls containing the entrails were carried on their heads.

It was customary for pagan gods to be celebrated with music and dance. For Elagabal again the participants were unusual. The Emperor himself, in priestly costume and wearing make-up, danced with Phoenician women, including his mother and grandmother. They not only danced but sang. Cassius Dio primly said he would not describe the 'barbarian chants'. According to Herodian, the music also was 'barbaric'.

Like a modern dictator, an ancient god enjoyed a big procession. That of Elagabal was exotic. The black stone rode in its chariot, the reins of the white horses tied round it, as if the god were driving. In fact, the bridles were led by the Emperor. As priest, Heliogabalus ran backwards, along a path spread with golden sand, supported on either side by bodyguards to stop him tripping. He was preceded by images of the other gods, imperial standards and heirlooms and the army. A crowd ran along the sides of the route, with torches and throwing wreaths and flowers. While important elements of the procession were alien – the stone driving and the Emperor running backwards – others were close enough to the specific traditional ceremony of a *Triumph* to allow damaging inferences to be evoked. We will return to these at the end of this chapter, when we look at what went wrong with the Emperor's religious innovations.

Heliogabalus arranged for his god to be married. According to Herodian, Elagabal first wed Pallas Athena, whose sacred object, the Palladium, was moved from the Temple of Vesta to his quarters. Modern scholarship links this to the first of Heliogabalus' two marriages to the Vestal Virgin Aquilia. As we have seen, Cassius Dio has Heliogabalus say, 'I did it in order that godlike children might spring from me, the high-priest, and her, the high-priestess.' In Herodian, the Emperor added that marriage between a priest and a priestess was 'fitting and sacred'. Athena proved too warlike for the Emesene deity. The black stone was given a second wife, the African goddess Urania, whose statue was shipped to Rome. Herodian says she was a moon goddess, known to Phoenicians as Astroarche, and that the Emperor declared a marriage between the sun and moon appropriate. Cassius Dio only mentions the second divine marriage. Modern scholars claim that the Emperor was attempting to create a divine triad to supplant Jupiter, Minerva and Juno as the summit of Roman state religion. As we will see in a moment, this rests on negligible and disputed evidence and has to dismiss Herodian's explicit statement about the god's displeasure and the clear implication of divorce. The gods had always been thought of as having families. Marital disharmony makes some of the best scenes in Homer. Divine marriage was perfectly acceptable if undertaken by the gods a long time ago. If arranged by the Emperor now, it was open to scorn. Herodian described it as 'a mockery' and Cassius Dio as 'extreme absurdity'.

We are told that, as priest of Elagabal, the Emperor was circumcised and prohibited from eating pork. Both were alien to Roman custom, and, like the procession of Elagabal, opened up avenues for very hostile interpretations.

So we know quite a lot about the externals of the religion – what it looked like, and how its rituals were conducted. When we turn to its internals – its myths, teaching and beliefs: what it all *meant* to worshippers – we find next to nothing. Etymology tells us that Elagabal was 'the god of the mountain', or maybe 'the mountain god'. The deity was a sun god, frequently given the additional name of *Sol* (in Latin) or *Helios* (in Greek). The stars sometimes depicted on the stone, its temple and the coins of its priest-Emperor, suggest possible wider heavenly interests. Cassius Dio implies that in Emesa Elagabal gave oracles. And that is all.

But not for modern scholarship, which has exercised extraordinary ingenuity in filling the gap. Cassius Dio and Herodian and the *Augustan History* are accused of failing to understand the eastern religion and convicted of the invidious western sin of 'Orientalism'. They are said to have uncoupled their stories of Heliogabalus' sex and social life and everything else from their religious significance. This has opened the way for a trawl through other 'eastern' religions for comparisons to import and explain. The results are certainly colourful: drunken sexual orgies, ritual homosexuality, transvestism, castration, sacred prostitution, ritual purity, tower-tombs, and, rather endearingly, a menagerie of animals dedicated to Elagabal.

This approach, of course, relies on the modern scholars knowing better than the ancient sources. Cassius Dio and Herodian and, for what it is worth, the *Augustan History*, saw the behaviour of Heliogabalus as motivated by perversity, extravagance and other personal vices. No, say modern commentators, the contemporaries (and the *Augustan History*) were wrong. They did not understand the eastern religious practices of the Emperor. There is an irony in this accusation, for the modern infilling – dragging in anything from the East – depends on all eastern cults being the same, their rituals and beliefs interchangeable. When manifestly they were not. The modern scholars themselves have fallen into the trap of 'Orientalism', misinterpreting the East in western terms, of which they accuse the ancient writers.

To take just one example: sacred animals. Various other cults in the Near East kept animals (albeit various different species, often fish) dedicated to the gods in their temples. You remember the dangerous animals (all actually tame) with which Heliogabalus liked to terrify his guests by releasing them into dinner parties? Not a practical joke at all, according to modern scholars, but a misunderstood aspect of the rituals of the cult of Elagabal. Unlikely, given that the beasts roaming among the couches are an invention of the author of the *Augustan History*. Equally fictional is the story in Cassius Dio of *secret* rites involving human sacrifice and throwing severed human genitals into a temple containing a lion, a monkey and a snake.

Sometimes scholarship goes even further, cutting loose from evidence altogether. Take these relief sculptures found in the Roman Forum.

You can just make out the black stone of Elagabal on the left. Actually, it is easier to spot the outstretched wings of the eagle standing in front. The god is flanked by two female figures. They stand on plinths, so are statues. Another female, very hard to see, reclines on the floor to the right. An infant, equally hard to discern, plays on her lap. Above them a bull is sacrificed by another female: this time she has wings. There are traces of three more winged figures at the top. And there is an awful lot of swirling vegetation.

Image 14: Relief Sculpture of Elagabal

Presumably all the figures are divine: certainly the ones with wings. The females flanking Elagabal have been identified as Athena and Astarte (Astroarche). This is the only evidence for the theory of a new triad at the head of Roman religion. The iconography of the figure on the left makes it almost certain that she is Athena: she wears the *Aegis*, an unusual item of clothing, usually worn by the goddess in art. The one on the right, however, is far too damaged for any identification. If she had not been mentioned by Herodian, there would be no reason to think Astarte is depicted here. The other figures have been seen as Gaia (reclining), Eros (playing), Nike (sacrificing) and three Griffins (almost obliterated at the top).

So far, so prosaic, if uncertain. But then imagination shifts into overdrive. We are told the sculpture gives insights into 'theology, cosmology, and ritual'. Apparently, it is all about energy. This is released by the sacrifice of the bull and flows down to Eros and Gaia, then up through the foliage and the wings of Nike and the Griffins, then down again to Elagabal. 'The black meteorite, warmed by that energy, recovers his original red, then white glow', the flanking goddesses absorb the radiated energy, and each of their statues 'comes to life, and speaks, glows, sweats, or moves'. Not content with animating a couple of statues, the deity goes on to possess the worshippers, who have been prepared by rhythmic dancing, feasting, drinking, sex and psychotropic herbs or fungi. In this account, the young Emperor is partial to smoking aromatic herbs. It is almost a shame that this bravura vision is supported by no evidence whatsoever.

Better by far to stick with what our ancient sources show – a lot about the externals and next to nothing about the inner life of the Emperor's religion.

How widespread was the cult of Elagabal beyond the region around Emesa before the reign of Heliogabalus? Very, according to one modern study: 'the cult of Sol Invictus Elagabal assumed major proportions and importance as early as the reign of Commodus' (AD 180–92). But this conclusion is reached by a completely unconvincing method: 'all the dedications to Sol Invictus that do not concern Mithras refer to the Syrian Sol Invictus Elagabal'. This is unacceptable. Elagabal was a sun god, but there were many others, apart from Mithras. Not all sun gods were Elagabal. Only direct references to Elagabal, or dedications to Sol Invictus by Emesenes, will do.

Examination with those criteria gives a very different answer. A cohort of Emesene archers set up a temple to Elagabal where they were garrisoned at Intercisa in Pannonia. At El-Kantara in Egypt another unit from Emesa dedicated a temple to Sol Invictus. Caius Julius Avitus Alexianus, Heliogabalus' maternal grandfather, built an altar to his 'ancestral god' when governing Raetia. A series of inscriptions from the Trastevere district of Rome identify one Tiberius Julius Balbillus, most likely a member of the Emesene dynasty, as a priest of Elagabal. The latest inscription of Balbillus dates to AD215.

So no missionaries and no converts. Instead, men from Emesa serving or living abroad and taking their god with them. Except for one piece of evidence. In the reign of Hadrian, one Lucius Terentius Bassus, standard bearer of the Third Cohort Breucorum, set up an inscription to Sol (H)Elagabal where he was stationed in Germania Inferior. The Breuci originally were recruited in Pannonia. Unless Terentius was a lone Emesene serving in an alien unit a long way from home – which is possible, but there is nothing to link him to Emesa – he appears to be the exception that proves the rule.

When Heliogabalus conveyed his god to Rome, apart from the occasional Terentius the vast majority of the inhabitants of the empire had never heard of the black stone of Elagabal.

IV *The Most High Priest of the Invincible Sun*

Heliogabalus was already high priest of Elagabal at the outset of his revolt. What effect did this have when he became Emperor? What were his religious innovations? What did the young priest-Emperor actually do?

The black stone was conveyed in its chariot, along with the eagle and standards/parasols, from Emesa to Rome. Did a priest run backwards leading the chariot all the way? Was it the Emperor himself? Even if this is not credited, a god was not to be hurried.

The stately progress should be added to Maesa's desire to show the new ruler to the armies of the Danube, to explain the length of time before the imperial party reached Rome.

Wintering at Nicomedia, Heliogabalus practised the rites of his god. The third of January, the Day of Vows, was an important date in Roman state religion. Sacrifices were made for the welfare of the reigning Emperor and for the eternity of the empire of the Roman people. Officiating as consul, Heliogabalus did not wear the traditional triumphal dress, Cassius Dio tells us, instead appearing in his priestly vestments. From Nicomedia the Emperor sent ahead to Rome the picture of himself performing as priest to the black stone. Herodian continues: 'Instructions were also issued to every Roman magistrate or person conducting public sacrifices that the name of the new god Elagabal should precede any of the others invoked by officiating priests.' As Cassius Dio puts it, Heliogabalus placed Elagabal in front of Jupiter. In the same sentence, the historian has the Emperor cause himself to be voted high priest. This must mean by the Senate, which occupies most of Cassius Dio's attention. Obviously, it was intended to embed the Emesene god in the Roman state religion. Some scholars like to place the senatorial vote later, in AD220, but its place in the text indicates the winter of AD218–19 and it fits with the other instruction and the picture.

Herodian has Heliogabalus clad in his priestly robes when he arrived in Rome. Emperor and god took up quarters in the imperial palace. Two temples were ordered to be built for Elagabal: one on the Palatine, the other on the outskirts of the city. Patient archaeological work has identified the site of the central temple on the *Vigna Barberini*, to the left of the main walkway up from the Forum and the Arch of Titus. Today there is little for the thousands of passing tourists to see. A later church to St Sebastian stands on part of the site. In antiquity, however, it was an imposing complex.

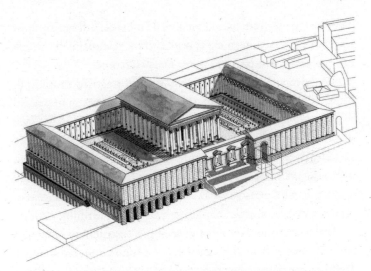

Image 15: Reconstruction of the Temple of Elagabal on the Palatine

A monumental staircase led up to three gateways through the surrounding porticos. Inside, the temple stood on a tall podium, approached by more monumental steps, ringed by altars and probably flanked by gardens. Two late sources give different dates for its dedication: AD 220 or AD 221. As the former is only a year after the arrival of the imperial party, it has been suggested that an existing temple was converted. No evidence – literary or archaeological – survives of the hypothetical previous structure. The scale of the new building has inclined opinion to the later date. This may be to underestimate the labour an Emperor could mobilise, especially as orders to begin the construction could have been sent ahead from Nicomedia in the winter of AD 218–19, along with the picture of the god and the order for his primacy in public oaths.

It has been thought that the suburban temple was across the Tiber in Trastevere, because that was where Tiberius Julius

Balbillus, the probable kinsman of the Emperor, had worshipped Elagabal. But Balbillus was a private citizen, celebrating his ancestral god in the temple of another deity. Far more likely was the imperial property at the Gardens of Old Hope (*ad Spem Veterem*). Although no trace of the temple has been found – an imperial basilica and baths were later built on the site – archaeologists have attributed to Heliogabalus alterations here to a circus, and the building of an amphitheatre. Interestingly, Herodian claims that the suburban temple had tall towers, from which the Emperor threw gifts to the crowd, and towers were added to the circus as part of the remodelling.

We have already seen the annual procession that conveyed the black stone from the Palatine to the suburbs at midsummer. Two further points can be made here. The procession can only have happened twice: Heliogabalus had not reached Rome by midsummer AD219, and by the spring of AD222 he was dead. Also, there must have been a procession going the other way: at midwinter would be a plausible suggestion.

The Emperor arranged two marriages for his god: first to Athena, then to Urania. Herodian records that the Palladium, the symbol of Athena, was transferred to the imperial palace. In one evidently fictitious passage, the *Augustan History* adds a string of other religious objects – the emblem of the Great Mother (Magna Mater), the fire of Vesta, the shields of the Salii and 'all that the Romans held sacred' – while in another a deception by the senior Vestal Virgin thwarts his depredations. When the too warlike Athena had been dismissed, the statue of Urania was brought from Carthage. Herodian says it was accompanied by all the gold in her temple, and Cassius Dio by just two golden lions, which were melted down. The divine marriages had a direct material impact on the inhabitants of the empire. Cassius Dio and Herodian agree that wedding gifts were collected from all subjects. Cassius Dio, optimistically, claims they were returned in the next reign. The exactions did have a mitigating factor in Rome and Italy, where festivities and banquets were held. Whatever their feelings about the 'absurdity' of the weddings, for most Italians free drink and a roast meal would have momentarily trumped any religious scruples.

Elaborate daily sacrifices at sunrise were instituted. Presumably they were held at whichever of the temples the black stone was in residence. As we have seen, the Emperor danced and sang at the ceremonies, along with Phoenician women, including his mother and grandmother. High-ranking officials acted as attendants, and 'the entire senate and equestrian order stood round them in the order they sat in the theatre'. To assume the latter only appeared on special occasions might be to underestimate the personal nature of power. The ambitious and anxious would have attended. To feign devotion to the religion of an autocrat might bring advancement or mitigate punishment.

Midway through the reign, in AD220, there was a dramatic change in religious policy, so it has been argued. Imperial promulgation of the cult of Elagabal, which had been quiet and subtle, became loud and insistent. Various causes have been advanced. Heliogabalus, now sixteen, was breaking free of the women of the dynasty. Or there was a power struggle within the court. The faction of Soaemias and Heliogabalus was asserting itself over that of Maesa and Mamaea. Or Maesa, having carefully prepared the ground, unleashed a new style of theocratic rule. When she realised its unpopularity, Maesa abandoned it, although her grandson did not.

The appeal of the idea is obvious. It gives us drama, and, above all, a narrative. We have strong storylines from the outbreak of the revolt in May AD218 to the Emperor's arrival in Rome in October AD219, and then again from the adoption of Alexander in June AD 221 to the death of Heliogabalus in March AD 222. But in between, the evidence does not allow any chronological reconstruction: not month by month, let alone day by day. Instead, the treatment has to be thematic. Heliogabalus chooses this or rejects that (as he did in the last chapter), but does so in no sequence.

Yet, despite its appeal, the religious reform and all its beguiling explanations should be rejected. Although many coins cannot be precisely dated, the modern theory is based on a demonstrable change in the types issued by the imperial mint in Rome. In the early years of the reign, the cult from Emesa barely featured. With an occasional exception, when alluded to it was in the Hellenised form of an anthropomorphic figure of Sol, and specifically not named as Elagabal. The coinage concentrated on traditional types: Roma, Safety (*Salus*), the Victory of the Emperor or of the god Mars, the Loyalty of the Army or Soldiers (*Fides Exercitus* or *Militum*) and Liberality or Public Happiness or Loyalty (*Laetitia* or *Fides Publica*). Jupiter, the head of the state pantheon, appears as *Conservator*, chief preserver, of the Emperor. The later years saw a flood of coins naming the Emperor as Priest of the Sun God Elagabal (*Sacerdos Dei Solis Elagabal*), High Priest Augustus (*Summus Sacerdos Augustus*), or Invincible Priest Augustus (*Invictus Sacerdos Augustus*). Although most traditional types continued, Jupiter as Conservator vanished, to be replaced in that role by Elagabal. From AD 221 Heliogabalus was depicted as a more mature figure with facial hair (the so-called Type Two Portrait, illustrated in chapter 7), sometimes with the enigmatic 'horn' sprouting from his wreath.

To see this as evidence of a change in religious policy it is necessary to believe that the coin types were always chosen by the Emperor himself and thus offer a direct window into the mind of the ruler. At the most extreme we are told, 'none of this variation is left to chance, or the die engraver's fancy, for it can be detected that Varius (Heliogabalus) has overseen his own depiction on coins, and in some cases ordered corrections in the early stages of minting'. This is completely unconvincing. Very occasionally, a literary source tells us that an Emperor, although not Heliogabalus, chose a coin type: Nero playing the lyre, Constantine at prayer. The question is: do these represent the usually unreported norm, or are they recorded precisely because they were exceptional? Almost certainly the latter. Unless an Emperor intervened, the choice of what appeared on coins minted at Rome was left to the *Tresviri Monetales*. This was a board of three junior magistrates, who were at the start of their careers and not yet senators. They chose content that they hoped would appeal to the Emperor. What appeared on coins were images offered up to the ruler. Of course, if the Emperor bothered to look at the offerings, and the type continued from one year to the next, they can be considered to have at least retrospective and passive imperial approval.

Let's put ourselves in the place of these young *Tresviri Monetales* in the years AD218–19, before Heliogabalus reached Rome. What did they know about the new Emperor? It was claimed he was the natural son of Caracalla. He had defeated Macrinus in a civil war. There had been revolts in the East. He was a devotee of an eastern sun god. Not much to go on, best to play safe. His Type One Portrait looked like Caracalla and his inscribed name and titles were the same. Victory, always a good thing, might reflect the battle which had brought him to the throne, and the loyalty of the armies was never more apposite than in times of unrest. For the rest, stick to traditional generalities – Safety, Liberality, Public Happiness – with just a nod towards the deity he was said to favour. Then, in October AD219, the Emperor arrived in Rome dressed as a Phoenician priest. The dawn sacrifices were instituted. Work was started on two temples. The air was full of incense, exotic music and brick dust. All impossible to miss. Evidently it was time to offer up a new image: Priest of the Sun God Elagabal.

Even when Heliogabalus was flaunting his religion in Rome the *Tresviri Monetales*, or, to be more precise, the die-cutters following their instructions, did not go full on depicting the Emesene cult. Look back at the coin showing the Emperor as a priest (Image 13, p. 212). On the right, the reverse, he makes an offering to his god. Although he is clad in oriental garb, he is not dancing in Phoenician style but standing still in a stately and conservative Roman way. On the left, the obverse, is a head and shoulders portrait. Herodian tells us Heliogabalus wore an eastern tiara. Here he wears a traditional Roman wreath. The only unusual element is the 'horn' jutting forward from the wreath. Probably it is something to do with his Emesene priesthood, but more speculation is futile. We have no idea what it represents. In both images the exotic is watered down. Why did those in charge of the mint show such reticence?

An obvious answer, quite probably correct, is that the moneyers were interpreting the alien cult through a filter of their own Roman preconceptions: 'this is how a priest makes an offering'; 'this is what an Emperor looks like'. They are not making a point but assimilating the foreign: merely trying to understand and to help viewers understand. This is the so-called *interpretatio Romana*: somehow it seems to have more authority if put in Latin.

Analogy with a very different image offered up to the ruler gives a more political, although extremely speculative, answer. Panegyrics were formal speeches of praise to an Emperor. The example surviving from the principate is the published version of that delivered to Trajan by Pliny in AD 100. It is now widely accepted that panegyrics offered not just praise but also tacit advice. Where the ruler recognised himself in elements of the eulogy, there was an unspoken admonition: 'keep behaving like this'. Conversely, where he did not: 'alter your ways'. On this line, just conceivably, the images on the coins were advising Heliogabalus to tone down the non-Roman in his cult practices. Of course, it might be objected that the *Tresviri Monetales* were very junior magistrates to have the temerity to admonish the Emperor. But the young are often more adamant in their views than their elders, and here they were addressing an Emperor even younger than themselves.

There was no religious reform in AD220, or any other year of the reign. Heliogabalus had converted to the cult of Elagabal when he went to Emesa. He was high priest of the black stone before the outbreak of his revolt. The role was celebrated on coins minted in the East, both imperial and local, from the start in AD218. In the West the well-informed, perhaps those who had returned from an embassy to the new imperial court, knew from near the beginning of the reign what to call the Emperor. An inscription found in the amphitheatre of Tarragona in Spain was by the second half of AD218 already describing him as *Sacerdos Amplissimus Dei Invicti Solis Elagabali*: Most High Priest of the Invincible Sun Elagabalus.

V *The Offence: What Went Wrong?*

The ancient Romans believed in their gods. They had many of them, but usually were not opposed to accepting new deities. That was how polytheism worked. Some old gods faded and were forgotten. New ones took their place. Often the newcomers were equated with deities already known. So what was wrong with the Emperor introducing his god Elagabal into Rome?

Much might seem at first sight unobjectionable. In 433BC Apollo had been introduced to Rome. One aspect of Apollo was a sun god, commonly identified with the Greek Helios. The Emperor Augustus (31BC–AD14) had boasted a special relationship with Apollo and built him a temple on the Palatine. In 204BC, during the war against Hannibal, the Roman Senate had summoned Cybele, the Mother of the Gods, from Asia to Rome. A temple was constructed to house the new deity on the Palatine. Her cult image was an unworked stone, which had fallen from heaven. Cybele came with a train of effeminate priests, often self-castrated, who wore exotic clothes and worshipped her with eastern music, wild cries and ecstatic dance. In the century before Heliogabalus, the worship of the Persian sun god Mithras, *Deus Sol Invictus Mithras*, whose priests wore distinctively eastern costume, had spread across the whole Roman Empire, including Rome itself.

These deities, and others like Isis or Jupiter Dolichenus, seem to be precedents for Elagabal. But there were crucial differences. Apollo was not eastern, in the sense of Syrian or Phoenician, but Greek. The Persian rituals of Mithras were limited to initiates and were private. The cult of Cybele was strictly controlled by the Roman state. Citizens worshipped her in traditional ways, with sacrifices and games overseen by a senior magistrate. The exotic elements – all the alien music, and leaping and chanting in outlandish costume, let alone the castration – were left to a foreign priesthood, which it was illegal for Romans to join. The individual elements of the cult of Elagabal might have been unobjectionable, but not when combined and performed in public by the Emperor, with members of the Roman elite forced to attend and participate.

Two aspects of Heliogabalus' priesthood encouraged especially negative evocations. The Emperor was circumcised and abstained from pork. These carried connotations of Judaism. Dark anti-Semitic stories circulated: hatred of mankind, fraud, sexual immorality, magic, cannibalism, cruelty and ritual murder. Cassius Dio claims Heliogabalus sacrificed boys in unholy secret rituals. The ever-inventive *Augustan History* elaborated this into the Emperor collecting children of noble birth from across Italy who had both parents living, to increase the suffering. Several Emperors, including Heliogabalus' 'father' Caracalla, were accused of necromancy. It was common knowledge that in the distant past Phoenicians had in reality sacrificed children. Heliogabalus was from Phoenicia. His ethnicity combined with the Jewish associations of his circumcision and avoidance of pork to encourage the dark rumours about him. Like the other Emperors accused, Heliogabalus was almost certainly innocent.

The Jews were notorious in the Roman world for denying the existence of all gods but their own. Heliogabalus too was accused of monotheism.

> *As soon as he entered the city, however, neglecting all the affairs of the provinces, he established Heliogabalus (Elagabal) as a god on the Palatine Hill close to the imperial palace; and he built him a temple, to which he desired to transfer the emblem of the Great Mother, the fire of Vesta, the Palladium, the shields of the Salii, and all that the Romans held sacred, proposing that no god be worshipped at Rome, save only Heliogabalus (Elagabal). He declared, furthermore, that the religions of the Jews and the Samaritans and the rites of the Christians must also be transferred to this place.*

The *Augustan History* returned to this congenial theme: *It was his desire to abolish not only the religious ceremonies of the Romans, but also those of the whole world, his one wish being that the god Heliogabalus (Elagabal) should be worshipped everywhere.* Of course, the passages are complete fiction – the name given to Elagabal is a hint, as are the Jews, Samaritans and Christians. Neither of our contemporary witnesses mention monotheism. As we will see in a moment, Cassius Dio says something very different. Other gods besides Elagabal had been worshipped at Emesa and continued to be in Rome. Glance back at the relief sculpture illustrated in section III (Image 14). Never mind the specific identity of the two figures flanking the black stone, there is no doubt they are goddesses. The Emperor was enrolled in the traditional priestly college of the Arval Brothers. When excited, Cassius Dio says, he exclaimed, 'By Jupiter!' Heliogabalus as a monotheist was an invention of the late fourth century AD, when Christianity had become the Roman state religion. It is a mystery why some modern scholars have supported the idea.

The most important evidence for understanding the contemporary outrage caused by Heliogabalus' religion is given by Cassius Dio.

> *The offence consisted, not in his introducing a foreign god into Rome, or in his exalting him in strange ways, but in his placing him before Jupiter himself.*

If we leave aside the debunked notion that Roman paganism was in its incredibly prolonged death throes, and that no one believed in the gods any more, then we can grasp how serious was the offence. In the *Aeneid* Jupiter had promised the Romans 'empire without end' (*imperium sine fine*), not limited by time or space. The importance of Virgil cannot be overstated. The *Aeneid* was a national epic, hardwired into the Roman consciousness. Every schoolboy learnt to write by copying, and often memorising, passages. Heliogabalus would have done this, although with him the lesson did not stick.

All Roman followers of the traditional gods knew that Jupiter's promise was contingent on human good behaviour.

This was the *Pax Deorum*, the Peace of the Gods, perhaps better understood in English as the Pact with the Gods. If the Romans did right by the gods, then the gods would do right by them. To supplant Jupiter as the head of the pantheon with a black stone from Emesa was not to do right by the gods. Every day, Jupiter Optimus Maximus (the *Best and Greatest*) could look out of his temple on the Capitol and see that of the Phoenician deity that had usurped his rule rearing up on the Palatine. It is hard to imagine a more profound threat to the *Pax Deorum*. At best it would lead to the withdrawal of the favour of the gods. At worst it exposed Rome to divine retribution. The very existence of Rome was put at risk.

The midsummer procession that took Elagabal from his temple on the Palatine to that in the suburbs symbolised the overthrow of Jupiter. The black stone in his chariot was preceded by 'images of all the other gods and valuable or precious temple dedications'. They in turn were preceded by the imperial standards and the cavalry and army. For contemporaries, it evoked an inversion of a Roman Triumph. Elagabal rode in the place of the general celebrating the Triumph (the *Triumphator*), who represented Jupiter. While Jupiter himself, and the other gods, took the place of the barbarian captives, and their temple dedications that of the spoils of war. Even the route was inverted. Coming down from the Palatine to the Arch of Titus, Elagabal turned right onto the Sacred Way (the *Via Sacra*), towards his temple at *ad Spem Veterem*: not left towards that of Jupiter on the Capitol. No one would forget that when a Triumph reached its destination the leading captives would be executed.

No wonder that, when Heliogabalus was dead, his god was packed off home to Emesa, and his Palatine temple was rededicated to Jupiter Ultor: Jupiter *the Avenger*.

CHAPTER 9   IN THE PROVINCES

AD219—22

1   *Talking about God in Anazarbus*

On 29 October AD219 the Emperor arrived in Rome. Heliogabalus
never visited the provinces again. In the service of his god, he
moved between the Palatine and the imperial property of *ad
Spem Veterem* on the outskirts. Sometimes he may have gone a
little further afield, staying in villas just outside the city. Then,
as now, the elite often left the city to escape the stifling heat
in August. A water pipe found at Alsium, a delightful spot
on the coast of Etruria about twenty miles west of Rome, is
inscribed with the words *dei Solis invicti magni Elagabal*: of the
invincible Sun great Elagabal. That the Latin is in the geni-
tive — *of* Elagabal — suggests a shrine at the villa. It may have
been an imperial property, or it may have been owned by a
member of the elite, who either out of conviction or to curry
favour had become a devotee of the god from Emesa (not that
the two motives had to be mutually exclusive). And as we saw
earlier, Heliogabalus' father — Sextus Varius Marcellus, not
Caracalla — had owned a villa at Velitrae in the Alban Hills
about twenty-five miles south-east of Rome. We do not know

if Heliogabalus even went that far. Maybe the suburbs were far enough. The Roman Empire had a population of perhaps fifty-four million. About a million lived in Rome itself. Out in the provinces, apart from the tiny minority along Heliogabalus' route from Emesa to Rome, no one had ever seen the young Emperor.

The regime projected the image of the new Emperor to the provinces via decrees and rescripts, portrait busts, pictures and coins. The latter, surviving in large numbers, are most useful for us. We have already seen how imperial coins, in origin, were images offered up by a few junior members of the elite to the ruler. Out in the provinces they were 'read' very differently. An Emperor was expected to be involved in every aspect of his reign. There was a popular anecdote told about various rulers. An old woman approached the Emperor with a petition. He said he had

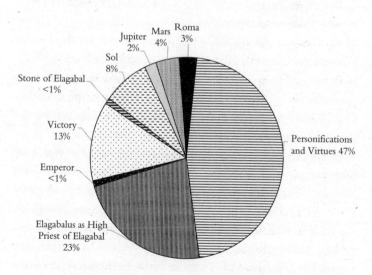

Image 16: Reverses of Silver Coins of Heliogabalus Found in Hoards

no time. So she told him to stop being Emperor. The Emperor heard her out. This expectation of personal involvement led to the idea that what was done in the Emperor's name was done by the Emperor himself. Provincials looking at imperial coins, like some modern scholars, thought the Emperor was talking to them directly.

What was Heliogabalus saying? Here we have a pie chart showing the reverse types of his silver coins found in hoards.

Much was entirely usual. Almost half were the accustomed personifications and virtues: the Loyalty of the Army, Liberty, the Happiness of the Time, Peace, Security, Abundance and so on. Rome, Jupiter and Mars were still there. But almost a quarter were new and exotic: the Emperor as high priest of Elagabal, and sometimes the Emesene god himself, made an appearance. How did provincials react to this unusual line of imperial conversation?

Before we go any further, a note of caution. Fifty-four million people, from modern Scotland to Iraq, from different cultural backgrounds, speaking different languages, were all Romanised or Hellenised to very different degrees. Almost all our evidence comes from Greek and Roman adult elite males, and the overwhelming majority of what follows is from the Greek-speaking East. When we talk about the thinking of 'provincials', we enter a world of the broadest and vaguest generalisations.

Some provincials reacted positively to the new line of imperial conversation. A number of provincial cities minted their own coinage. What appeared on the coins was chosen by members of the local elite. In the reign of Heliogabalus, the black stone of Elagabal featured on surviving coins issued by seven cities: Alexandria in Egypt, Neapolis in Samaria, Aelia Capitolina (Jerusalem), Laodicea ad Mare in Syria, Hierapolis (Castabala) and Anazarbus, both in Cilicia and Juliopolis in Bithynia.

Elagabal in the Provinces

It is tempting to think these coins were minted to celebrate the arrival of Elagabal and the Emperor on their journey to Rome. But three of the cities – Alexandria, Aelia Capitolina and Neapolis – were far from that route. Also, some were issued after the imperial entourage had reached Rome. Much more likely, the coins advertised the adoption of the cult of Elagabal by these cities.

Another coin records a festival called *Elagabalia* at Sardis in the province of Asia. The festival was linked to the introduction of the cult of the Emesene god.

Inscriptions add two more cities to the list. At Attaleia in Pamphylia the city council and the people dedicated an inscription to Elagabal: an official act, probably part of a religious cult. At the other end of the empire – our only example from the Latin-speaking West – at Altava in Mauretania in AD221, those 'holding land' (*possessores*) built a temple to Elagabal, with money raised by collections.

A literary source gives an eleventh, and final, example. Unfortunately, that source is the *Augustan History*. Faustina, the wife of Marcus Aurelius, had died in Cappadocia. According to the *Augustan History*, Marcus 'made the village where Faustina died a colony, and there built a temple in her honour. But this later was consecrated to Heliogabalus.' The author returned to the topic in his biography of Caracalla, who 'has a board of Salii, an Antonine Brotherhood, who took from Faustina, not only her temple, but also the name of a goddess – that temple, at least, which her husband had built her in the foothills of the Taurus, and in which this man's son Heliogabalus Antoninus afterwards made a shrine, either for himself, or for Syrian Jupiter, or the Sun; the matter is uncertain.' As always, invention embroiders fact. There was a temple of Faustina in the colony bearing her name. Caracalla never had colleges of priests called Salii or Antonine. If Heliogabalus rededicated the shrine, it would not have been to himself, or to the 'Syrian Jupiter', but to Elagabal.

Not all provincial reactions were positive. We have evidence for just eleven cities instituting the cult of Elagabal in an empire which boasted over a thousand Greek *Poleis*, as well as all the cities in the West. We should not assume that many others are hidden by a lack of evidence, or had not yet got round to it before the death of the Emperor. A reign of four years was more than enough time to set up a civic cult. The condemnation of the memory of the Emperor sometimes stretched to his god, but it did not necessarily destroy all traces. An attempt was made to erase the name of the god on the inscription at Attaleia, but it remains readable. Most significantly, for all but two of the eleven cities we can find very specific reasons for their setting up the cult: reasons that would not have been replicated at many other towns.

Hierapolis, Anazarbus, Faustinopolis and Juliopolis lay on the route from Emesa to Rome. Later, these four second-rate cities had every reason to celebrate that brief moment when the arrival of the Emperor and his god made them the epicentre of the Roman world. At backwoods Altava, the collections of money to pay for the temple may well have been the *possessores* giving thanks for a grant by the Emperor giving them *possession* of their land. Something similar might have happened at the important city of Sardis. The major cities in the Greek East competed for titles of status. One was Temple Warden (*Neokoros*). The city would petition the Emperor for permission to build a temple to the imperial cult. The more it had the better. Under Heliogabalus, Sardis became Temple Warden for the third time. The festival of *Elagabalia* may have been an act of gratitude. It is worth noting that Anazarbus had received from Heliogabalus the right to call itself 'the first, biggest, and most beautiful' city in Cilicia. At two cities – Neapolis and Laodicea ad Mare – worship of Elagabal fitted neatly with an existing civic cult. Neapolis already celebrated a mountain god. The local Mount Gerizim appeared alongside Elagabal on its coinage. Laodicea added a crescent moon to coins featuring Elagabal, a local lunar goddess making a natural pair with the sun god from Emesa. Alexandria in Egypt was always a special case. Its mint was controlled by that at Rome. Only two cities – Jerusalem and obscure Attaleia in Pamphylia – are left without a particular catalyst for adopting the cult. Despite all the 'talk' coming from the Emperor, the take-up of his god across the empire was extraordinarily low.

If we focus on the Greek East, and those seven cities that issued coins of Elagabal, we find something very significant about their attitude to the religion of Emesa. The imperial mint at Rome concentrated on interpreting, or maybe offering advice about, the (evidently problematic) role of the Emperor as high priest. Less than one percent of coins depicted the god. The situation is reversed in the Greek cities. All depicted the stone of the god, but none ever showed the Emperor clad in his Phoenician robes and sacrificing. While Elagabal the god was acceptable, there was a reluctance to engage with the concept of the Emperor as 'oriental' high priest.

Where the portrait of the Emperor was on the obverse of the civic coins, one distinctive feature of his iconography in Rome was never shown: the mysterious 'horn' of Heliogabalus. Perhaps the appendage was avoided because whatever it symbolised, almost certainly something to do with his priesthood, was unacceptable to the Greek cities. Or perhaps, like us, the local elite were completely baffled by this tubular object attached to the Emperor's wreath.

If we turn to inscriptions, not only is the reluctance of the Greek East to think about the Emperor as high priest of Elagabal reinforced, but a similar unwillingness appears across all the provinces of the empire. *Sacerdos Amplissimus Deo Invicti Solis Elagabali* – Most High Priest of the Invincible Sun God Elagabal – was how the Emperor styled himself from the beginning of his reign. From Nicomedia in the winter of AD218–19 he had written to Rome, instructing the formal vote of the title by the Senate. Heliogabalus intended everyone to know him as high priest. There are 153 surviving inscriptions dating to his reign (139 in Latin, 14 in Greek). Of these only thirteen bear the sacerdotal title, in whole or in part. All of these are in Latin. Almost half are diplomas issued in the name of the Emperor to veterans on discharge from the army. Although the number of examples is very small, the title is never used in the Greek world. Interestingly, it is not even used by the governor of Arabia, suggesting that this official was aware of local sensibilities.

Herodian tells us that from Nicomedia the Emperor issued instructions 'to every Roman magistrate or person conducting public sacrifices that the name of the new god Elagabal should precede any of the others invoked by officiating priests'. This order finds no reflection in any surviving inscription. In none of the nine inscriptions mentioning Jupiter is he preceded by Elagabal. To get round this, it has been claimed that Herodian was wrong: either the order was never given, or it only applied to Rome and Italy. There is nothing to suggest the contemporary was mistaken, especially as his statement is supported by Cassius Dio saying that the Emperor desired Elagabal to be placed in front of Jupiter. It is better to accept that the imperial order was widely ignored.

How could subjects just ignore an order by the Emperor? This brings us to a paradox of Roman imperial power. In theory, the Emperor was all-powerful. No one doubted, and legal authorities insisted, that his will was law. In the wilder fringes of Greek political philosophy – the haunt of wizards and vegetarians, who called themselves Pythagoreans – he was the embodiment of the law, or the 'living law' (*nomos empsychos*). But in reality an Emperor's power was limited. He could only compel or intervene in the areas of which he was aware. That amounted to the things he could see and what he was told. Sometimes even then his power could be flouted. This becomes clear in an anecdote about a governor and Marcus Aurelius.

A persecution of Christians in Gaul during the reign of Marcus Aurelius is recorded by the later Christian historian Eusebius. Some of these Christians were people of wealth, who had servants and possessed Roman citizenship. The date was about AD177, a generation before Caracalla, in AD212, gave citizenship to almost all inhabitants of the empire. Among these well-off citizens was Attalus, 'a man of note'. When Attalus was paraded in the amphitheatre prior to being thrown to the beasts, the governor was informed that he was a Roman citizen. The governor had Attalus put in gaol, along with others of the same status, and wrote to the Emperor for instructions. The Emperor replied that those without citizenship were to be given to the beasts, but those who were citizens were to be beheaded, as was their legal right. Nevertheless, the governor sent Attalus to the beasts, this time fatally, 'to gratify the mob'. Here we see a high government official ignoring a direct and personal order from the Emperor.

So far, the language of this chapter has been almost painfully cautious and measured. Provincials had 'a reluctance to engage with' or 'an unwillingness to think about' the new religion introduced by Heliogabalus. It is time to state their attitudes and feelings with more force. Despite all the imperial orders and communications, most cities did not start worshipping the black stone from Emesa. The few that did had very specific, and usually self-interested, reasons. In the Greek East the god might be worshipped in some places, but the Emperor as 'oriental' high priest was acceptable nowhere. The majority in the Latin West likewise rejected the sacerdotal role of their ruler. The imperial commandment to invoke Elagabal before all other gods was blithely and uniformly ignored across all the provinces of the empire. The attempt of Heliogabalus to introduce his religion was unwelcome and ran aground on the rocks of provincial passive resistance.

If they resisted his religion, what effect did Heliogabalus have on the lives of his provincial subjects?

II *Money, a Daemon and a Scribe*

On 24 June AD222, three months after his accession, the new Emperor Alexander Severus wrote to his subjects.

> ... *in order that through their desire to express the joy they feel at my accession to the empire* [on 13 March AD222, he had become

sole Emperor] *they not be forced into contributions greater than they can afford… if the poverty of the government in these times had not prevented me, I should have offered a much more conspicuous proof of my magnanimity, and should not have hesitated to remit likewise whatever arrears were still owing from the past for contributions of this sort, and whatever sums had been already voted under the title of crowns for my proclamation as Caesar* [on 26 June AD 221, he had been adopted, and made heir by Heliogabalus], *or should still be voted for the same reason by the cities. But though I fear that I cannot remit these for the reason which I have just stated, yet I have not failed to observe that these, as far as I can see, under present circumstances, are all that the cities can afford to pay. Therefore let all persons in all the cities, both in Italy and all other regions, know that I remit to them the sums due in place of golden crowns on the occasion of my accession to the empire, to which I have attained in accordance with the wishes and prayers of all, and that I do this not owing to a superfluity of wealth, but to my personal policy, recognising the need ever since I was made Caesar, powerless though I was, to restore our fortunes, not by extortion of taxes, but by economy only, avoiding expenditure for my private ends.*

Across the empire copies of the letter were posted up in each city where they were most easily visible. There would have been crowds: the letter was about tax relief. Our copy was found on a papyrus from Egypt.

Although he is not named, the letter is an implicit attack on the previous Emperor, Heliogabalus. The cities have been bled dry. They owe taxes to the government and cannot afford any new ones. Despite the exactions, the imperial treasury is empty: drained to pay for Heliogabalus' personal extravagances.

Of course, Alexander – or the imperial secretary who actually composed the letter: Alexander was thirteen – was not an unbiased reporter. He was making an ideological statement: I am different from my predecessor. Note the way Alexander was dissociated from the actions of the previous regime, when he was Caesar: 'powerless though I was'. But it was not all empty political spin. The exactions and the debts must have been public knowledge, and perhaps also the impecunious state of imperial finances.

Payments of Crown Gold in origin were literally wreaths of gold voluntarily offered by cities and provinces to the ruler on special occasions, such as accession and victories. Over time they had transmuted into compulsory payments in cash, which could be demanded for a wide variety of circumstances. Large sums were involved. In 29BC Augustus declined gold crowns offered by the cities of Italy weighing no less than 35,000 pounds. That had been a very special occasion: a triple Triumph. Perhaps more usual was the crown weighing fifteen pounds given to Galba by the province of Tarraconensis in Spain. When the stingy Emperor had it melted down, it was found to be light. Galba demanded Tarraconensis cough up the missing few ounces. Fifteen pounds does not sound a huge amount, but multiply that by the more than thirty provinces, and then by whatever was the average weight of crowns from perhaps two thousand cities, and every payment of Crown Gold becomes a substantial sum.

Alexander was only remitting the Crown Gold due for his accession as Augustus. All the arrears, imposed by Heliogabalus, still had to be paid. Heliogabalus clearly had remitted nothing. There had been his accession in AD218 and three anniversaries (AD219–21: by May AD222 he was dead). The elevation of Alexander to Caesar, as in the letter, added a fifth payment. Yet these were less than half the additional imposts the cities and provinces had to pay in the reign of Heliogabalus.

When Heliogabalus married his god to the Carthaginian goddess Urania, Herodian tells us: 'he also issued orders that a very large sum of money should be contributed, supposedly as a dowry'. From Cassius Dio we learn this was not an isolated incidence: 'he collected wedding-gifts for her from all his subjects, as he had done in the case of his own wives'. To the Crown Gold for accessions and anniversaries can be added exactions for two divine weddings and four imperial ones, taking the total to eleven. There may have been yet more, if Cassius Dio is right that the Emperor fitted in three more marriages between his third named wife Faustina and remarrying the Vestal Aquilia. Judging by the change to a more mature (Type Two) portrait of the Emperor in AD220, Heliogabalus offered the bristles of his first shave and took the toga of manhood at the conventional age of sixteen. Once again, almost certainly, his subjects were expected to give pecuniary evidence of their loyalty for the ceremony.

In a reign of only four years, there were at least eleven special exactions, perhaps as many as fifteen. An average of some three to four a year. These were in addition to regular taxes: both direct (poll tax and land tax) and indirect (sales taxes, import duties, taxes on the manumission of slaves and the like). As well as bringing an unsettling new religion, Heliogabalus imposed drastic financial demands on his provincials.

Where did all the money go? Alexander twice complains about the poverty of the treasury. To be fair, it might have been in straitened circumstances when Heliogabalus came to the throne. Septimius Severus and Caracalla had both raised the soldiers' pay. The Parthian War of Caracalla had to be paid for, as had Macrinus' humiliating peace treaty. Heliogabalus was lucky enough not to have had to finance a war. But he found many other ways to drain the exchequer.

There were all those weddings, human and divine: at least six, maybe as many as nine. Sometimes connected to them were the lavish feasts and spectacles with which he entertained the populace of Rome. There were his buildings: the temple on the Palatine and that at *ad Spem Veterem*, along with remodelling the circus there, repairs to the Colosseum, additions to the Baths of Caracalla, a golden statue of himself. Then there were the formal gifts of cash to the plebs of Rome (*congiaria*). We do not know how much each individual received from Heliogabalus. In AD202 Heliogabalus' 'grandfather' Septimius Severus had given one gold piece for each of the ten years of his reign. Whatever the amount, like all *congiaria*, those of Heliogabalus were paid to the 200,000 on the register for free grain. Coins advertise these occasions with the word *Liberalitas* and are numbered to IV. Four distributions in four years – 800,000 recipients – was the greatest frequency of any reign in the history of the empire. *Congiaria* to the civilians, donatives to the soldiers. We saw Heliogabalus give 2,000 sesterces to each soldier in the army that entered Antioch. There would have been others: as he passed along the Danube, and after that concentrated on the troops stationed around Rome. Late in his reign, Heliogabalus said to the senators: 'Yes, you love me, and so, by Jupiter, does the populace, and also the legions on the frontiers, but I do not please the Praetorians, to whom I keep giving so much.' At least Heliogabalus was right about the attitude of the Praetorians. Finally, as signalled in Alexander's letter, there were Heliogabalus' personal expenses: all those dinners, silks, exotic animals and gifts to favourites. And if we believed the *Augustan History*, jewels on the soles of his shoes. Actually, the fictions of the *Augustan History* encourage the modern marginalisation of the subject: 'it is much exaggerated', or 'it is nothing but rhetoric made up later'. Living in a modern democracy makes it difficult to appreciate just how much an autocrat can spend for his personal gratification. In 1977 the inhabitants of the Central African Empire would not have had that problem. Jean-Bédel Bokassa had just spent, at the most conservative estimate, one third of the annual budget of the country, plus all the financial aid from France, on his coronation as Emperor: including a two-ton gilded throne, a fleet of sixty new Mercedes, twenty-four thousand bottles of Moët & Chandon and forty thousand other bottles of wine, including Château Lafite and Mouton Rothschild.

After reaching Rome, Heliogabalus never set foot in the provinces again. But the regime of the absent Emperor had a profound impact on them in two ways: endless financial exactions and the attempt to introduce the cult of the black stone of Emesa. Both were unwelcome and unsettling. An extraordinary story in Cassius Dio suggests the result was unrest.

A *daemon* appeared on the Danube, sometime before summer AD221. Proclaiming himself Alexander the Great, whom he resembled in looks and dress, he gathered an escort of 400 men, equipped with the thyrsi and fawn skins of devotees of Dionysus. He then processed through the provinces of Moesia Superior and Thrace to the city of Byzantium, celebrating Bacchic rites as he went. Each day, like an Emperor, he sent messengers ahead announcing his coming. At every stop accommodation and provisions were provided at public expense. 'Not a soul, neither governor nor soldier nor procurator, nor the magistrates of the local communities, dared to withstand him, or say a word against him.' From Byzantium he took ship across the Bosphorus, 'crossed to Chalcedon, carried out some rites at night, made a hollow wooden horse, and disappeared'.

To try and make some sense of this bizarre event we need to set it in two contexts: one specific, the other more general. First, the route taken by the *daemon* is close to, if not exactly the same as, that taken some seven or eight years earlier by the Emperor Caracalla on his final journey to the East. It was on that trip that Caracalla had begun to emulate Alexander the Great, 'or rather Dionysus', as Cassius Dio says at one point. So the *daemon* was performing a sort of double identity theft: imitating Caracalla imitating Alexander. Second, 'False Princes' were not an unknown phenomenon in the Roman Empire. There had been at least three 'False Neros', and two false imperial princes: Agrippa Postumus and Drusus. These followed a common pattern. In a time of political uncertainty, a man of lowly origins, sometimes a slave, traded on a physical resemblance to announce that he was a deceased member of the imperial house, who had somehow or other escaped death. The 'False Prince' dressed himself in the appropriate costume, gathered an impressive entourage and travelled in official style towards some symbolic destination: Rome or the armies or the eastern frontier. After initial success, the adventure always ends in capture, revelation of true identity and execution.

The *daemon* fits the model of the 'False Prince' in several ways – suitable appearance and costume, large entourage, stately procession with 'official' recognition, symbolic destination (the wooden horse suggests Chalcedon was a substitute for Troy), ultimate failure – but adds distinctive features. The *daemon* had only an implicit link to a recently dead member of the Roman imperial house. Instead, he claimed to be the great Macedonian king, dead for more than half a millennium. The *daemon* introduced a new religious dimension: thyrsi and fawn skins, Bacchic ceremonies, nocturnal rites at Chalcedon. And his 'failure' was uncertain. He was not captured, unmasked and killed, but just vanished. After all, Cassius Dio had no doubt: he was not a man, but a *daemon*.

The strange story illustrates the disturbed nature of life in the provinces under Heliogabalus. Imperial officials – soldiers, equestrian financial officers, even senatorial governors – fail to intervene, city magistrates and councils give aid, and hundreds of locals flock to join the entourage of the *daemon*. Central government's control over all levels of society in the provinces was weak. 'False Princes' appeared only at moments of political uncertainty. The flow of extraordinary religious innovations from the imperial court encouraged the appearance, behaviour and reception of the apparition.

Heliogabalus was unpopular in the provinces. In March AD 220, in the Egyptian backwater of Oxyrhynchus, a scribe wrote a report on how much earth (cubic foot by cubic foot) had been shifted in the embankments of the town's canals between the twelfth and the sixteenth of the month. The report, dated by the regnal year of the Emperor, was duly filed. Two years later, news reached Oxyrhynchus that Heliogabalus was dead. Someone (the same scribe?) went back through the records, found the report and drew a black line through the Emperor's name. There was no need to take such trouble. No passing member of the Greco-Roman elite, no one connected to the new regime of Alexander, was going to search the archives of the Superintendents of the Dykes in the obscure City of the Sharp-Nosed Fish. Bureaucracy seldom went so far. The excision speaks not of efficiency but of loathing.

Hang on a minute, the astute reader may well be thinking, at the start of this chapter there were some sensible words about the dangers of generalisation, and now, towards the end, an anonymous scribe from the middle of nowhere in Egypt is representing the feelings of some fifty-four million provincials. What can I say? History is an art, not a science. Sometimes you have to trust your instincts when filling in the gaps in our evidence. If it makes you feel any better, after Heliogabalus' death had been announced in the great Bithynian city of Nicaea, a man fished a coin out of his wallet and vented his feelings on the tiny, engraved face of the Emperor with a chisel.

Heliogabalus lived on in popular memory in Oxyrhynchus. Sometimes it was not enough to strike out his name and pretend he had never existed. Astrology demanded precise dates. Some decades after the death of the Emperor, he appeared in two papyri. In a set of planetary tables he was 'unholy little Antoninus'. A series of horoscopes used a word of local dialect, *koryphos*, which means either 'catamite' or 'rapist of virgins'. The provincials remembered Heliogabalus, and despised him, for his religion and his sexuality.

Let's turn our attention to his sexuality.

CHAPTER 10 SEX

I *Paralysed by Prohibitions?*

Sex in ancient Rome was one big orgy, where you could do anything with anyone. So modern popular culture likes to imagine.
Absolutely not, says an eminent French scholar. *Pas du tout.*
Instead, they were 'paralysed by prohibitions'. *Paralysed?* As we
will see, that is going way too far. Roman sexuality had norms
and limits – every culture does – although they were very different from those of the contemporary western world. Heliogabalus
was thought to have transgressed almost every boundary.

First, we need to accept that our framework for thinking about
sex is not universal. Heterosexual and homosexual and bisexual
are not concepts or self-images that fit the sexuality of elite males
in the Roman Empire. Nothing in Latin or Greek neatly trans-
lates our words. The gender of the people they enjoyed having
sex with was not an essential element in how Roman men constructed their self-identity. Many (perhaps most?) found pleasure
in sex with both males and females. Instead, the key distinction
was being active or passive: to penetrate or to be penetrated. The
passive partner in male–male sex, penetrated even just the once,
was considered unmanned and became an object of contempt.
There was no redemption. The taint was permanent. This was

one of the things held against freedmen – they had been slaves and thus had been available to be penetrated by their former masters. An elite male was free to penetrate slaves and the non-elite of either gender, but other categories were excluded. Apart from his wife, elite females (who should be either virgin daughters or chaste spouses of other elite males) were off limits, as, of course, were all elite males.

Yet the Romans were always slightly uncomfortable with male–male sex. They liked to believe it was an import from the Greeks, along with such things as luxury, talking too much, sitting down at shows and financial untrustworthiness. Sex with another soldier was illegal in the Roman army. The penalty was death. The hostility to 'Greek love' is often thought to have gathered strength in the first three centuries AD, as part of a generally more condemnatory attitude towards non-normative sexual activity. In a virulent and extended attack on morally corrupting, and thus 'bad', sex the philosopher Dio Chrysostom included pederasty along with prostitution, adultery and sex before marriage. To try to explain this change to a tighter and more prescriptive morality, we have to move into a realm of high theorising. There are two modern explanations, which are not necessarily incompatible. Both seek an answer in changes in elite political and social power.

One hypothesis (French and very theoretical, created by Paul Veyne and espoused by Michel Foucault), locates the cause in the change from the free Republic to rule by the Emperors. The Roman elite, no longer able to define themselves by open political competition in the Senate House and Forum, turn inwards towards families and marriage and self-discipline. Only a handful of radical philosophers advocated sexual fidelity for the husband, but the new stress on marriage, and so male–female sex, led all the elite to an increased marginalisation of male–male sex.

The other theory (Anglophone and pragmatically starting with the sources) notes that the majority of the evidence for the change in attitudes comes not from Roman senators but from elite male Greeks: men like Plutarch and Dio Chrysostom. Such elite Greeks had not lost their political autonomy. They had not ruled the empire under the Republic, and they did not do so under the principate. One thing that had changed was that, backed by the *Pax Romana* imposed by the Emperors, they were more firmly in control of their own Greek cities. These *poleis* were called democracies, but in fact were oligarchies. There were fees to pay to be a magistrate or a councillor. Only the wealthy could serve. Everyone knew these were not democracies in the sense of the Classical Athenian democracy. The Greek elite needed to find new justifications for their exclusive rule. They looked to the Classical Greek past. They invested heavily in knowledge about Classical Greek history. They spoke and wrote the Attic Greek of the fifth and fourth centuries BC to distinguish themselves from the *Koine* (Common Greek) used by the contemporary non-elite. They colonised the past by inventing the Greek novel, which projected contemporary elite attitudes and values back into a Classical setting. And they claimed they were direct descendants of the great figures of the Classical age, happily forging family trees as proof. The latter merged with the effects of another change, this time not one for the better. The imposition of Roman rule, above all the acquisition of Roman citizenship, gave greater legal and social freedom to Greek women. To maintain control over their wives, Greek elite men invested more cultural capital in their bloodlines and marital fidelity, and thus began to disapprove of other sexual activity, including male–male sex.

II 'Call me not Lord, for I am a Lady'

Heliogabalus drove a chariot through the acceptable sexual behaviour of his time (perhaps literally, as we will see). It was one of the reasons he would be killed.

The Emesene family may not have been strong on conventional sexual morality. Maesa openly branded both her daughters as adulteresses to claim Caracalla's paternity for her two grandsons. Soaemias and Mamaea went along with the assertion. A claim to the throne was more important than a reputation for chastity. And Soaemias' affair with Eutychianus, a freedman of the family, was public knowledge. Although it was much later when the *Augustan History* turned this into her behaving like a whore, with multiple partners, the elaboration would have been available to contemporaries. Yet the family were not strangers to the norms of sexual activity. If it is true that Domna was accused of adultery, it did not convince her husband, Septimius Severus. In a speech in a surviving fragment of Iamblichus' second-century AD novel *A Babylonian Story*, a husband who suspects his wife has cuckolded him prosecutes her for the 'insufferable crime' of adultery, made all the 'more disgraceful' because it was with a slave of the family. If Iamblichus belonged to an earlier generation of the Emesene house (as argued in chapter 2), it forms an ironic contrast with Soaemias and Eutychianus. It also shows a member of the family subscribing to conventional sexual morality, or, at least, ascribing it to a character. Or does it? The husband is pompous and superstitious, and his only proofs are his wife's dreams. It is clear that he finds the slave sexually attractive himself. Perhaps we are meant to be laughing at him.

The sexuality of Heliogabalus is of varied interest to our sources. Herodian in general writes little about sex. Maesa worries that the population of Rome might consider Heliogabalus' priestly costume 'more appropriate for women than men'. The soldiers are revolted by his make-up, which is more elaborate than that of a modest woman. It is implied that his interest is limited to male–male sex. He pretended to fall in love with a Vestal to 'provide a semblance of virility'.

Cassius Dio has Heliogabalus having a lot of sex with females. He married many times, including the Vestal Virgin Aquilia twice, and had intercourse 'without legal sanction' with many more women. In his marriages 'he conducted himself in the most licentious fashion'. What does this mean? A wife was meant to be modest in bed. Sex during daylight was only socially acceptable for newly-weds. Sex with the light on was very daring. Erotic poets were breaking the 'rules' when they wrote of how their sexual partners looked. The varied positions depicted in Roman art were provided by prostitutes or slaves, not a demure wife. Even prostitutes sometimes kept their breasts covered. If Heliogabalus flouted these conventions with his wives, how could anyone have known? The answer is the extraordinary (to us) lack of privacy in the ancient world. In many scenes of lovemaking in Classical art the couple are not alone. A servant watches from the door, or is actually in the room ready with refreshments.

But, Cassius Dio says, all this male–female sex turns out to be a means to an end of having better male–male sex, so Heliogabalus could learn the techniques of playing the woman's role with men. To further that end the Emperor deployed numerous agents (presumably the *frumentarii*) to find those who could best please him. A passage of Cassius Dio implies they searched locations where men were naked – the baths, gymnasia and athletics stadia – and the essential requirement was a very large penis.

Heliogabalus might be condemned for his interest in big penises. The Romans had inherited from the Greeks a very different attitude to penis size than the modern western one. A small penis was good: it represented self-control, rationality and civilisation. A big penis indicated the opposite: wild, irrational barbarity. Except the Romans did not buy into this all the time. The poet Martial wrote that if you heard a round of applause from the baths, it was caused by the sight of a huge cock.

Heliogabalus, however, encountered his most notorious lover by chance. Hierocles was a slave from Caria in Asia Minor, who had been trained as a charioteer by his master Gordius. In a race he fell from his chariot just in front of Heliogabalus. His helmet came off, revealing his beardless face and a crown of blond hair. The Emperor rushed him to the palace. If the accident happened in the Circus Maximus, it was a short journey, as the palace overlooked the track. The nocturnal feats of Hierocles captivated the Emperor, who took him as a husband. Transgressive marriages, which lacked any legal force, were not unknown among the elite. Nero was said to have taken the role of bride with his freedman Pythagoras, and that of groom with a boy called Sporus. Messalina went through a wedding ceremony with her lover Silius while still married to the Emperor Claudius. Presumably the very transgressive nature of the act added to the sexual thrill. Hierocles became so influential that his mother, while still a slave, was given a military escort to Rome and granted the status of the wife of an ex-consul. Heliogabalus went further, wanting to appoint his husband Caesar. When this was opposed by Maesa, the Emperor threatened his grandmother, but Hierocles did not become Caesar.

The agents found Heliogabalus' other well-known lover. Aurelius Zoticus was an athlete from Smyrna. His father had been a cook, but Zoticus was a freeman. The perfection of his body and the enormous size of his cock were his recommendations. He was brought to Rome accompanied by a retinue suitable for an oriental prince. Before he arrived, he was given the post of chamberlain (*a cubiculo*) and the name of Heliogabalus' grandfather, Avitus. The latter is puzzling. Modern scholars have seen it as evidence that he was a freedman of the Emesene family. But athletes were not ex-slaves, the family has no link to Smyrna and Cassius Dio is explicit that Zoticus was given the name by Heliogabalus. What was Heliogabalus doing? Was it a perverse sex thing: preparing to have sex with his grandfather? Or was it, like treating Eutychianus as a father, another bizarre attempt to rebuild a family decimated by death?

Zoticus, garlanded and lit by many torches, processed into the palace and made the customary salutation: 'My Lord Emperor, Hail!' Heliogabalus sprang to his feet with rhythmic movements, bent his neck in a feminine pose, and fixing Zoticus with a melting gaze, said, 'Call me not Lord, for I am a Lady.' They bathed together – when stripped Zoticus' physique proved worthy of his reputation – dined, and retired to the bed chamber. And then things went wrong.

Hierocles rightly saw Zoticus as a rival and a potential threat. Rivals in male–male affairs were believed to be particularly vindictive. By now well established in the palace, Hierocles had won over some of the *Familia Caesaris*. He induced the cupbearers to administer a drug to the newcomer that, as Cassius Dio put it, 'abated his manly prowess'. Various foods were thought to be antaphrodisiac: the seeds of cannabis and the Chaste-Tree, rue, cress and lettuce. Wine in which a red mullet had been drowned was also held to be effective. Whatever the drug, 'Zoticus, after a whole night of embarrassment, being unable to secure an erection, was deprived of all his honours.' Zoticus was banished from the palace, then Rome and finally Italy. As Cassius Dio points out, it was to save his life. Zoticus has been identified with an athlete on a mosaic from Puteoli and a member of the *Familia Caesaris* in the next reign. Maybe he returned, but the name is not uncommon.

Fidelity was not for Heliogabalus. He made sure Hierocles caught him with other men and let his husband beat him. In an alarming insight into ancient domestic violence, Heliogabalus loved him all the more, as the black eyes he sported proved the reality of his role as a wife.

The odium heaped on Hierocles and Zoticus does not fit with the idea that it was always acceptable to be the penetrator in male–male sex. Either they are condemned because of their association with Heliogabalus, or such censure is evidence of the hardening of attitudes towards all male–male sexual activity.

Although Cassius Dio claims that Heliogabalus indulged in many sex acts that no one could endure to tell or hear, it would be 'impossible to conceal' that at night he left the palace, wearing a wig, and frequented taverns and brothels, driving out the sex workers and taking their place. Similarly, he equipped a room in the palace as a brothel. There he would stand naked behind a curtain, soliciting passers-by. The customers were men specially selected for the role. Afterwards, he would boast of his takings and the number of his lovers.

Similar stories had been told of other 'bad' Emperors: including Caligula, Nero and Otho. They are usually dismissed as *topoi*, standard literary clichés: mere fiction invented after the death of the ruler. But, as we will see in a moment, that might be to misunderstand the role of *topoi* in the Roman world.

Cassius Dio has Heliogabalus dressing and acting as a woman: wearing make-up, a hairnet and working wool. It is claimed he desired to go beyond cross-dressing and have a sex change. He wanted to be castrated and asked physicians about the possibility of having an incision to create a vagina. Cassius Dio is explicit that the former had nothing to do with his religion but was prompted by effeminacy.

The normal modern scholarly response to many of the above stories is to dismiss them as mere *topoi*: conventional accusations applied after death to Emperors disliked by the next regime, and thus at best their truth is unknowable, or they are complete fiction. Yet if that was the case, they should be applied indiscriminately. That is not how they are deployed. Some are altered. Caligula and others are said to have visited brothels as customers, or to have forced females from elite families to prostitute themselves. Heliogabalus prostitutes himself. Some supposed *topoi* are new. No other Emperor is accused of exploring the possibility of the insertion of a vagina. And, most significantly, some *topoi* are not used. Emperors were accused of incest: Caligula with his sisters, Nero with his mother. Soaemias had a bad sexual reputation: adultery with Caracalla and sex with the freedman Eutychianus. If *topoi* were meaningless and indiscriminate pieces of invective against the dead, we would expect Heliogabalus to be condemned for incest with his mother. Yet even the lurid fiction of the *Augustan History*, to which we will turn next, does not make that claim. *Topoi* played a powerful symbolic role in the Roman imaginative economy. They were selected for their appositeness, their plausibility. They were shaped to fit the perceived truth. *Topoi* were powerful conceptual tools, providing quick and easy, but not necessarily misleading, orientation.

Looking back from the best part of two centuries later, the *Augustan History* claims that many filthy anecdotes about Heliogabalus have been put in writing, but as they are not worthy of being recorded it will concentrate on his extravagance. The disclaimer is disingenuous, the theme is congenial and the text is at its creative best on the sex life of Heliogabalus. Like a good historical novelist it draws on contemporary sources. For this subject Herodian was no use, so it turned to Cassius Dio. (Let's not get bogged down with Marius Maximus, whose putative *Life of Heliogabalus* only exists through the distorting lens of the *Augustan History* itself.) It both plays with the material found in Cassius Dio, adding layers of inventive detail, and uses it as an inspiration for amusing free fiction.

The idea of imperial agents hunting men with big cocks appeals to the author. They scour the whole city and the docks. A Bath House is built to lure the well-hung. They are given a collective name: *Onebeli*, 'Hung like an ass'. The Emperor awards lots of them high office. In the palace, embittered men with smaller cocks spread damaging rumours.

It goes on to say that Zoticus is elevated to take the role of Hierocles as husband to the Emperor. There is much about his influence: even his words are quoted. The heads of government departments (which actually only came into existence a century after the reign) treat him as an official consort. He suffers no erection problems. While being penetrated Heliogabalus shouts, 'Get to work, Cook!' That joke probably accounts for the switch. Although ousted from centre stage, Hierocles performs fellatio on the Emperor.

As an aside, getting oral sex was good, doing it very bad: either fellatio or cunnilingus. As we have seen, the poet Martial frequently expressed distaste at having to kiss such people socially. Along with being anally penetrated, oral sex lies behind an opaque statement of Cassius Dio that Heliogabalus 'used his body both for doing and allowing many strange things'. Of course he did, many would have said – he was a Phoenician, and in Greek and Latin 'to act like a Phoenician' was to perform cunnilingus.

Heliogabalus and the prostitutes get a whole new range of interactions in the *Augustan History*. He tours brothels in disguise to give them gifts; buys one for a fortune but does not touch her; buys others to set them free; summons male and female prostitutes and gives them encouraging speeches, addressing them as 'Fellow-Soldiers'.

The death of his favourites is made more symbolic: killed before the Emperor, their innards are torn out or they are pierced up the arse.

The scene in Cassius Dio of the Emperor naked behind the curtain is transformed into Heliogabalus falling to his knees and thrusting his buttocks out as he plays the role of Venus on the stage. Given the imperial order that all sex depicted in the theatre had to be real, we know what the actor playing Mars will do next.

Heliogabalus' odd religion now stretches to include infibulating himself (tying his penis back between his legs) as he dances among the castrated priests to worship the Great Mother.

Mocking invention accrues around philosophers. After being fucked by Zoticus, the Emperor asks philosophers if they have experienced such pleasure. To curry favour with Heliogabalus, some philosophers take to wearing hairnets and boasting they too have husbands.

In perhaps its finest creation – maybe even better than the flowers smothering the dinner guests – the *Augustan History* has Heliogabalus harnessing the most beautiful women naked to pull his chariot – sometimes two, or three, or four, or more – then driving around, often naked himself.

Or might it actually be historical? That is always the nagging question with the *Augustan History*. Here a cameo (a carved gemstone) held in the Bibliothèque Nationale in Paris makes it particularly acute.

Image 17: Cameo of Heliogabalus?

A naked young man drives a chariot pulled by two women, who are also naked except for breast-bands. He holds the reins in his left hand and a whip in his right. He wears a *corona* (a crown associated with the sun), has a short beard and sports a magnificent erection (he is ithyphallic, as art historians say). The enigmatic Greek Text runs EPIXENI NEIKAS, which might mean 'The Stranger Triumphs'.

No other individual in antiquity is credited with this eccentric mode of travel. It seems to refer to Heliogabalus. But how? Several interpretations are available (this is the sort of thing that makes me love ancient history!). First, is it a modern fake? By their nature cameos lacking a secure archaeological provenance cannot be dated scientifically. On stylistic grounds it has been dated to 'mid-Severan'. But would that have been the case without the link to Heliogabalus? Anyway, style can be copied. The cameo appeared in the second half of the nineteenth century. This was when the Decadent Movement in France was drawing on the *Augustan History* to remodel the image of Heliogabalus (as we will see in the final chapter). Of course, that could be a coincidence.

Two interpretations, which consider it a genuine antiquity, harness the cameo directly to the *Augustan History*. The cameo, or rather others of the same design, which had nothing to do with the Emperor, inspired the fiction in the biography. As the cameo is unique, this is unconvincing. The argument might work better the other way round. The passage in the *Augustan History* could have inspired a late antique gem-cutter.

From another view, the cameo 'may represent some rite associated with the worship of the sun god Elagabal'. Not a shred of evidence supports this idea, and it deserves no more credence than the sacred prostitution, hallucinogenic drugs and other stuff modern scholars ascribe to the religion.

The final two ways of understanding again mirror each other. They link the cameo to Heliogabalus, but uncouple it from the *Augustan History*. 'It may have been created after the Emperor's murder as a kind of posthumous denigration of his memory.' A cameo was both very expensive and very small. After the death of the Emperor, many individuals might want to distance themselves from his regime: Cassius Dio was an example. Why choose such a costly and inefficient medium to proclaim their public condemnation of the dead Emperor? And where on the cameo is the denigration? Not in the jutting, large cock – remember Martial and the applause in the baths. More likely the wealthy patron found the image amusing and/or arousing and commissioned the cameo to celebrate the unusual sexuality of the Emperor: *The Stranger Triumphs*!

This positive reading of the cameo opens the possibility that it was not just discreet individuals who privately rejected conventional attitudes to sex. There may have been groups in Roman society who openly flaunted what was generally considered a 'deviant' sexuality. Let us look at some more evidence.

The photo shows one of a pair of statues of the Emperor. They were erected in Carnuntum, the provincial capital of Pannonia Superior and the home of *Legio XIV Gemina*, perhaps to commemorate a visit by Heliogabalus when touring the Danubian army on his journey to Rome. The other statue depicts the Emperor in traditional military dress but this one shows him in his robes as Most High

Image 18: Heliogabalus in Carnuntum

Priest of the Invincible Sun Elagabal. The eastern apparel evoked effeminacy, and thus the passive role in male–male sex, for traditional western viewers. It has been suggested that the statue deliberately goes further. The pose and the see-through costume, both emphasising the exposed thighs, have been thought to sexualise the image. The thighs were a zone of keen erotic interest in ancient male–male sex.

If this understanding is correct, whoever commissioned the statue must have believed that the evocations would not have been offensive to all its viewers; that there would have been more than just a few isolated individuals in Carnuntum to whom the image of the Emperor as passive partner in male–male sex would have appealed. This group may have included soldiers as well as civilians. Herodian tells us that back in Emesa, before the start of the revolt, the soldiers enjoyed watching Heliogabalus dancing in this costume. That the statue was deliberately beheaded after his death does not invalidate this reading: so was the one that showed him in military costume.

Interestingly, it is precisely from Carnuntum that we find an inscription that has been interpreted as unique evidence of the open celebration of a same-sex relationship between two soldiers. One is called FVTVTOR, the penetrator. Which labels the other the passive partner. Unfortunately, in all probability FVTVTOR was no more than a rough military nickname: he was a 'Fucker'. Nothing else on the inscription points to a sexual relationship.

Finally let's turn to a letter of Philostratus.

> *You offer yourself for sale; yes, mercenary soldiers do the like. You belong to anyone who pays your price; yes, so do pilots. We drink of you as of the streams; we feel of you as of the roses. Your lovers like you because you stand naked and offer yourself for examination – something that is a peculiar right of beauty alone – beauty fortunate*

> *in its freedom of action. Pray, do not be ashamed of your compliance,*
> *but be proud of your readiness; for water too is public property, and*
> *fire belongs to no individual, and the stars belong to all, and the sun*
> *is a common god. Your house is a citadel of beauty, those who enter*
> *are priests, those who are garlanded are sacred envoys, their silver is*
> *tribute money. Rule graciously over your subjects, and receive what*
> *they offer, and, furthermore, accept their adoration.*

Philostratus 'the Athenian' was the most prominent of a family of Greek public intellectuals, who wrote in many genres. Today he is best known for his biographies *The Lives of the Sophists* (in which he invented the term 'Second Sophistic', now used to describe the whole Greek cultural renaissance of the first three centuries AD), and his historical novel *The Life of Apollonius of Tyana*. A member of the Severan imperial court, he claimed Domna prompted him to write about Apollonius, and his *Heroicus*, a brilliant short novel retelling Homer, was shaped by the concerns of the regime of Alexander Severus. The quoted letter indicated he was active at the court of Heliogabalus.

The sun god and the priests, the envoys and the tribute, the kingship and the adoration, the passive role in male–male sex: there can be no doubt it is about Heliogabalus. On the few occasions on which the letter is mentioned in modern scholarship, it is seen as mocking the young Emperor after his death. But read it again, without preconceptions.

Indeed, the poem starts with the addressee as a boy-prostitute, and the comparisons drawn are negative: mercenaries and pilots, both had bad connotations. But then the imagery moves to streams, roses and beauty, to water, fire, the stars and the sun: all good. His house is a citadel, his customers priests or sacred envoys, their payment tribute money. The negative tone has become positive. The prostitute has become a king (not an autocrat, let alone a tyrant, but a *Basileus*), who is urged to rule graciously, accepting the adoration of his subjects.

Unless you have made up your mind before you start reading, the letter does not simply 'mock' Heliogabalus. Instead, it plays a clever literary game. It starts as if to condemn and urge a change of behaviour. But it has wrong-footed the reader. The letter shifts to admiration and praise and ends by urging the Emperor to continue his flamboyant and unconventional lifestyle. The letter shows a contemporary could spin Heliogabalus' sex life in a positive way.

Of course, a published literary letter was not intended to be read by its recipient alone. Philostratus was a creative writer. The letter forms a pair with one written to a female prostitute. Philostratus may not have shared the interests of Heliogabalus, but he could write for those who admired and enjoyed such sexuality.

No one can doubt that the majority of his subjects did not approve of the Emperor's sexual activities. As we shall see in the next chapter, the ancient historians say they contributed to his death. Yet taken together, the cameo, statue and letter suggest that a minority responded enthusiastically to what most saw as his utter decadence.

CHAPTER II DEATH

26 June AD221 to 13 March AD222

I Finding a Son

In the spring of AD221 Maesa was worried. Some eighteen months after the imperial entourage arrived in Rome she suspected that the various constituencies that could overthrow an Emperor were turning against Heliogabalus. Herodian specifies the soldiers, who were 'revolted' by the Emperor's religious practices, his *levitas* in throwing gifts to the plebs and driving as a charioteer and his effeminacy. Cassius Dio says he was 'hated' by the plebs as well as the soldiers, for his sexuality: above all, his marriage to Hierocles. We can assume that the Senate and the *Familia Caesaris* were also alienated 'by this kind of behaviour', perhaps especially by the influence of the charioteer Hierocles.

It begs the question of how Maesa knew. The imperial women in the palace did not live in seclusion. This was not the Ottoman harem in Istanbul. Maesa lived surrounded by the *Familia Caesaris*. As we will see in a moment, she could choose those who served her. As Augusta, Maesa had a guard of Praetorians. Ceremonial as well as practical, they also acted as a channel of communication. A woman should not enter the Senate, but as a person of influence at court, perhaps thought of as the power behind the throne, her company would have been sought by senators. Her connections to the *Plebs Urbana* were more tenuous. Yet the plebs often made their views known at the public spectacles. They called out and chanted. Relying on safety in numbers, they were more outspoken than any other group in society. Unlike in other reigns, we hear of no popular demonstrations under Heliogabalus. The relationship between the Emperor and the populace of the city is one of the most intriguing of his life, to which we will return in the next chapter.

Maesa had not contrived her grandson's accession just for his behaviour to risk everything. If Heliogabalus was overthrown by some outsider, at best she would be reduced to the status of a private citizen. She had experienced this before in Emesa, after the assassination of Caracalla. It was uncongenial. If there were to be a coup, most likely she would be killed. So she formed a plan.

She had another grandson. Alexianus, the son of Mamea, was twelve and appeared more biddable than his cousin. Heliogabalus had to be persuaded to adopt Alexianus and declare him his heir, as Caesar. Maesa employed the persuasion most likely to succeed with Heliogabalus: religion. If Alexianus was Caesar, he could perform the mundane ceremonies of the imperial role, leaving Heliogabalus free for the more exalted worship of Elagabal. The Emperor agreed. Herodian characterises him as 'a thoughtless, silly young man'. Certainly, he was no match for Maesa.

The twenty-sixth of June was a hot day in Rome. The temperature at the end of the month often reaches the eighties in Fahrenheit (the high twenties Celsius). On the packed benches of the Senate House the Conscript Fathers, as the senators were known, were sweltering in the voluminous folds of their togas. The doors were open to allow non-senators to observe proceedings from the threshold. They let in what breeze there was. The windows, set high in the walls, were also open. Birds often flew in. During dull sessions the bored might watch them. Today, the superstitious might indulge in augury – some indeed were members of the priestly college of Augurs – observing their flight to determine the will of the gods.

Heliogabalus arrived, not only with Alexianus but also Maesa and Soaemias. His grandmother and mother sat on either side of him. This was an extraordinary breach of protocol. Even Maesa's sister Domna had not attended the Senate. Back in the dark days of Nero, Agrippina had only watched from behind a screen. Soaemias and Maesa sat in the place of the consuls. Maesa must have been aware of the offence this would cause. Perhaps she thought it more important to put on a show of imperial unity, to demonstrate that there were older and wiser heads in the dynasty, not just a seventeen-year-old youth and a twelve-year-old boy. There again, she might have been determined to see the thing through. After all, she had overseen the acclamation at Raphaneae and personally intervened at the battle at Immae.

Alexianus was formally adopted, took the toga of manhood and the name Alexander, and was declared Caesar. Although Heliogabalus stated that 'he had no need of any other child to keep his house free from despondency', he undercut the solemnity of the ceremony with a joke that made explicit the falsity of the Roman custom of adoption, congratulating himself on 'suddenly becoming the father of such a large boy'.

According to Cassius Dio, Heliogabalus claimed that he was acting on the orders of Elagabal. Although he did not believe a word of that, the historian still detected the hand of the divine. Years later, Cassius Dio interpreted the enigmatic *daemon* that had processed through Moesia and Thrace as an omen of the adoption. There is no need to give credence to the modern theory that the *daemon* was organised by Maesa. On the other hand, if the 'someone' who prophesied to Heliogabalus that 'an Alexander should come from Emesa to succeed him' was one of the priests of Elagabal who had travelled with the god to Rome, that might betray the hand of Maesa. At the outset of the revolt, we can assume she was behind the favourable oracles emanating from the deity, and we have just seen religion was her way of convincing Heliogabalus.

Alexander was given a strange title. One undamaged inscription records it in full, although with some words abbreviated: NOBILISSIMUS CAES IMPERI ET SACERDOTIS COS. It can be understood as 'Most Noble Caesar of the Emperor and Priest (i.e. of Heliogabalus) and Consul', or alternatively 'Most Noble Caesar Consort in the Imperium and Priesthood'. Our uncertainty reflects that of contemporaries. No other Caesar ever held such a title. The vast majority of the inhabitants of the empire would have been unsure exactly what it signified. The unique title points to the abnormality of the reign. The legal powers granted to Alexander are debatable. He may or may not, depending on which of the above reconstructions is accepted, have been invested with *imperium*. The numbering of the years of tribunician power on Alexander's later coins seem to show that he did not have the *tribunicia potestas* as Caesar. But it is wrong to get too hung up on constitutional niceties. Clearly the twelve-year-old Caesar was both heir of and subordinate to the seventeen-year-old Emperor.

Heliogabalus soon came to regret the adoption. But not immediately. On 1 July Alexander was designated to be *consul ordinarius* with Heliogabalus the following year. They would take up office on 1 January AD222, and the year would be named after them. On 10 July, Alexander was co-opted into the *Sodales Antoniniani* college of priests. Something else happened in the summer of AD221; perhaps in June, at the same time as the adoption of

Alexander. Heliogabalus' unpopular marriage to the Vestal Virgin Aquilia Severa was ended. We have already read the letter the Emperor circulated to his subjects explaining his reasons (chapter 7, section III): it was at the request of the Praetorians, for the public good, because Aquilia could not provide an heir. If this was a move to restore public approval of the regime, one possibly initiated by Maesa, it misfired completely. Heliogabalus immediately chose another wife, Annia Aurelia Faustina. As we saw earlier, she was already married to the aristocrat Pomponius Basus, who was summarily executed. Such behaviour would have alienated not only the Senate, but also the general public. It was the stuff of tyrants.

Heliogabalus turned against his cousin and became 'suspicious of all men', according to Cassius Dio, when he learnt that popular favour was moving to Alexander. Herodian gives another reason. Heliogabalus wanted his cousin trained in the priesthood of Elagabal. When introducing the boys back in Emesa, Herodian claimed both were already dedicated to the god. Our sources have nothing about Alexander participating in any rituals. Perhaps he was too young, or perhaps his mother held him back. Now Mamaea – for the first time appearing with an active role in the story – removed him from such contact and appointed teachers of conventional Greek and Roman culture.

Heliogabalus was furious, and drove Alexander's teachers from court, exiling some, executing others. Herodian gives no names. The *Augustan History* gives a long and fraudulent list: either real intellectuals who had been long dead, or complete inventions. Only one of them might in reality have tutored the young Caesar, as Emperor Alexander referred to the distinguished jurist Ulpian as 'my parent'. Yet it was merely an expression of respect to an older man. The *Augustan History* liked to spin its fiction round the figure of Ulpian. In the last months of Heliogabalus' reign

Ulpian probably was in charge of the grain supply of Rome as *praefectus annonae*. It is unlikely that he combined this role with that of palace tutor.

Herodian's religious motivation can be doubted. It fits neatly with the central scheme of his history: judging Emperors by their attitude to Greek culture (*paideia*). Devoted to the alien culture of his god, Heliogabalus is the enemy of conventional *paideia*. When he becomes Emperor, Alexander is presented as a case of undermined *paideia*, as his mother, who attempts to instil it, herself lacks the quality. However, Herodian's shaping of the material does not prove its falsity. Indeed, the actuality of the relations of Heliogabalus and Alexander could in part have inspired Herodian's creation of the scheme.

Before sunrise on 1 January AD222 the senators, like great white moths in their gleaming togas, followed their torch bearers through the gloomy streets of Rome to the Senate House. All public ceremonies had to be carried out in daylight. The inauguration of the consuls at New Year was a lengthy process. There were only nine hours to dusk.

In the event, the senators had a long wait. Heliogabalus refused to go to the ceremony. Maesa and Soaemias reasoned with him. It is the last time we hear of mother and daughter acting in unison. This time their argument was not religion but self-preservation. The soldiers were threatening to kill him if they did not see harmony between him and his cousin. Eventually, Heliogabalus put on the formal *toga praetexta* and entered the Senate at the sixth hour of the day (about midday in our time). The Emperor invited Maesa to the session and escorted her to a seat.

It was customary for a *consul ordinarius* taking office on 1 January to make a speech of thanks to the Emperor. To experience such sycophancy dressed up as free speech we can read the *Panegyric* of Pliny. It is not recorded if the twelve-year-old

Alexander was schooled to deliver an oration. Maybe there was not time.

The new consuls were expected to leave the Senate House, turn right through the Arch of Septimius Severus and process up to the Capitol, where they took their vows and sacrificed to Jupiter Optimus Maximus in front of the temple of the god. Heliogabalus again refused. If the Emperor did not go, nor could his Caesar. A praetor, the next rank of magistrate down, was left to officiate on the Capitol.

Why did Heliogabalus refuse? The question is seldom asked. The answer seems so obvious – he did not want to be associated with his cousin. Very true, but another reason can be found. The Most High Priest of Elagabal had no intention of participating in a ceremony that symbolically reaffirmed the primacy of Jupiter as the head of the Roman pantheon.

Religion induced the adoption of Alexander, struck a novel and perplexing note in the Caesar's titles, caused the rift between the cousins and curtailed their inauguration as consuls. In the reign of Heliogabalus, behind everything loomed the great black stone of Elagabal.

Had Maesa already decided to embark on a second coup when she persuaded Heliogabalus to adopt Alexander in June AD 221? Was she prepared to risk everything again to plot another regime change? Probably not. She still acted to preserve Heliogabalus the following January. So far Alexander was an insurance policy. She was soon to have a change of heart.

II *The Power of Women*

In Rome, a woman could not hold civic or military office. She could not be a magistrate, a senator, or, even though its membership was by personal invitation, sit in the imperial *Consilium*. Most certainly she could not rule as empress in her own name. Any political power a woman might possess was informal influence exercised through the men in her family, as wife, mother or grandmother.

Roman was not the only identity available to Maesa and the other women of her family. Emesa was a Greek city. There is a paradox here. Before Caracalla's grant of almost universal Roman citizenship, Greeks regarded Roman women as less restricted than in their own culture. Yet, unlike in Rome, we find women holding magistracies in Greek cities under the empire. In one modern survey of magistrates named on coins in the East, 17 out of 231 are women. The paradox is more apparent than real. The *poleis* in which these women served as magistrates tended to be small, out-of-the-way places. Presumably the need for suitably wealthy office holders led to a relaxation of the normal rules, much like allowing ex-slaves to become magistrates.

The women from Emesa also were descended from a royal dynasty of the Hellenistic world. From before the reign of Alexander the Great in monarchic Macedon, under exceptional circumstances women had acted as regents, even led armies. From the late Hellenistic period Cleopatra (VII) of Ptolemaic Egypt remained a dangerous exemplar throughout the rest of antiquity.

Emesa was founded by Arabs. Although its dynasty seems to have preferred to adopt a Phoenician or Syrian identity, it is worth noting that Arab culture was more accepting than Roman of the open political power of women: as demonstrated by the famous Zenobia of Palmyra, a generation after Maesa and Queen Mavia in the following century.

Maesa may have drawn encouragement from these other heritages – civic Greek, monarchic Macedonian and Arab – but the fact remained that in Roman imperial politics her only avenue to power was through influencing the males in her family.

That Maesa, and the other women of the Severan dynasty, had any serious political influence at all has been denied by some scholars. This interpretation rests on two lines of argument. The first looks at formal expressions of status. Maesa and her daughters were granted no titles that had not been held by their predecessors. Maesa was 'Mother of the Camps and of the Senate and Grandmother of our Augustus'. Soaemias was 'Mother of the Camps and of the Augustus', but seemingly not of the Senate. Domna had held all these titles under Septimius Severus. Likewise, the percentage of coins issued in their names was normal (about seventeen percent of imperial coinage), and what featured on these coins in the main was completely conventional. The second argument is that as Cassius Dio does not emphasise the influence of Maesa, it is a fiction of Herodian, which was later altered into the influence of Soaemias by the *Augustan History*.

The argument that Maesa's influence was a literary invention is unconvincing. We have already seen (chapter 1, section 1) that Cassius Dio had more reason to write Maesa and Mamaea out of his story than Herodian had to create a fiction about their role. Similarly, an argument that judges political power from formal status in Rome misrepresents the realities of life under the Emperors. It is easy for modern scholars, writing in safe western democracies, to forget that under an autocracy power comes not from grand titles, but from having the ear of the ruler. Remember the slave holding the Emperor's piss-pot. Nevertheless, one public expression by an Emperor does reveal the contemporary perception of the strong influence of the women from Emesa. During the revolt Macrinus had the Senate declare war not just on Heliogabalus and his cousin as *hostes* (enemies of the state) but also on Maesa and her daughters.

When did Maesa exercise her influence? On what occasions did she, or her daughter Soaemias, have access to Heliogabalus? Not in the Senate (except in rare circumstances) or in court, nor when he was giving audience to embassies, or in the *Consilium*. Of course, Heliogabalus was not keen on any of those activities. He enjoyed driving chariots. Although we know his grandmother and mother were in the audience, the track itself was a male preserve. The imperial box at the games was too public a venue. At dinner might seem more promising. In the Alma-Tadema painting, Maesa and four other women recline with Heliogabalus at the high table, watching the other diners being smothered with rose petals. In reality, the imperial women normally seem to have dined separately. When Caracalla arranged the killing of the praetorian prefect Plautianus, someone plucked a tuft from the dead man's beard. He took it to the room where Domna and the prefect's daughter, Plautilla, were dining, and, brandishing the hairs in Plautilla's face, exclaimed: 'Behold your Plautianus!' Heliogabalus devoted much time to sex. It was not somewhere the women of his family went. We have already explored the implications of the standard tyrant *topos* of incest *not* being applied to Heliogabalus. Similarly, when the young Emperor slipped out of the palace at night to visit brothels, he would not have invited his grandmother. All of which leaves just religion. No wonder the elderly Maesa in Rome continued to dance and chant at dawn in honour of Elagabal, long after she had begun to have doubts about the political wisdom of the ceremonies back in Nicomedia.

It is always difficult, if not impossible, to judge with any accuracy the degree of behind-the-scenes influence at the court of an autocrat. The best we can do is assemble a checklist, in chronological order, of Maesa's recorded interventions. In Nicomedia, she failed to persuade Heliogabalus to change out of his priestly costume into conventional Roman clothing. In Rome, despite being threatened by her grandson, she succeeded in preventing him from appointing Hierocles as Caesar. Instead, she convinced him to adopt Alexander. On 1 January AD 222, aided by Soaemias, she eventually prevailed on Heliogabalus to put on the *toga praetexta* and attend the Senate, but then could not get him to sacrifice to Jupiter on the Capitol. A strike rate of three out of five. Maesa won more than she lost. Not an overwhelming control, but a very influential voice. Soon she would have a greater success in a yet more dangerous venture.

III   *To the Tiber*

When we enter the last months of the reign of Heliogabalus, we encounter a strange reversal of normal scholarly attitudes. Usually, on a sliding scale of trustworthiness, Cassius Dio is rated above Herodian, with the *Augustan History* a distant third. For most of the reign of Heliogabalus a few scholars reverse Herodian and Cassius Dio, but the *Augustan History* still brings up the rear. Until we get to the endgame. When suddenly we find that the account of the *Augustan History* 'forms a coherent and seemingly correct narrative', which 'has long been considered excellent'. This extraordinary turnaround is based on the belief that here the *Augustan History* is closely following the account of the contemporary biographer Marius Maximus. A *Life of Heliogabalus* was probably included in the imperial biographies written by Marius Maximus, although that is not certain. The work of Marius Maximus is only known from citations by later authors. All but one of them are in the *Augustan History*. If we look at the use of Herodian by the *Augustan History*, we find a masterpiece of misrepresentation. The information in Herodian is altered, as are his historical interpretations. Herodian is credited with things he never wrote. Fragments of Herodian are used as the jumping-off point for passages of complete fiction. Given the way in which the *Augustan History* treats a text we can check, it is naïve to believe that, for the fall of Heliogabalus, it accurately reproduces one we can't.

The *Augustan History* gives an extended narrative of the last months of Heliogabalus, complete with names of people and places. Probably some of it is historical, quite possibly derived from Marius Maximus. But passages are evident fiction. Let's take a couple of examples.

Heliogabalus commanded the Senate to leave Rome: 'Even all those Senators who had no carriages or slaves were ordered to set out at once.' As Sabinus, to whom Ulpian had dedicated some of his books, remained, Heliogabalus whispered to a centurion to kill him. Luckily for Sabinus, the centurion, who was rather deaf, misheard the instruction and merely threw him out of the city. Even if we could believe there were senators (property qualification one million sesterces) who lacked carriages and slaves, the close shave with the deaf centurion gives away the fiction. Ulpian's *ad Sabinum* was not dedicated to a contemporary senator, but was a fifty-one-book commentary on the work of a first-century lawyer named Sabinus. An extraordinary mistake, or a sly joke?

Another fiction involving the Senate. Heliogabalus summoned the Senate and ordered them to remove Alexander's title of Caesar. The senators refused, meeting the Emperor with silence. If true, this would be unique in Roman history. Again, if it were true, Cassius Dio would not have failed to vaunt the courage of his order. Herodian was not a senator, but was alert to acts of rare senatorial independence in his account of the later reign of Maximinius Thrax. This prequel would also have found a place in his story.

To reconstruct the last months of Heliogabalus, it is unwise to uncritically accept the *Augustan History*. Instead, all three major sources should be canvassed, scrutinising the information they provide and testing each step, like a climber crossing loose scree.

All three sources agree that the rift between the cousins was caused by Heliogabalus moving against Alexander and that these moves came in two phases. The *Augustan History* places the first plot before the joint consulship. Although the dating is commonly accepted, there are problems. In the text of Cassius Dio, Heliogabalus makes his first move after the cousins are consuls. Would Maesa have acted to prevent the soldiers from killing Heliogabalus on 1 January if she had known that the Emperor was already attempting to remove Alexander? More likely both plots were played out in early AD 222, between 1 January and 13 March.

Cassius Dio is frustratingly vague about the form the first plot took. When the Emperor 'attempted to destroy Alexander, he not only accomplished nothing, but came near being killed himself'. Alexander was guarded by Maesa, Mamaea and the soldiers. When the Praetorians heard of the attempt, they raised a tumult. Heliogabalus took Alexander to their camp, and the Praetorians demanded the surrender of some of Heliogabalus' 'companions in lewdness'. The Emperor begged to retain Hierocles: 'Grant me this one man, whatever you may suspect about him, or else slay me.' For now, the Praetorians were appeased, at least in part. The fate of the other 'companions in lewdness' is not recorded.

If Cassius Dio gives us nothing of the details of Heliogabalus' initial plot, the *Augustan History* provides too many variants. The Emperor despatched assassins to kill Alexander, issued a written order to the soldiers to take away Alexander's rank as Caesar, sent men to the Praetorian camp to smear mud on the inscriptions on

Alexander's statues and told Alexander's 'guardians' (*nutritores*) that if they hoped for rewards and distinctions they should murder him in any way they could: in the bath, by poison or with the sword. Either Heliogabalus was exploring all options, or the author of the *Augustan History* was having fun imagining methods of removing a Caesar.

The *Augustan History* has a different story from Cassius Dio about the aftermath of the plot. Heliogabalus had withdrawn to *ad Spem Veterem*, claiming the need for privacy to seduce a youth, where he awaited the result of the assassination attempt. When the Praetorians saw the mud on Alexander's inscriptions, they were incensed. Although the majority remained in the camp, where Aristomachus, a tribune loyal to Heliogabalus, held back the standards, one group of soldiers went to the palace. There they took Alexander, Maesa and Mamaea under guard, and brought them back to the camp. Soaemias, fearing for the life of her son, trailed after them on foot. Meanwhile, a few discontented Praetorians set off for *ad Spem Veterem*. When they arrived, Heliogabalus, who had been preparing for a chariot race, hid behind a curtain. The Emperor sent out one of the praetorian prefects, Antiochianus, to calm the soldiers at hand, and the other across Rome to the camp. Antiochianus was successful, reminding the troops of their military oath. In the camp, the soldiers told the unnamed prefect that they would spare Heliogabalus' life if he sent away his 'filthy creatures' and returned to a 'decent way of life'. Eventually the Emperor did dismiss Hierocles, Cordius, Mirissimus and two other favourites, although he kept pleading for the return of Hierocles.

A few details in the account raise suspicion. It is unlikely that Cordius or Mirissimus ever existed, and it seems from Cassius Dio that Hierocles was not sent away. Heliogabalus hiding behind a curtain is reminiscent of the Emperor Claudius. A little later, the *Augustan History* has Heliogabalus hiding again, this time in a suitably degraded place, probably deliberately altering something in Cassius Dio.

Yet it is important not to be hypercritical of the *Augustan History*. Other circumstantial details here are plausible. There was a circus for racing chariots at the imperial property of *ad Spem Veterem*. Antiochianus and Aristomachus are common enough names of the period. The author liked to reuse his fictional creations, often repeatedly playing with the same names, and neither of these names reappears in a fictional context in other biographies.

The first plot barely surfaces in Herodian. The soldiers, when they realised the Emperor was plotting against his cousin, kept a watch over him. But then the historian adds a significant detail. Mamaea would not allow Alexander to taste any food or drink sent by the Emperor. Perhaps Heliogabalus first attempted to rid himself of his unwanted Caesar by poison.

However it had played out, Heliogabalus' first plot against Alexander had failed, the soldiers were alienated and the Emperor was fortunate to escape with his life. But he was not going to give up.

'Even his grandmother hated him because of his deeds, which seemed to show that he was not the son of Antoninus [Caracalla] at all, and was coming to favour Alexander, as really sprung from him,' as Cassius Dio has it.

At the start of the revolt, Maesa had told the soldiers that both her grandsons were the natural children of Caracalla. Herodian's statement is made likely by the Senate declaring both boys enemies of the state. From the beginning, Maesa had seen Alexander as a potential claimant to the throne.

Alexander had gone through more changes of paternity than his cousin. First the son of the Syrian equestrian Gessius

Marcianus, then Caracalla, then, after adoption, of Heliogabalus, then Caracalla again. With the remarkable fluidity of an elite Roman family, it also meant that Septimius Severus, the founder of the dynasty, had moved from being his grandfather to his great-grandfather and finally back to his grandfather.

Was either really the illegitimate child of Caracalla? The question might seem long deferred, and in a sense it is unimportant. But it can be answered briefly and with a high degree of probability. For what it is worth, both Soaemias and Mamaea lived at court in the reign of Septimius Severus. Both Caracalla and Soaemias can be placed in Rome in AD204, the year of Heliogabalus' birth. Two late sources state that Heliogabalus was the son of Caracalla. On the other hand, the contemporary Herodian said it 'may or may not have been true', and at Raphaneae the soldiers detected a family resemblance, because that was 'what they wanted to see'. Cassius Dio did not believe a word of it: Heliogabalus' father was Varius Marcellus. As for Alexander, it was rumoured that Caracalla was impotent in his later years. It is extremely unlikely that either was fathered by Caracalla. Maesa made the claims for political reasons. The truth was unimportant. Without his paternity there was no reason for either to become Emperor.

In the weeks or months between the initial plot and 13 March, doubtless the imperial court was divided into two factions: one centred around Heliogabalus and Soaemias, the other around Alexander, Maesa and Mamaea. We can perhaps catch glimpses of this, but lack the material for a thorough reconstruction.

There was an abnormally high turnover of prefects of the city under Heliogabalus. A tentative list might run as follows (although all bar the first and last dates are uncertain and the inclusion of Censorinus and Sacerdos is highly speculative):

Marius Maximus – AD218
Censorinus – AD218–19
Sacerdos – AD219
Comazon – AD220
Leo – AD220–1
Comazon II – AD221–2
Fulvius – AD222

What happened on 13 March lets us deduce some individuals' adherence to the two factions. Comazon, risen from the ranks and a cunning survivor, was a supporter of Maesa. He was replaced by Fulvius, an adherent of Heliogabalus. Most likely he is the outspoken Fulvius Diogenianus, who during the revolt in AD218 had shouted in the Senate that all hoped for Macrinus' death. That, combined with his allegiance to Heliogabalus, could account for Cassius Dio, years later, describing him as 'hardly of sound mind'.

We know the identities of four of Heliogabalus' praetorian prefects. Quite possibly these account for all those who held office in the reign. Comazon was appointed in AD218. On the journey to Rome, he had been given Julius Flavianus as a colleague. Both were Maesa's men. Comazon, when first appointed prefect of the city in AD220, relinquished his praetorian prefecture. Perhaps then he was replaced by ...ATVS, who had been Heliogabalus' *a studiis* (Director of Studies) and who remained close to the Emperor to the end. At some point, possibly in the tense atmosphere in the early months of AD222, the place of Flavianus was taken by Antiochianus, another Heliogabalus loyalist.

Some drag the exiles of Zoticus and Ulpian into the faction fight: two more supporters of Maesa removed by Heliogabalus and Soaemias. The inclusion is unjustified. The exile of Ulpian was a fiction of the *Augustan History* and, as we have seen, Zoticus, who was not a freedman of Maesa, was sent away because of his inability to get an erection. As so often, modern scholars seek to impose a 'rational' motivation on the wildly idiosyncratic politics of an autocratic court.

Amid the fraught manoeuvring of the factions in early AD 222, Heliogabalus divorced Annia Aurelia Faustina and remarried the ex-Vestal Virgin Aquilia Severa. As the Emperor's motive for his original marriage to the priestess was to produce 'godlike children', we can see this both as a doubling down on his religious policy and as a threat to Alexander's position as Caesar. When some advocates, or maybe clients (the Greek is ambiguous), remarked how fortunate he was to be consul with his son, Heliogabalus replied, 'I shall be more fortunate next year, when I will be Consul with a real son.'

The influence of Soaemias in all this is unclear. The *Augustan History* claims that she dominates Heliogabalus throughout his reign. No real examples are given. Instead, it generalises from her attendance in the Senate for the adoption of Alexander and creates much fiction – complete with its favoured antiquarian details and a lengthy list: here various means of transport – round a 'Women's Senate' supposedly established on the Quirinal Hill. Clearly it exaggerates the role of Soaemias. In Herodian she plays second fiddle to Maesa. It is Maesa who elevates her grandson to the throne and tries to alter his behaviour in Nicomedia. In Cassius Dio, it is Maesa who dissuades him from making Hierocles Caesar. Even in the *Augustan History*, when Soaemias joins with her mother on 1 January to get him to attend his inauguration as joint consul, Heliogabalus takes only Maesa to the Senate House.

There is a very unusual feature on Soaemias' coins. The coinage issued in the name of the other imperial women in the reign features a range of conventional messages. That of Soaemias is dominated by one goddess. Venus Caelestis had not featured on Roman coinage previously. But about ninety-six percent of Soaemias' coins found in hoards bear the image of the goddess. It has been suggested that Venus Caelestis was identified either with Urania, the goddess brought from Africa to wed Elagabal, or with a female deity worshipped at Emesa. If either was the intention of the officials in charge of the mint, it was a public statement of Soaemias' adherence to the religion of her son. Although, it must be said, the statement was not explicit and likely to be missed by many of those who handled the coins in the provinces.

Soaemias had no choice about which faction to join. As Augusta and 'Mother of the Augustus', Soaemias had both status and potential influence. Were Heliogabalus to be overthrown, even if she survived and perhaps managed to keep the title of Augusta, both would be drastically reduced. Soaemias' fate was inextricably bound to that of her son. Her lover, Eutychianus, had been stabbed to death in public by Heliogabalus. Soaemias' feelings would not have been straightforward.

Mamaea only has an active role in our sources when Heliogabalus begins to plot against her son. At first she is passive, a passenger carried along by events. Maesa took her and Alexander to Raphaneae, in the process sacrificing several of Mamaea's closest family: her daughter and son-in-law, and most likely her elder son, as well as her husband. Maesa announces that Mamaea committed adultery with Caracalla. The Senate declare her a public enemy. After that Mamaea vanishes. She is not recorded in the Senate House at any point: not even when her son is appointed Caesar. She re-emerges to defend Alexander, choosing morally improving tutors and carefully selecting cooks and cupbearers for their 'complete loyalty'. Both of which show that the imperial women had a certain independence in the palace. After Heliogabalus' first plot had been foiled, Mamaea took a daring step. She 'privately handed over some money for a clandestine distribution to the soldiers', hoping to 'capture their loyalty'. We are not told to whom she handed the money – probably to some of the *Familia Caesaris* of 'complete loyalty' – but the loyalty she hoped to induce in the soldiers was to Alexander. It was the tactic that Maesa had employed before the revolt against Macrinus. It was treason. All the more dangerous now in Rome, as the Emperor was at hand. There was no way back: either Heliogabalus or Alexander had to die.

In the run-up to the final showdown on 13 March, Cassius Dio and Herodian essentially tell the same story. The fuller account in Herodian can be supplemented with details from Cassius Dio. The brief version in the *Augustan History* is different, and, as we will see, consists of a fictional reworking of what the author found in Herodian.

Heliogabalus discovered that Mamaea was giving money to the soldiers. Someone must have told him: a soldier or one of those members of the *Familia Caesaris* that Mamaea trusted. Not everyone had turned against the Emperor. Yet, after his recent experience with the Praetorians, Heliogabalus evidently lacked the confidence to order the arrest and execution of his aunt and cousin. Instead, Herodian and Cassius Dio tell us he once more plotted to kill Alexander. Neither historian says how. Tiberius was rumoured to have been smothered with a pillow; Commodus had been strangled in the bath; magic had been one of the methods used against the imperial prince Germanicus; and most assassinated Emperors had met their end with the sword: but perhaps Heliogabalus again tried to suborn someone close to Alexander to administer poison. The renewed plot was frustrated by Maesa. 'She missed none of the machinations of Antoninus (Heliogabalus), since his behaviour was naturally unsubtle, and he was totally indiscreet about his plans in words and actions.' Maesa had experienced a murderously divided imperial court before: that of Caracalla and Geta. Of course, Heliogabalus had been there too, but he had been a child. Evidently, unlike his grandmother, he had not learnt the necessary lessons of discretion in such an untrustworthy and deadly environment.

With the failure of this new contrivance, Heliogabalus tried a different tactic. Alexander was 'no longer to be seen at public salutations or at the head of processions'. The Emperor had not lost control altogether. Although the soldiers were angered, there was no immediate insurrection. Heliogabalus further tested their responses by spreading a rumour that Alexander was on the point of dying.

This was a serious miscalculation. The Praetorians refused to mount their usual guard over the Emperor. Shutting themselves up in their camp, they demanded the presence of Alexander at their shrine. This was the Temple of Mars, which housed the standards of the Praetorians and the statues of the deified Emperors. As such, the demand was a symbolic affirmation of the traditional religion and a rejection of the god from Emesa.

This was a challenge that could not be ignored. Heliogabalus got hold of Alexander. Together they travelled in the imperial litter from the Palatine to the camp. At walking pace, the journey takes time: a prolonged and unwanted intimacy, charged with extreme tension.

To bolster his *auctoritas*, the Emperor was accompanied by a retinue of the highest officials, including Fulvius, the prefect of the city, and both of the praetorian prefects, Antiochianus and ...ATVS. Totally misreading the mood of his subjects, Heliogabalus included both Hierocles and Aurelius Eubulus, the financial officer from Emesa, in the entourage. Soaemias and Mamaea also went to the camp. Our sources do not record the

presence of Maesa. Given the crucial situation, and her intervention at all other important moments in the reign, it is inconceiv-
able that Maesa was not there.

The camp was fortified. The Praetorians opened the gates for
the imperial party. Alexander was welcomed with enthusias-
tic shouts of goodwill. Heliogabalus was ignored. Furious, the
Emperor retired to the shrine, where he spent the night 'fuming
and raging at the soldiers'.

Although the soldiers had specified the Temple of Mars to
make a point, the location was welcome to Heliogabalus. It was
where his 'father' Caracalla had withdrawn the night after the
murder of Geta. In the morning, the Praetorians had acclaimed
Caracalla. Heliogabalus could draw reassurance from that
example. Also, it was in the shrine at the camp of *III Gallica* at
Raphaneae that almost certainly he had passed part of the night
before his own acclamation as Emperor. In the Praetorian shrine
were images of him and his cousin on the military standards.
When young he had seen those of Geta torn down. Heliogabalus
hoped that the same would soon happen to those of another
junior partner in the imperial power.

As they had four years before at Raphaneae, the Emesene
women spent the night talking to the troops, trying to win them
over. Except this time, Cassius Dio tells us, the women were
divided. 'The mothers of the two youths, being more openly at
variance with each other than before, were inflaming the spirits
of the soldiers.' Maesa would have added her voice to the cause
of Alexander.

Where was the thirteen-year-old Alexander during this long
and anxious night: cowering in the shrine, or being exhibited to
the soldiery by his mother and grandmother?

In the morning, Heliogabalus issued orders for the arrest
of those soldiers who had most enthusiastically acclaimed

Alexander. The charges were sedition and riot. At first all went well. The orders were obeyed, and the ringleaders were taken into custody. Momentarily, it looked as if the authority of the Emperor would be maintained.

It did not last. The Praetorians, already antagonistic to Heliogabalus, says Cassius Dio, 'thought they should help those who were being held as prisoners'.

When did the awful realisation strike? At what point did Heliogabalus become 'aware that he was under guard and awaiting execution'? Perhaps when he saw those arrested begin to be released. Now his only hope was to escape from the camp.

Not everyone had deserted him. The young Emperor was 'placed in a chest' to be smuggled out of the gates. A jolting, claustrophobic journey, which ended in failure. The chest was opened and the fugitive discovered. Soaemias 'embraced him, and clung tightly to him'.

The display did not soften the hearts of the Praetorians. 'Believing the opportunity was right, and their case just', Herodian says, they killed both mother and son. We are not told who struck the first blows, or if they were fatal. Nor do we know if either tried to defend themselves. Our sources summarily despatch Heliogabalus and Soaemias. They are more interested in what happened next.

More were to die. The Praetorians slaughtered Fulvius, the prefect of the city, and both of their commanding officers: the prefects Antiochianus and ...ATVS. It is unlikely that Aristomachus, the tribune who had held back the standards in the first revolt, survived. Hierocles and Aurelius Eubulus were killed with their Emperor. The latter was 'torn to pieces by the populace and the soldiers'. Either the gates had been opened, or Eubulus had managed to get out of the camp, and the hunt for 'the attendants and confederates' of the Emperor extended across the city.

In the *Augustan History*, the Emperor's 'accomplices' die first. The Praetorians formed a conspiracy to 'free the *Res Publica*'. In this story, set implicitly in the palace, the killings are symbolic: 'some by tearing out their vital organs, and others by piercing the anus, so that their deaths were as evil as their lives. Next they fell upon Heliogabalus himself, and slew him in a latrine, where he had taken refuge.'

Killing the Emperor and his mother was not enough. Their heads were cut off and their corpses stripped naked. The bodies, according to Herodian, 'were handed over to those who wished to drag them around and desecrate them. After being dragged through the city for a long time and mutilated, they were thrown into the sewers that run down to the Tiber.' Cassius Dio has the corpse of Soaemias cast aside 'somewhere or other', and that of Heliogabalus thrown straight into the river. The *Augustan History* elaborates what its author had found in Herodian: the route through the streets included the Circus Maximus – the sewer was too small, so Heliogabalus' corpse was pulled out and taken to the Aemilian Bridge, from which it was cast into the Tiber with a weight attached, so it could never be buried. The Pons Aemilius was a real bridge, but the name Aemilius featured elsewhere in fictional passages of the *Augustan History*.

'Their heads were cut off, and their bodies, after being stripped naked, were dragged all over the city.' It took a certain sort of woman to watch that happen to her daughter or sister. Yet Maesa and Mamaea had won. Now they had to secure the rule of Alexander.

CHAPTER 12   THE RECKONING

13 to 14 *March* AD222

| *The Trappings and the Name of Emperor*

While the corpse of his cousin was still being dragged through the streets of Rome, Alexander was acclaimed Emperor by the soldiers. In the confusion, it might not have been until the next day that the Senate voted him the necessary legal powers: the *maius imperium* and the *tribunicia potestas*. Certainly, later in his reign, the 14 March was celebrated as the day he had become *Pontifex Maximus*.

The new Emperor reigned as Marcus Aurelius Severus Alexander. He was thirteen. According to Herodian, 'he possessed the trappings and the name of Emperor, but the control of administration and imperial policy was in the hands of his womenfolk'. Maesa and Mamaea moved to secure the regime. Loyal men were appointed to the vital positions. The arch-survivor Comazon returned for an unprecedented third stint as prefect of the city. The Praetorians were given two new prefects. Julius Flavianus had held the post before, as Comazon's colleague at the start of Heliogabalus' reign, when that Emperor had left government in the hands of his grandmother. Similarly,

Geminius Chrestus had been selected by Maesa as prefect of Egypt back in AD219. Most likely all three were on hand and ready on 13 March. Between them they now commanded all the troops that mattered in Rome: the urban cohorts, the Praetorians, the imperial horse guards (*equites singulares Augusti*) and the feared secret service (*frumentarii*). Any shortage of grain would cause the plebs of Rome to riot. The jurist Ulpian either was appointed or retained as prefect of the grain supply (*praefectus annonae*).

The first reform of the new regime was a significant act of political theatre. The Senate was allowed to select from its membership sixteen councillors and advisers to the Emperor. Herodian says they were 'men who presented the appearance of greatest dignity of years and the most moderate way of life'. Of course, this group had no more power than the usual imperial *Consilium* (which, given its ad hoc membership, continued to exist), but it was a strong public statement: this regime is not like the last; the traditional elite will be honoured and respected and its views heeded.

Punitive measures further distanced Alexander's rule from that of his predecessor. The memory of Heliogabalus was formally condemned, and the public responded with enthusiasm. We have seen that an individual in Nicaea defaced the Emperor's image on a coin with a chisel. Greek cities also took official measures, countermarking their local coinage featuring Heliogabalus with either the letter A or a small male bust, both 'claiming' the coins for Alexander. Across the empire, some or all of Heliogabalus' official names were chiselled off inscriptions. On some statues the sensory organs – eyes, nose, mouth and ears – of his face were defaced. These statues were either cast down, or left in place, rather like the corpse of a condemned criminal on the cross. Other statues were unharmed, but taken down and hidden away in storage, with the intention that they would later be recut as another Emperor. The intention was not always carried out, as with the famous 'Type Two' portrait bust from the Capitoline (Image 9).

One well-known statue allows us to recreate its 'biography' and see an unusual variation of the process of condemnation in action.

There are several things wrong with this statue of Alexander Severus, now in the Museo Nazionale Archeologico in Naples. The features of the face do not quite fit with the turn of the head. The head itself looks unnaturally wide in profile. The full curls of the hair at the back of the head contrast with the short locks at the front. If you look carefully, you can see the line of a join running from under the chin, in front of the ears and across the crown of the skull.

Image 19: A Statue of Heliogabalus Remodelled as Alexander

The features of Alexander have replaced those of his predecessor. The statue was discovered in the Baths of Caracalla, to which Heliogabalus had added a portico. Originally it would have stood on a plinth and been placed in a niche. Carved from one block of marble, it presented Heliogabalus larger than life, heavily muscled and in heroic nudity, wearing just the short cloak of a general and holding a staff of military office. The palm tree, which supports the Emperor's weight-bearing right leg, was a symbol of military victory. This hyper-masculine image – don't worry about the seemingly tiny penis: the original has been removed, possibly to facilitate the addition of a modesty-preserving fig leaf at some point – may have been designed as a counter to contemporary stories about his effeminacy. Although, given the rumours that he employed the *frumentarii* to discover well-endowed men to be taken to the palace for his pleasure, encountering a naked image of Heliogabalus in the baths may have evoked a measure of disquiet. Well, at least, among those who thought themselves suitably qualified.

After Heliogabalus was killed, someone climbed a ladder and attacked his features with a hammer and chisel. The eyes, nose and mouth suffered. The ears are undamaged. For at least three years the statue was left on display in its mutilated state. In AD225, or sometime thereafter, a sculptor climbed up and chiselled smooth what was left of Heliogabalus' face. Another piece of marble was sculpted into a mask of the face of Alexander, complete with vestigial moustache and more luxuriant sideburns. Alexander was first depicted with facial hair in AD225, which gives us the earliest date for the remodelling. The mask was fitted onto the head and one Emperor replaced another. The incongruities of the fit were less apparent to contemporaries, as the statue could only be viewed from directly in front and gazing upwards. Also, it would have been painted, which disguised the line of the join.

Ironically, the tough martial image suited Alexander no better. In AD235 the soldiers mocked him as a weak little boy tied to his mother's apron strings – he was about twenty-seven! – before killing him because of his failure to fight the Germanic tribes. The memory of Alexander also was condemned. This time the statue was removed, presumably to some storeroom in the baths complex, to await another repurposing that never came.

The indignities inflicted on the corpse of Soaemias were unprecedented. Previous imperial women had been executed, even beheaded, but none had been dragged naked through the streets of Rome. The memory of Heliogabalus' mother was condemned. The obliteration of her image was so thorough that no sculptural portraits of Soaemias have been securely identified. In the Greek East her coins, like those of her son, were counter-marked. On only three surviving inscriptions is her name undamaged. A statue base stood in the Forum honouring Soaemias, her mother and her son. When Heliogabalus fell, it was removed. Thirteen years later, when Alexander in turn had been killed and the dynasty was ended, the names of all three were defaced. As an added denigration the stone was reused face down as a step behind the Senate House.

Aquilia Severa, the ex-Vestal and last wife of Heliogabalus, may well have been killed with her husband. Again, her name is defaced on inscriptions, and her eastern coins countermarked. A bronze portrait from Sparta, identified as Aquilia, was mutilated in antiquity, although probably this was the work of the later campaign of vandalism against pagan art carried out by Christian iconoclasts. Heliogabalus had boasted that the following year he would be consul with a natural son. Maesa and Mamaea were ruthless. If there was a risk that Aquilia was pregnant, she could not be allowed to live to produce a potential heir to the murdered Emperor.

An inscription survives on which the name of Annia Faustina has been defaced. She was the penultimate wife of Heliogabalus, divorced so that he could remarry Aquilia. It is unlikely that her memory was condemned with that of the Emperor. Reprisals did not go that far. There are two other possibilities. One is that provincials were not always well informed about the imperial court. When news arrived of the death of Heliogabalus, the inscription of Annia Faustina was attacked by those unaware of her divorce. Or, perhaps, during the intense faction fight in the imperial court in the last months of the reign, she was not only divorced but also executed, at the command of her ex-husband.

Heliogabalus and all his prominent supporters were dead and their memories condemned. Except one – the god Elagabal. Any god, even one of whom you disapproved, by definition was immortal. In pagan thought a deity could not be killed by mortals, nor could its memory be extinguished. But its worship in Rome and Italy could be banned. Although the name of the Emesene god was chiselled off some inscriptions, an official ban is uncertain. There was no question of the Emperor or Senate declaring a formal *damnatio memoriae*. They lacked the power. But the movements of a deity could be controlled. A god could be constrained in one place. Two cities in Asia had ordered statues of Ares, the god of war, bound in chains to prevent him going to the aid of their enemies, the Isaurian tribesmen in the hills. And a god could be summoned. The Romans had a ritual called *evocatio*, to bring over the gods of their enemies and other people. Just as a god could be brought to Rome, so it could be sent away. The great black stone was despatched back to its home in Emesa. The temple of Elagabal on the Palatine was rededicated to Jupiter Ultor, *Jupiter the Avenger*.

The worship of Elagabal continued in Emesa, as did the local influence of the extended dynasty. A generation later, Uranius

Antoninus, a short-lived pretender from the city, who almost certainly claimed to be a descendant of the royal house, featured the black stone on his coins. Half a century after the death of Heliogabalus, the Emperor Aurelian, attributing his victory in battle at Emesa to divine aid, would reintroduce the deity to Rome, although without the huge black stone, and not under the name Elagabal, but the more general, and more acceptable, title of Sol Invictus, the *Invincible Sun*.

That all lay far in the future. For now, in March AD222, Heliogabalus was dead and Elagabal was gone. Alexander was secure on the throne and Maesa and Mamaea controlled the compliant young Emperor. Normality was restored and Jupiter had achieved his *Vengeance*.

II *The Hatred of Everyone*

Being Emperor was a vertiginous balancing act, trying to satisfy the mutually exclusive and fiercely competitive desires of Senate, army, *Familia Caesaris* and plebs of Rome. No other Emperor failed quite as spectacularly as Heliogabalus. Almost two centuries later, the author of the *Augustan History* (not mentioning the staff of the palace, to whom he was especially hostile) sententiously summed it up: 'those who do not win the love of the Senate, the people, and the soldiers do not win the right of burial'.

The Senate had no reason to love Heliogabalus. He failed to show due respect for the venerable institution: using the imperial titles before they were voted; on at least two occasions bringing women into the House; and on 1 January AD222 keeping them waiting for six hours. He promoted to high office individuals from outside the traditional elite: granting the ex-centurion Claudius Pollio the status of a consul, and employing him, between two prestigious governorships, as spokesman for the regime to the Senate; and twice appointing the ex-auxiliary ranker Comazon as prefect of the city. As we saw earlier, it was believed that he first wanted to appoint as Caesar the freedman Eutychianus and then the charioteer Hierocles. No attempt was made to play the *Civilis Princeps*. Instead of spending his time with senators of 'moderate way of life' and 'dignity of years', Heliogabalus preferred the company of young charioteers and athletes, like his sexual partners Hierocles and Zoticus. The Emperor displayed an unbecoming levity: personally throwing gifts to the plebs and driving in chariot races, where he saluted the president of the games and begged for gold coins as if he were an ordinary contestant. Heliogabalus was feared as well as loathed. Senators were executed, and their estates confiscated, throughout his reign. In senatorial eyes many of the victims had done no wrong: they were men like Claudius Attalus, sacrificed to the revenge of Comazon, or Pomponius Basus, who died because of the beauty of his wife. To men so painfully conscious of their *dignitas*, perhaps even worse than the fear of execution were the humiliations. The *Augustan History* has Heliogabalus forcing elderly senators to drive chariots as after dinner entertainment and making a joke of their virility at a wine festival. Even if such stories are not believed, various senators were in the audience when he raced chariots, and the whole Senate had to attend the dawn rituals and the annual procession of Elagabal. Participation in the Emesene religion was not only a degrading humiliation but also a threat to the *Pax Deorum*. It posed a risk to the very safety or health (*Salus*) and thus the existence of Rome. Cassius Dio singled out placing Elagabal before Jupiter as the worst of the Emperor's many wrongdoings.

Heliogabalus and the army got off to a good start. Dressed as a young Caracalla, at Raphaneae he made an effective speech to the troops. On horseback, brandishing a sword, he rallied his army at Immae. Generous cash donatives were frequently distributed during the reign. Yet already by the first winter in Nicomedia, if not that autumn in Antioch, things were going wrong. There was a wave of military revolts in the East before he left. The Third Gallic Legion, which had first come over to him, and was the unit most attuned to the worship of Elagabal, was cashiered after its second uprising. In Nicomedia, when Heliogabalus ordered the soldiers to kill Eutychianus, they did not obey until the Emperor himself had struck the first blow. Heliogabalus toured the garrisons along the Danube on his way to Rome, although the highly sexualised statue from Carnuntum may indicate that his self-presentation as high priest of Elagabal was not universally welcomed. Once the Emperor had entered Rome, we never hear of him visiting or addressing the garrison of the city, until the crises of the last months of the reign forced him to the Praetorian camp. In the first unrest, initially he tried to leave it to their prefects to calm the Praetorians. The soldiers demanding the surrender of the Emperor's 'companions in lewdness' demonstrates that they did not approve of his sex life. Their insistence that Alexander appear in the Temple of Mars in the camp symbolises their commitment to the traditional gods and their alienation from the black stone of Emesa.

As always, the feelings of the *Familia Caesaris* have to be inferred, rather than vouchsafed by adducing specific items of evidence. The imperial staff will have disapproved of the introduction of outsiders, like Hierocles and (briefly) Zoticus, to positions of influence on the Palatine. Similarly, if it is true that he opened a brothel in the palace, that will have outraged their sense of the stately decorum that should surround the figure of the Emperor. They will have been appalled when Heliogabalus slipped out of the palace, escaping their oversight, to roam the streets at night.

Most importantly, the ceremonies they controlled, such as the morning *Salutatio*, where they carefully choreographed admission to the imperial presence, were overshadowed by those of Elagabal, which were orchestrated by the Emperor himself and the priests he had brought from Phoenicia.

The urban plebs of Rome should have loved Heliogabalus. He did all the things that won their favour. First – and so obvious it is easy to overlook – he remained in Rome. The plebs wanted their Emperor on hand, not touring the provinces, or inspecting the armies on the frontiers, or fighting wars in distant barbarian lands. They wanted him on hand to give them things: more things than just the regular 'Bread and Circuses'. Heliogabalus obliged. Four cash handouts (*congiaria*) in four years: a higher frequency than in any other reign. 'He instituted many different festivals,' Herodian says, 'and constructed circuses for horse racing, and theatres, imagining if he provided chariot races, and all kinds of spectacles and entertainments, and if he feasted the people all night long, he would be popular.' A late source, Hydatius, whose value is uncertain, claims that he burnt the records of debt to the imperial treasury. It is said they were so numerous that the bonfires lasted thirty days. If true, it would have been very welcome: the plebs always seem to have been deep in debt. Heliogabalus' building programme – especially the temple on the Palatine, the repairs to the Colosseum and the renovation of the Baths of Caracalla – provided much-needed paid employment.

The desires of the plebs were ideological as well as material. They wanted their Emperor to enter into their pleasures, to show a popular *levitas*. Heliogabalus drove a chariot in the colours of the green circus faction, threw tokens to the crowd at the spectacles, snuck down from the Palatine to visit brothels and perhaps established a brothel in the palace. The plebs warmed to an Emperor who escaped the protocols of the *Familia Caesaris*, ignored the soldiers and humiliated the Senate.

Yet, when Heliogabalus was dead, there were no signs of grief. Unlike with Nero, no slave with a physical resemblance gathered a following by announcing that he was the Emperor returned, somehow having escaped death. Again unlike for Nero, no one left flowers on his grave. Okay, the latter would have been difficult, as Heliogabalus had no grave, but they could have left some flowers somewhere, say scattered on the waters of the Tiber, or at the foot of the gigantic mutilated statue in the Baths of Caracalla.

Far from sorrow, the urban plebs appear to have felt a fierce joy. After the Emperor was killed, his partner in debauchery, the Emesene Aurelius Eubulus, whose surrender had been demanded previously, was torn to pieces by 'the populace and the soldiers'. The Praetorians handed over the corpses of the Emperor and his mother to 'those who wished to drag them around and desecrate them'. It was the urban plebs who hauled them on hooks through the streets and mutilated them, and who hurled that of Heliogabalus into the sewer that ran down to the Tiber.

What had gone wrong? Perhaps the *levitas* had gone too far. If people in reality were killed in the crush when Heliogabalus threw tokens to the crowd, it would be easy to assume that had been his intention. Heliogabalus' sex life alienated the plebs: his enjoyment of a passive role in male–male intercourse and his penchant for transgressive role play. An Emperor visiting brothels as a customer was one thing, but taking over the duties of the sex workers was quite another. Likewise, Caligula staffing a brothel in the palace with women from elite families brought the plebs double pleasure: sex combined with the degradation of the rich. It was a vastly different affair if it was the Emperor himself who was being degraded. Then there was religion. The plebs were devoted to the traditional gods, as the Christians were to discover to their cost in the persecutions later in the century. In Rome they had an especial regard for Jupiter Optimus Maximus. On 14 September AD217, at chariot races put on to celebrate the birthday of Diadumenianus, the plebs called upon Jupiter, declaring that he alone should be their leader. When the senators and equestrians praised Macrinus and his son, rather than join in the plebs raised their hands towards heaven and exclaimed: 'There is the Augustus of the Romans; having him we have everything!' As with all the other constituencies, placing Elagabal above Jupiter had turned the plebs from Heliogabalus. The final factor was the plebs' sense of natural justice. An Emperor who flouted this by attacking a member of his own family, who was popular with the plebs, brought odium on himself. The plebs were never reconciled to Augustus banishing his daughter Julia and continued to demand her return. Tiberius was hated for persecuting the family of Julia's daughter, Agrippina the Elder. The banishment, subsequent exile and execution of his wife Octavia for a time estranged Nero from the plebs. Alexander is said to have been popular, and as long as Heliogabalus 'continued to love his cousin he was safe'. It was the Emperor's attacks on his cousin, and adopted son, that dragged him to the Tiber.

The Senate, the army, the *Familia Caesaris* and the urban plebs – Heliogabalus had alienated all four of the crucial 'constituencies'. Every choice made by the Emperor backfired. Yet Heliogabalus was never passive, at least outside the bedroom or brothel. His innovations, above all in religion, undermine the modern scholarly orthodoxy that the role of an Emperor was essentially passive. They also cost him his life.

CHAPTER 13

THE AFTERLIFE OF HELIOGABALUS

Tyrant, Aesthete, Queer Icon,
Fashionista, in Art Criticism and as a
Roman Lady, AD222 *to* AD2022

Soon after Heliogabalus was killed, Aelian, the sophist and historian, was reading aloud. That was nothing unusual. Almost everyone at least moved their lips when reading. But Aelian was indignant and emphatic. When questioned by his fellow sophist Philostratus of Lemnos, Aelian said, 'I have composed *An Indictment of Gynnis* [the 'womanish-man'], for by that name I call the tyrant who has just been put to death, because by every sort of wanton wickedness he disgraced the Roman Empire.' The Lemnian replied, 'I should admire you for it, if you had indicted him while he was alive.'

As soon as Heliogabalus was safely dead, contemporaries portrayed him as a monstrous tyrant. Yet there is no reason to think that either Aelian or Philostratus of Lemnos was trotting out some 'official narrative', or propaganda, of the new regime. Now they were free to express emotions it had been unsafe to voice under Heliogabalus. Philostratus the Athenian, great-uncle and father-in-law of the Lemnian, perhaps recounted the anecdote not just to demonstrate the wit and sagacity of his relative but also implicitly to exculpate his own role under the dead Emperor: *everyone was scared, and no one dared speak out, so don't blame me for that poem in which I applauded Heliogabalus.*

After holding the consulship with the Emperor Alexander Severus in AD229, Cassius Dio retired to his properties at Nicaea in Bithynia to finish writing his *Roman History*, a monumental work in eighty books from the earliest times to his own day. Cassius Dio was much like Tacitus, except without the insight or the literary genius: a senator who accepted the need for the rule of Emperors – *pray for good Emperors, but serve what you get* – yet who looked back fondly to the senatorial independence of the free Republic. Both blithely ignored the fact that in the Republic, with their provincial origins, they would not even have been Roman citizens, let alone senators.

As we have seen, Cassius Dio thought Heliogabalus the very worst of Emperors. Although he stated that placing the black stone of Emesa in front of Jupiter was the most serious transgression, he devoted more space to condemning Heliogabalus' sexuality and his bad treatment of the Senate: all those violations of precedent and those executions on trumped-up charges. There was no need to follow any official line: Cassius Dio had a very personal reason to distance himself from the regime of Heliogabalus.

Cassius Dio firmly locates himself in Rome in the spring of AD218 – seated in the Senate, listening to despatches from the East – during the revolt that brought Heliogabalus to the throne. He stresses that it was Macrinus who had appointed him as *Curator* of the cities of Pergamum and Smyrna. Then he becomes reticent, glossing over the fact that he actually held the post under Heliogabalus. Cassius Dio travelled to the province of Asia later in AD218. By the end of that year, Heliogabalus had taken up residence at Nicomedia in the neighbouring province of Bithynia, close to Cassius Dio's hometown of Nicaea. If there was a visit to the imperial court, it is not mentioned.

Cassius Dio gives a summary of his later career after recounting the death of Heliogabalus: *after going from Asia into Bithynia, I fell sick, and from there I hastened to my province of Africa; then on returning to Italy I was almost immediately sent as governor first to Dalmatia and then to Pannonia Superior, and though after that I returned to Rome and Campania* [when, as he tells us a few paragraphs later, he held the consulship in AD229], *I at once set out for home.* The reader is meant to assume that after leaving Asia, Cassius Dio was indisposed in his hometown for the remainder of the reign of Heliogabalus, and that all the posts from Africa onwards were held under Alexander. But this is not explicitly stated, and the normal tenure of these posts argues against the assumption. The proconsulship of Africa technically was a post awarded by the Senate, and so was held for one year. The governors of Dalmatia and Pannonia Superior, however, were legates (deputies) of the Emperor, who usually remained in office for three years. Yet, in the normal run of things, these three posts would occupy more than seven years, as it was rare to move from one governorship to another without an interval, and virtually unprecedented to then go directly to a third. From the death of Heliogabalus in March AD222 to the end of December AD228 (before Cassius Dio became consul on 1 January AD229) was just under seven years.

The historian seems to have given the game away just before the summary of his career: *Thus far* (to the death of Heliogabalus) *I have described events with as great accuracy as I could in every case, but for subsequent events I have not found it possible to give an accurate account, for the reason that I did not spend much time in Rome.* Although intended to imply that the offices he goes on to list were all under Alexander, it looks like an inadvertent admission that he was in Rome for more than just those first months of the reign of Heliogabalus, when the Emperor was still absent. It is almost certain that Cassius Dio was appointed to Africa by Heliogabalus, and quite possibly the same was true of Dalmatia. Cassius Dio had good reason to distance himself from a regime he had loathed and now condemned, but in which he had held high office and been deeply complicit.

Despite confident modern assertions, the life of Herodian is a mystery. The Alps, he writes, are bigger than 'anything in our part of the world'. So, as we would expect, he came from the Greek half of the empire, but no greater precision is possible. A single phrase about his 'imperial and civic service' is the only evidence for his career. The word for 'service' he uses elsewhere for those of quite low rank. On this has been built the modern orthodoxy that he was an ex-slave. That is a lot of weight to put on one word, and, of course, he could have been self-deprecating. His lack of interest in the Senate indicates that he was not a senator. Beyond that we really do not know, and, as we will see in a moment, his world view was very much that of the Greek elite. One certainty is the date *after* which he was writing. He says he will write the history of seventy years. As his work starts in AD 180, that means to AD 250. Herodian wrote those words after that date. What survives of the text actually ends after fifty-eight years in AD 238. This has encouraged modern scholars to exercise enormous ingenuity in trying to explain away the 'seventy years', and, for reasons I find incomprehensible, put the composition of his *History after the Emperor Marcus* in the AD 240s, or even AD 230s.

Herodian constructed his *History* in an interesting way. Roman Emperors were judged on their attitude to Greek culture (*paideia*). Heliogabalus wanted to send away Alexander's tutors in *paideia*, and have his cousin trained in his own leaping and dancing in worship of Elagabal. For Herodian, Heliogabalus was the enemy of Greek *paideia*, being the follower of an alien and barbaric culture. Again, there is no reason to believe that in this interpretation, so pleasing to the Greek elite, and written at least fifteen years after the death of Alexander, Herodian was wheeling out an 'official narrative' put out by the regime that succeeded Heliogabalus.

Herodian was much closer to a modern historical novelist than to a modern historian. Which is not to say that he was indifferent to the historical truth, or working to some understanding of historicity radically different to ours. Instead, like a novelist, he operated on a system of 'true enough'. He was happy to alter, omit or invent, if it suited the story he was telling. Remember Macrinus' exciting attempt to escape by boat – the fugitive Emperor gets within sight of Byzantium before a contrary wind gets up and sweeps him back to his fate.

Another near contemporary, the author of the *Twelfth Sibylline Oracle*, is usually overlooked (indeed this is his first mention in this book!). The surviving *Sibylline Oracles* are not to be confused with those consulted by priests in Rome. The texts we have are popular history, pretending to be oracular prophesies of the future. They were written in the eastern half of the empire, in often not very good Greek hexameter verse. Although deliberately obscurantist, their general tone is anti-Roman. They are resistance literature, often mixing the viewpoints of different alienated groups – pagan, Jewish and Christian – within one oracle.

The latest historical figure in the *Twelfth Sibylline Oracle* is Alexander Severus. So it was written sometime after his death in AD235. Its main message appears to be Jewish – 'do not be an idolater' – and hostile to Rome, which will 'make amends for all that it alone did formerly in many wars'. Here Heliogabalus is a priest with barbarian customs, who acts deceitfully towards his infant Caesar. After he is killed in war, the populace tear his corpse apart. The Emperor was a thoroughly bad ruler – as 'Temple-warden' he would have been a keen worshipper of idols – who gets what he deserves. His death in war is an odd mistake – the memory of Heliogabalus was already slipping out of control – but the *Twelfth Sibylline Oracle* is also wrong about the deaths of the Emperors Tiberius, Vespasian, Titus, Domitian, Nerva and Verus.

Later antiquity shared the view of Heliogabalus as an abominable tyrant. That is how he appears in the three brief and often inaccurate late fourth-century Latin histories of Eutropius, Aurelius Victor and the anonymous *Epitome*, preserved in the works of Victor. But it was their contemporary, the author of the *Augustan History*, who created the extraordinary monster of all depravity that became the dominant image of the Emperor in later ages.

A series of biographies of Emperors pretending to be written by six men around AD 300, but actually composed by one man about a century later: so much is agreed about the *Augustan History* by all sensible and well-informed scholars. The anachronisms and the personal names from late antiquity confirm the date; the unchanging interests and literary tone, as well as the cross references, do the same for the solitary author. It is a long text – three volumes in the Loeb edition – and would have taken time. Why undertake such an effort? No one knows. My favourite explanation was offered, with a slyness worthy of its subject, by Sir Ronald Syme. The writer was a schoolmaster – the infantile humour fits, as does the didactic pedantry – who, sick of the mockery of his pupils, and the contempt of the wider world, decided to get his own back with an inventive literary fraud.

The *Life of Heliogabalus* played a significant, and often overlooked, role in the literary development of the unknown author.

The 'Lives' can be divided into two types. There are the 'Major Lives' of important Emperors, which are underpinned by real history, enlivened by flashes of invention. And there are the 'Minor Lives' of imperial princes and often ephemeral rulers, which are entirely fiction, except for the occasional fact. All the 'Major Lives' happen before Heliogabalus: afterwards there is nothing but 'Minor Lives'. The change happens halfway through the *Life of Heliogabalus*: at section 18.1 out of 35.7 to be precise.

There are two ways of looking at this. First, the downbeat view. Heliogabalus broke the author. Faced with the bizarreness of the Emperor, he just gave up. What was the point in going to all the trouble of research to anchor his biographies in historical fact, when you ended up with this sort of stuff? Second, the positive interpretation. Heliogabalus freed the author. In the eccentricities, even madness, of the Emperor the writer discovered his true metier – wildly inventive alternative fiction. No reader can doubt the exuberant creativity of the lives after Heliogabalus. Snatches of autobiographies of the 'six authors' frame the biographies, official documents and imperial letters provide authentication, scholarly digressions discuss sources, while literary poems and jokes enliven these stories featuring a cast of dozens of courtiers, generals and imperial relatives – almost all of whom are invented. Even some of the Emperors themselves are the products of the author's imagination: Celsus, devoured by dogs, but unique in sharing with Christ his image appearing on a cross; or Firmus, that prodigious drinker, who swam with crocodiles and 'rode about sitting on huge ostriches, so that he seemed to be flying'.

After the West had fallen in the fifth century, the memory of Heliogabalus remained alive in the surviving eastern half of the empire, conventionally known as Byzantium. He appeared in the histories of Zosimus (around AD 500) and Zonaras (in the twelfth century). But by now he was a minor character from the very distant past. Mistakes were made. The thirteenth-century chronicler Theodorus Skoutariotes must have confused him with another Antoninus, maybe Marcus Aurelius, to describe him as 'eloquent, an excellent man, fierce in battle, gentle, wise, swift, conciliating all and justifiably loved by all'.

In the Middle Ages in the West, Heliogabalus was completely forgotten. He returned with the Renaissance rediscovery of Classical texts and the introduction of the printing press. The image of the Emperor in the *Augustan History* held the floor. It was published first (in 1475, Herodian appearing in 1490, and the relevant books of Cassius Dio not until 1551). More people could read its original Latin than the Greek of the other texts, although vernacular translations of all three were soon published. Above all, its fiction, especially the second half of the biography (all of which was taken as fact), was far more temptingly sensational.

A direct line of descent can be drawn from the *Augustan History*-led popular image of the tyrant in the Renaissance to that of today. Take *Being an Account of the Life and Death of the Emperor Heliogabolus*, an online comic written and drawn by Neil Gaiman in twenty-four hours in 1992 (maybe that is why he spelt the Emperor's name that way). An awful lot of the *Augustan History* gets crammed into a few pages – the guests smothered by flowers, the wild animals in the dinners, the meals of flamingo brains, the schoolboys calling him Varius, the men hung like asses, the marriage to Zoticus, the chariot pulled by naked women and dogs and stags and lions… Even a few things get added: Heliogabolus (*sic*) makes his horse a consul, becomes the penetrator in male–male sex and adds crocodiles to the list of animals pulling the chariot. About the latter, Gaiman says, 'However, I can find no reference to this anywhere.' Which is just the sort of joke the author of the *Augustan History* loved.

There is an alternative to condemning the tyrant. Back in the second half of the nineteenth century, a rather different version of Heliogabalus was created. The Emperor's contempt for convention, his androgyny and perversity, even his cruelty: all these had an allure for the Decadent Movement with its profound antipathy to bourgeois morality. Mainly using the *Augustan History*, they reimagined him as one of their own: a sensual hedonist and aesthete. Although only mentioned once, Heliogabalus joins the real Count Robert de Montesquiou lurking behind the hero, des Esseintes, in the ultimate Decadent novel *À Rebours* (usually translated as *Against Nature*) by Joris-Karl Huysmans (1884): all that artifice – endless things dressed up to seem like something else – all that obsession with colours, never mind the rejection of societal norms.

It was against the background of the Decadent Movement's remodelling of the Emperor that Alma-Tadema painted *The Roses of Heliogabalus*. So, near the end of this book, we end up back where we started: looking at people being smothered by flower petals. Alma-Tadema was a thoughtful painter, who did prodigious amounts of research. Things do not appear in his paintings without a reason. It is worth looking carefully.

Let's start with the bronze statue group that stands at the back, but at the highest point in the centre of the painting. Alma-Tadema often made his viewers think 'where am I meant to be concentrating?', 'who is the main character?', by arranging his human subjects off-centre. The statue is the god Bacchus with a faun and panther. It clearly indicates that this is a Classical scene, as opposed to biblical, or oriental. But it also carries another meaning. Alma-Tadema copied a real sculpture from the Vatican Museum, of which he had a photograph in his extensive collection. The original, in marble, is Bacchus with his lover Ampelus. This version is a coded reference to the homosexuality of the Emperor.

The use of the statue group is clever, yet straightforward. Things get more uncertain and speculative, and thus more interesting, when we turn to the humans. Not the ones being suffocated – they are just extras – but the ones on the high table with Heliogabalus. A recent study sees two men and four women. Referencing a line in the *Augustan History* which states that the Emperor liked to place perverts beside him at dinner, it suggests the man nearest to the Emperor is Zoticus. Except this is not a young and beautiful athlete, but someone older and plain. The figure wears female dangling gold earrings. Well, Heliogabalus wears small gold earrings, so maybe this is another, and less subtle, nudge towards his homosexuality? But compare this figure's face with that of the Emperor. They look similar, perhaps close enough to suggest a family resemblance? Heliogabalus only had one living male relative. This is not the twelve-year-old Alexander. The resemblance becomes clear if we compare it to another painting of the same family by Alma-Tadema: *Caracalla and Geta* (1907).

Image 20: *Caracalla and Geta* by Alma-Tadema

Look at the oldest woman in *Caracalla and Geta*, the one sitting next to Septimius Severus, turning to look out at us: Julia Domna. Her long-nosed, severe face closely resembles the person next to Heliogabalus in *The Roses of Heliogabalus*, because the latter is not a man at all, but Domna's sister Julia Maesa, the Emperor's grandmother. A younger, prettier version of Maesa stands in *Caracalla and Geta* with her hand on Geta's shoulder, hinting at her future role as maker of young Emperors. If you want further proof, look back at the contemporary portrait of Maesa in Image 3. Alma-Tadema had drawn the physiognomies of the imperial women from their coins.

If the nearest figure is Maesa, who on earth is the next one along? Holding up a cup, a flushed and fat face, no earrings – this is a drunk man, well past youth. Certainly not Zoticus or Hierocles then. Given there are three other Emesenes in the picture (we will get to number three in a moment), it is tempting to suggest Aurelius Eubulus, from Cassius Dio, the Emperor's financial officer and 'companion in lewdness'. But Alma-Tadema primarily was working from the *Augustan History*. 'He frequently invited the Prefect of the City to a drinking-bout after a banquet, and also summoned the Praetorian Prefects.' That is where we are: the fruit is on the table, the meal is over, everyone on the high table has a cup in hand. This is one of those prefects, who will share the fate of Heliogabalus: most likely the prefect of the city, Fulvius Diogenianus.

Of the four women on the right as we look at the high table, the one nearest to us is older than the others, and again has a family resemblance to the Emperor. Probably it is the Emperor's mother, Soaemias. She may also be shown, as the younger woman on the viewer's left, in *Caracalla and Geta*. If that is her, it adds a sexual charge to the painting. As she innocently, or not so innocently, leans over the balustrade, Caracalla gazes intently at her accentuated buttocks. The adultery that conceived Heliogabalus is in the air. In *The Roses of Heliogabalus*, if the dark-haired woman is Soaemias, who are the rest? Most likely the three named wives of Heliogabalus.

If these identifications are correct, in the painting Alma-Tadema has given us a symbolic scale of the realities of power under Heliogabalus: closest to the Emperor is his grandmother Maesa, composed and shrewd, then the officers of state, represented by a drunk and corrupt prefect, and finally his frivolous and ineffectual mother and wives.

It is easy to think of the wives of Heliogabalus as victims: married and divorced, even humiliated at his whim – remember his 'indecent' behaviour in his marriages. That is not how Alma-Tadema depicts them. In the painting they watch the killings with interest: two of them twist round to get a better view, and one is smiling. Yet with their pale skin, and pink cheeks, they look like Victorian society beauties. Perhaps they represent a warning, or a moral lesson, about innocence corrupted?

Where characters are looking is often important in paintings. Everyone on the high table is looking at the roses falling from the ceiling or at the guests being suffocated. Except the Emperor, who is gazing at an extraordinary figure at the bottom right. (Actually, one of the 'wives' seems to be peering round the column at him too.) This figure – in no danger, only a few petals have drifted that far – returns the gaze. Neither betrays any obvious emotion. The figure is clad in barbaric splendour, with multiple gold chains around his neck. Because he has fair hair, he has been identified as Hierocles, the charioteer from Caria in Asia Minor who became the Emperor's husband. But Hierocles, in the first bloom of youth, had smooth cheeks. This is a mature man with a full beard. His exotic hairstyle gives a clue. Alma-Tadema was widely read in Classical history and deeply informed about archaeology. He would have known this was a 'Suebian top-knot', worn by ancient Germanic warriors, mentioned by Tacitus, and found on some of the 'bog bodies' discovered in Scandinavia in the nineteenth century.

None of our ancient sources place a northern barbarian at the court of Heliogabalus. The only link to *Germania* is the fiction in the *Augustan History* that the Emperor failed to start a war with the Marcomanni. Perhaps that was inspiration enough for Alma-Tadema. Consider the original viewers, and their (and our) viewpoint. *The Roses of Heliogabalus* was first exhibited at the Royal Academy in London in 1888. The British Empire liked to look back to that of Rome, often as an admirable precursor, sometimes as a moral warning. At the same time the nineteenth-century English liked to stress the fine moral qualities they had inherited from their Anglo-Saxon, and thus northern Germanic, ethnicity. For well-informed English contemporaries, in *The Roses of Heliogabalus* Alma-Tadema had placed one of their distant forebears at the heart of the decadence of the Roman Empire. It could have been intended to prompt reflection on the two empires. Especially as those viewing the painting were further implicated. They watch the roses fall from a raised, and safe position, opposite the high table where Heliogabalus reclines. As, of course, we do as well.

Finally, look out beyond the dining room. The story in the *Augustan History* implicitly is set in Rome. Why has Alma-Tadema moved it to the countryside? If it was not just that he enjoyed, and was good at, painting landscape backgrounds, there are two ways of thinking about those rolling hills. Maybe the corruption of Heliogabalus has spread from the city to endanger nature itself. The pictured hills, however, are untouched by man. Maybe there is a positive message: the hills are still there, but the decadence of the foreground has long since passed.

It is impossible to overstate the importance of *The Roses of Heliogabalus* in shaping subsequent popular understanding of the Emperor. Where the image of Heliogabalus appears in the modern world it is always that of the *Augustan History* filtered through the huge (seven foot by four foot) painting by Alma-Tadema.

Although a *heliogábalo* is a hedonist in Spanish, the modern image of Heliogabalus is extremely limited. His name means nothing to most people in the English-speaking world. The Emperor has vanished from mainstream culture. He has retreated to the margins. Yet now and then he can be glimpsed in unexpected places.

Heliogabalus has become an unlikely cult hero, or 'queer icon', in some quarters of the LGBT+ community. Type *Heliogabalus Gay*, or *Trans*, *Hero* into a search engine. Among the endless porn – novels, videos and art – you find earnest sites hailing him on such lines as 'one of the most prominent and cultivated transsexual women of antiquity'. Aspects of his appeal are obvious: his liking to be penetrated, wearing female clothing and inquiring about a physical sex change. But making him a hero involves eliding, or ignoring altogether, everything else about his character: the irresponsibility and extravagance, the killings, and, above all, the religious fanaticism. As a scholar said, 'Queer icons are nothing if not malleable.'

Occasionally, Heliogabalus is summoned up (always *à la* Tadema) in the vacuous publicity of fashion houses. Here is the creative director of a collection inspired by Heliogabalus: *Each rose petal resembles a dot that aligns with one another to form geometric shapes on the fabric, just like how the painting highlights exuberant contrasts between the colors, the romantic ideas, and the narratives*. The contrasts, romantic ideas and narratives are all a bit puzzling. More straightforward is this comment on a show featuring a runway strewn with petals: *The earthly Paradise Collection was inspired by The Roses of Heliogabalus by Sir Lawrence Alma-Tadema, 1888. The opulence of a bed of roses… what could be more romantic.*

Yet fashion houses can't hold a candle to modern art criticism when it comes to pretentious and meaningless prose. Here is an exegesis of an awning called *The Roses of Heliogabalus*, designed to be installed over the Ponte Sisto in Rome and scatter petals on passing pedestrians.

> *Using 'the beautiful' to establish the dynamics of attraction and repulsion, a texture (the flower petal) is plucked from ubiquity to saturate the scene in excess… By consuming the proscenium of the everyday, the disproportion of opportunities for 'the beautiful' will inevitably subvert the ordinary scripts of the bridge and engender any number of possible playful outcomes, perhaps even unhinging pre-existing feelings – annoyance to joy, flirtation to loneliness.*

No one deserves this, not even Heliogabalus.

Yet perhaps Heliogabalus had the last laugh. Hidden away in an obscure collection at Newby Hall in Yorkshire is an antique portrait labelled, 'Bust of a Roman Lady, Roman imperial period'.

Image 21: 'A Roman Lady'?

The bust was heavily restored in the eighteenth century. Only the central 'mask' from below the hairline to above the nose is original and unaltered. It is enough to see that she has sideburns. These and the shape of the eyes match Type Two portraits of Heliogabalus, such as the one in the Capitoline Museum. After fifteen hundred years Heliogabalus finally got what he wanted: 'Call me not Lord, for I am a Lady'.

AUTHOR'S NOTE

The origins of this book go back a very long way. I first met Heliogabalus in the pages of Alfred Duggan's novel *Family Favourites* when I was an undergraduate at Lancaster University. My MPhil thesis at Manchester University was a commentary on Herodian on the Emperor. 'So, you want to be Suetonius to Heliogabalus?' The Cambridge don who asked the question was not unsympathetic, but made it clear that a biography was not suitable for a doctoral thesis. The research for my DPhil at Oxford took other directions, but my interest in Heliogabalus remained. Over the years it led to several scholarly articles on Herodian and Cassius Dio. It was more acceptable for an ancient historian trying to make a career to write about the sources rather than the Emperor himself.

Forty years after my first encounter with Heliogabalus, Sam Carter at Oneworld commissioned me to write the Emperor's biography. Over the decades my ideas had changed. Now I not only wanted to recreate the extraordinary life of the Emesene youth who ruled the Roman Empire, but, inspired by Georges Duby's *The Legend of Bouvines*, I realised that one discrete event could be used as a window through which to view the big themes of history. A biography of Heliogabalus was the ideal jumping-off point to explore issues such as political power, religion, ethnicity and sex. The transgressions of Heliogabalus in all these areas clearly illuminated what was considered normal. These things are vital for our understanding of ancient Rome, and all still have strong resonance now.

Throughout the book the reader is shown, rather than told, the research. The sources – literary, material and visual – are put in context, looked at from different angles, and variant interpretations are canvassed. The aim is to demonstrate *what ancient historians actually do*, and what makes it so enjoyable.

Discontent with two trends in modern scholarship added a spur to writing.

Biography has long had a bad reputation among scholars, especially Classical lives. 'Biography offers the easy approach to history, and some go no further than biography', as it was put by Sir Ronald Syme, the Camden Professor of History at Oxford (1958). That ignores its several virtues. Biography brings a sense of human scale, the lived events of one lifetime, to the often overwhelming *longue durée* of the past, where generations and whole centuries collapse into a couple of chapters, or just a few pages, and the experience of the individual disappears.

Like a novel, biography both injects a narrative drive and engages the emotions of the reader. The saying is often trotted out that we know enough about only two men of antiquity to produce a true biography. The maxim is defeatist. Gaps in the evidence of lives other than Cicero and Saint Augustine are there to be filled with carefully labelled imagination: what anthropologists term 'thick description'. Again, biography has never had to avoid big themes. Plutarch and Suetonius used their subjects to examine what they believed were universal fundamentals of character. A modern biography of Heliogabalus offers a perfect way to think about issues, like sex, race, power and religion, which resonate as much today as they did in antiquity.

The other discontent is more recent – the retreat by many Classical scholars from reality to rhetoric. In the case of 'bad Emperors', like Heliogabalus, it runs like this. All the literary sources were written after his reign, and do nothing but repeat the 'official narrative' put out by the next regime. This makes it difficult, or impossible, to ascertain the truth. Everything they write are *topoi*, literary commonplaces, divorced from reality. If another Emperor is accused of doing something similar, somehow this *proves* it was done by neither. Any action that seems irrational is dismissed as clearly fictional, presumably just because a modern scholar would never behave that way. This sort of thinking makes the rehabilitation of 'bad Emperors' easy, maybe even compulsory. At its most extreme, history ends up as no more than just the rhetoric of historians.

There are two main flaws in this approach. First, as we have seen earlier, in Classical literature *topoi* were not arbitrary signs devoid of any relationship to reality, which could be applied to any Emperor. If they had been, Heliogabalus would have been depicted as an incestuous drunk, addicted to gambling and fighting as a gladiator. *Topoi* were carefully selected and nuanced to reflect the perceived truth. They were a shorthand to aid understanding, which provided quick and easy orientation. That they were formulaic does not necessarily mean they were untrue.

Second, an 'official narrative' did not exist. It is a modern invention. A few anecdotes record rulers, or their associates, encouraging authors to write works which might influence public opinion. Not all the writers took up the suggestions. When they did, they seldom seem to have produced what those in power wanted. Maecenas might have hoped for pro-Augustus propaganda, but what Virgil wrote was the deeply ambiguous *Aeneid*. Ancient writers were far less ready to toe the official line than modern scholars, even though the stakes were so much higher – wealth and influence or book burning, exile and death, rather than a Research Assessment Exercise.

'History as the rhetoric of historians' is lazy: dressing up avoiding the hard work of doing research in fancy methodological clothes. It is defeatist: it is difficult to get anywhere near the truth, so don't try. Yet it is also arrogant: it presupposes we know so much better than those contemporary writers. Worst of all, it represents a complete failure of historical imagination and empathy, as it judges the behaviour of ancient Roman autocrats by the cosy rationality of modern western academics.

History was not just the rhetoric of historians. It was lived. Those who were there had a life full of actions and thoughts. They went through a full range of emotions: love and hate, fear and pleasure, ambition and disappointment. Sometimes they seem very much like us, at other times totally alien. The past was another country, but it is worth making the effort to imagine how they did things there.

FURTHER READING

Comprehensive endnotes and bibliography are available online at oneworld-publications.com/work/the-mad-emperor/. Here I just point the reader to some of the more important works, ancient and modern: as far as possible, those available in English.

Indispensable to starting any study of ancient history are *The Oxford Classical Dictionary*, edited by S. Hornblower, A. Spawforth and E. Eidinow (4th ed., Oxford, 2012), and the *Barrington Atlas of the Greek and Roman World*, edited by R.J.A. Talbert (Princeton and Oxford, 2000).

By far the most enjoyable and informative place to begin thinking about sources and methods is L. Pitcher, *Writing Ancient History: An Introduction to Classical Historiography* (London and New York, 2009).

The best overview of this period of Classical history, as well as any other, remains the relevant volume of *The Cambridge Ancient History*: in this case volume XII, *The Crisis of the Empire, AD 193–337*, edited by A.K. Bowman, P. Garnsey and A. Cameron (2nd ed., Cambridge, 2005). Others are D.S. Potter, *The Roman Empire at Bay AD180–395* (London and New York, 2004); O. Hekster and N. Zair, *Rome and its Empire, AD 193–284* (Edinburgh, 2008); and C. Ando, *Imperial Rome AD 193 to 284: The Critical Century* (Edinburgh, 2012).

The three crucial ancient sources for Heliogabalus are available in English translations, with the original text on the facing page, in the Loeb series (Cambridge, Mass. and London): Cassius Dio (books 79 and 80 in Dio volume IX) by E. Cary (1927), Herodian (book 5 in Herodian volume II) by C.R. Whittaker (1970) and the *Augustan History* (*Heliogabalus* in *Scriptores Historiae Augustae*, Volume II) by D. Magie (1924). There is a better translation of the latter in *Lives of the Later Caesars* by A.R. Birley in Penguin Classics (Harmondsworth, 1976), who also provides an excellent introduction to this strange series of biographies. Introductions to Cassius Dio and Herodian can be found in H. Sidebottom, 'Severan Historiography: Evidence, Patterns, and Arguments', in: S. Swain, S. Harrison and J. Elsner (eds), *Severan Culture* (Cambridge, 2007), 52–82.

There are useful commentaries on the relevant books of Cassius Dio by A.G. Scott, *Emperors and Usurpers: An Historical Commentary on Cassius Dio's Roman History* (Cambridge, 2018), and the *Augustan History* by S.C. Zinsli, *Kommentar zur Vita Heliogabali der Historia Augusta* (Bonn, 2014). Whittaker's edition of Herodian has extensive notes.

F. Millar, *A Study of Cassius Dio* (Oxford, 1964) was the seminal study. J.M. Madsen and C.H. Lange have edited two important collections of recent articles: *Cassius Dio: Greek Intellectual and Roman Politician* (Leiden and Boston, 2016), and *Cassius Dio the Historian: Methods and Approaches* (Leiden and Boston, 2021). J.M. Madsen, *Cassius Dio: Ancients in Action* (London and New York, 2019) offers an overview (although with a controversial slant) aimed at non-specialists. See now M.O. Lindholmer, 'The Time of Composition of Cassius Dio's "Roman History": A Reconsideration', *Klio* 103 (2021), 133–59.

After long neglect, the late 1990s saw the start of a resurgence of interest in Herodian: H. Sidebottom, 'Herodian's Historical

Methods and Understanding of History', *ANRW* 2.14.4 (1998), 2775–2836; M. Zimmermann, *Kaiser und Ereignis: Studien zum Geschichtswerk Herodians* (Munich, 1999); T. Hidber, *Herodians Darstellung der Kaisergeschichte nach Marc Aurel* (Basel, 2006); L.V. Pitcher, 'Herodian', in: I.J.F. de Jong (ed.), *Space in Ancient Greek Literature* (Leiden and Boston, 2012), 269–82; A.M. Kemezis, *Greek Narratives of the Roman Empire under the Severans: Cassius Dio, Philostratus and Herodian. Greek Culture in the Roman World* (Cambridge, 2014); L.V. Pitcher, 'Herodian', in: T. de Koen and E. van Emde Boas (eds), *Characterization in Ancient Greek Literature* (Leiden and Boston, 2017), 236–50; A.G. Scott, 'Conspiracy as Plot Type in Herodian's Roman History', *Mnemosyne* 71 (2018), 434–59; S. Chrysanthou, 'Herodian and Cassius Dio: A Study of Herodian's Compositional Devices', *GRBS* 60 (2020), 621–51.

In 1889 Hermann Dessau, alerted by the many anachronistic names and titles in the text, proposed that the *Augustan History* was not, as it claimed, written by six men around AD 300, but by one unknown author about a hundred years later: 'Über Zeit und Persönlichkeit der Scriptores Historiae Augustae', *Hermes* 24 [1889], 337–92. Over a century of intensive scholarship has confirmed his argument. Most influential in English-speaking scholarship are the works of Sir Ronald Syme: *Ammianus and the Historia Augusta* (Oxford, 1968) and *Emperors and Biography* (Oxford, 1971).

Heliogabalus is illuminated in two recent scholarly books which employ very different approaches. L. de Arrizabalaga y Prado, *The Emperor Elagabalus: Fact or Fiction?* (Cambridge, 2010) contains many insights, but takes an extremely idiosyncratic line on historical evidence and 'truth'. M. Icks, *The Crimes of Elagabalus: The Life and Legacy of Rome's Decadent Boy Emperor* (London, 2011) furnishes a splendid analysis of the Emperor's afterlife, but subscribes to the current orthodoxy (also in Scott, above) that the history of his reign is impossible to reconstruct with any accuracy as our sources are no more than posthumous literary commonplaces.

Articles on the Emperor and his afterlife by numerous authors are collected in *Varian Studies* (3 volumes, Newcastle-upon-Tyne, 2017) edited by L. de Arrizabalaga y Prado.

The historical background to the reign is given in two superb biographies, A.R. Birley, *Septimius Severus: The African Emperor* (rev. ed., Abingdon, 1988); and B. Levick, *Julia Domna: Syrian Empress* (Abingdon, 2007); and a thesis, A.G. Scott, *Change and Discontinuity within the Severan Dynasty: The Case of Macrinus* (State University of New Jersey, 2008).

Emesa and Elagabal can be approached via F. Millar, *The Roman Near East 31 BC–AD 337* (Cambridge, Mass. and London, 1993); or, more eccentrically, by W. Ball, *Rome in the East: The Transformation of an Empire* (London and New York, 2000).

Turning to the main themes.

The evidence for Roman racism was presented by J.P.V.D. Balsdon, *Romans and Aliens* (London, 1979); now augmented by B. Isaac, *The Invention of Racism in Classical Antiquity* (Princeton and Oxford, 2004); but disputed by E.S. Gruen, *Rethinking the Other in Antiquity* (Princeton, 2011).

On power F. Millar, *The Emperor in the Roman World (31BC–AD337)* (2nd ed., London, 1992, 1st ed., 1977) dominates modern scholarship; but see K. Hopkins, 'Rules of Evidence', *JRS* 68 (1978), 178–86.

The sea change in thinking about Roman religion was caused by R. McMullen, *Roman Paganism* (New Haven and London, 1981); and R. Lane Fox, *Pagans and Christians in the Mediterranean World from the Second Century AD to the Conversion of Constantine* (Harmondsworth, 1986). Also important, in a different way, was S.R.F. Price, *Rituals and Power: The Roman Imperial Cult in Asia Minor* (Cambridge, 1984).

J.R. Clarke, *Looking at Lovemaking: Constructions of Sexuality in Roman Art 100 BC–AD 250* (Berkeley, Los Angeles and London, 1998), provides a brilliant introduction, both to ancient attitudes to sex and modern thinking about art, and is a joy to read. P. Veyne (ed.), *A History of Private Life: From Pagan Rome to Byzantium* (English translation, Cambridge, Mass. and London, 1987) had the Romans 'paralysed by prohibitions'.

Other particularly useful works include: B. Campbell, *The Emperor and the Roman Army 31BC–AD235* (Oxford, 1984); E.R. Varner, *Mutilation and Transformation: Damnatio Memoriae and Roman Imperial Portraiture* (Leiden and Boston, 2004); M. Gleason, 'Identity Theft: Doubles and Masquerades in Cassius Dio's Contemporary History', *CA* 30, no. 1 (2011), 33–86; I. Mennen, *Power and Status in the Roman Empire, AD193–284* (Leiden and Boston, 2011); C. Rowan, 'The Public Image of the Severan women,' *PBSR* 79 (2011), 241–73; C. Rowan, *Under Divine Auspices: Divine Ideology and the Visualisation of Imperial Power in the Severan Period* (Cambridge, 2012); C. Davenport, 'The Provincial Appointments of the Emperor Macrinus', *Antichthon* 46 (2012), 184–203; D. Okon, *Imperatores Severi et Senatores: The History of the Imperial Personnel Policy* (Szczecin, 2013), 77–105.

Comparative material comes from: R. Kapuscinski, *The Emperor* (English translation, London, 1983); C. Coughlin, *Saddam: King of Terror* (New York, 2002); B. Titley, *Dark Age: The Political Odyssey of Emperor Bokassa* (Quebec, 2002); D. Kalder, *Dictator Literature: A History of Bad Books by Terrible People* (London, 2018).

R.J. Barrow, *Lawrence Alma-Tadema* (London, 2001) is a superbly illustrated introduction to the painter and his work. D. Watkin, 'Sir Lawrence Alma-Tadema's Painting The Roses of Heliogabalus', in: L. de Arrizabalaga y Prado (ed.), *Varian Studies. Volume Three: A Varian Symposium* (Cambridge, 2017), 105–24 is a detailed study that comes to different conclusions from mine.

ACKNOWLEDGEMENTS

Writing a book is a solitary occupation, but I am fortunate to have a lot of support. It gives me pleasure to thank the following. James Gill at United Agents for helping me turn the initial idea into a sensible proposal. At Oneworld Sam Carter and Holly Knox have been indefatigable. Leonardo de Arrizabalaga y Prado and Consuelo Ruiz Montero were kind enough to send me electronic copies of their work when lockdowns prevented access to libraries. I am very grateful to Luke Pitcher for making the time to read the text; not that he necessarily agrees with any specific bit.

As ever, my main debt is to my family. That is why the book is dedicated to my wife Lisa, my mother Frances and my aunt Terry.

INDEX